PÂTÉ

The New Main Course for the '80s

A MENU COOKBOOK

Books by Carol Cutler

Haute Cuisine for Your Heart's Delight
The Six-Minute Soufflé and Other Culinary Delights
The Woman's Day *Low-Calorie Dessert Cookbook*
Cuisine Rapide

PÂTÉ

The New Main Course for the '80s

A MENU COOKBOOK

Carol Cutler

Illustrations by Joan McGurren

RAWSON ASSOCIATES • New York

Library of Congress Cataloging in Publication Data

Cutler, Carol.
   Pâté: the new main course for the '80's.

   Includes index.
   1. Pâtés (Cookery)   2. Terrines.   I. Title.
TX749.C87   1983   641.8'12   82-42691
ISBN 0-89256-232-3

Copyright © 1983 by Carol Cutler
Illustrations copyright © 1983 by Joan McGurren
All rights reserved
Published simultaneously in Canada by McClelland and Stewart Ltd.
Composition by P & M Typesetting, Inc., Waterbury, Connecticut
Manufactured by Fairfield Graphics, Fairfield, Pennsylvania
Designed by Jacques Chazaud
First Edition

To Mother,

*for patiently tolerating a stubborn daughter
who refused offers of cooking instruction
and for graciously not gloating when,
years later, the daughter came home
and solicited her culinary expertise*

Contents

LIST OF ILLUSTRATIONS   ix

PART ONE

The Secrets of Creating Successful Pâté   1

CHAPTER ONE: Why Pâté as a Main Course   3
CHAPTER TWO: The Techniques of Pâté Making   6
CHAPTER THREE: Tips for Better Cooking   21

PART TWO

The Pâtés, Terrines, and Their Accompaniments   23

CHAPTER FOUR: The Menus and Recipes   25

A Simple Dinner with International Flavors   26
An Informal Gathering Featuring Hearty Food   32
A Celebration of Delectable Delicacy   40
Dinner à la Française   45
An Adventurous Medley   51
Smoothly Sophisticated   58
A Robust Repast   65
Easy Elegance   71

Duck Dinner with a Stylish Difference   79
A Menu Full of Piquant Pleasures   85
Sumptuous Springtime Dining   92
A Surprise Party of Unexpected Pleasures   100
A Salute to Summer   108
Come by After the Theater   116
Come for a Celebration   122
A Warming Supper After the Game   130
A Three-Act Play of Palate Pleasures   136
Decidedly Different and Delicious   142
A Striking Palette of Savory Pleasures   148
Easy Panache   157
Brunch with an Emphatic Difference   163
Regally Russian   170
Stellar Sunday Lunch   179
A Dinner Salute to Italy   185
Artistic Flair Frames a Stylish Menu   192

PART THREE

Serendipities   199

CHAPTER FIVE: More Innovative Pâtés and Terrines and One Old Favorite   201

CHAPTER SIX: Basic Recipes for Use in Many Menus   215

CHAPTER SEVEN: Sauces, Sweet and Savory   223

INDEX   235

List of Illustrations

1. Handling Caul   6
2. Cutting Caul   6
3. Lining with Fatback   6
4. Cutting Lardons   7
5. Creating an Interior Pattern   7
6. Grinding Meats   7
7. Mixing Meats   8
8. Tasting Forcemeat   8
9. Composing a Terrine   8
10. Aluminum Foil Seal   9
11. The Essential Water Bath   9
12. Weighting Pâtés and Terrines   10
13. The Beginning of a Pastry-Wrapped Pâté   11
14. Covering the Meats with Pastry   11
15. Finishing the Pastry-Wrapped Loaf   11
16. Metal Molds for Pâtés   12
17. Lining a Mold with Pastry   12
18. Finishing the Pâté in a Mold   12
19. Aspic to Fill Spaces   13
20. Tasting Mousseline   13
21. Cutting Paper for Molds   14
22. Filling with Mousseline   14
23. Careful Handling of Mousseline over Garnishes   14
24. Loosening a Baked Terrine   15
25. Hot Water to Loosen Bottom of Terrine   15
26. Removing Top Paper   15
27. Shaking the Mold   16
28. Reversing the Mold   16
29. Removing Second Paper   16
30. Lining a Mold with Crêpes   17
31. Covering a Pâté with Spinach   17

32. Aspic as a Garnish   18
33. Decorative Vegetable Flowers   18
34. Pastry Decorations   19
35. Cutting Pastry Leaves   19
36. Fashioning Scalloped Pastry Rounds   19
37. Molds for Pâtés and Terrines   20

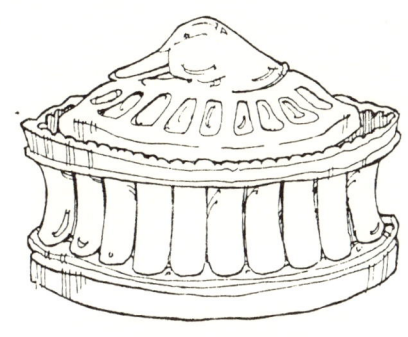

PART ONE

⇊⇊⇊

The Secrets of Creating Successful Pâté

CHAPTER ONE

Why Pâté as a Main Course

There are three commonly held beliefs about pâtés: that they are rich, expensive, and difficult to make. All three are wrong, and the reason for this book is to share with readers the good news that pâtés are lower in calories than you think, moderate in cost, easy to prepare, and a boon to contemporary entertaining.

The last decade has seen significant changes in the way Americans cook, eat, and ply guests with food. With more concern about good health and fitness, lighter foods are on the table. Although at first it may seem like a paradox, pâtés and terrines can play an important role in this trend, in fact, a starring role as the main course. It probably will come as a surprise to most readers to learn that a four-ounce serving of plain grilled beef sirloin has more calories than the same amount of, say, Terrine de Canard à l'Orange: 440 calories versus 258.

Though pâtés are most often served as a first course, they are in fact too filling for such use. The introductory plate is supposed to whet the appetite for more to come, as a small tasty offering, a frivolity, or even a luxury of sorts. Sparkling consommé, icy shrimp cocktail, oeufs en gelée (eggs in aspic), even caviar and toast are classic entrances to a special dinner. But except for pâtés I can think of no other instance where a substantial serving of meat or fowl has become a traditional menu opener. (For the same reason—their ability to satisfy the appetite—I do not think pâtés belong at the predinner cocktail hour, nor does cheese.) I want to make it clear that this is not a diet book. Nor am I offering pâtés as a sensational fad diet, but I must emphasize that they are not as sinful as you think. To alleviate any guilty feeling about the alleged richness of pâtés, each recipe includes a calorie count per one quarter-pound serving.

Pâtés and their cousins, terrines, have many virtues as main courses. Now that two-paycheck families are more the rule than the exception, styles of entertaining are different. A whole day devoted to making hollandaise sauce, veal Orloff, and crêpes suzette has gone the way of the penny post card. Once again pâtés come to the rescue. Because of their very nature, they must be completely prepared in advance, usually two to five days before serving. This means that the biggest cooking chore for a dinner party is out of the way early. There is no risk of overcooking or undercooking in a last-minute flurry of activity. In fact, pâtés can be prepared in several stages after you return home from work—trimming, chopping, and marinating meats one evening and baking them the next. A fish or vegetable terrine can be readied in its mold and wait in the refrigerator for baking the next evening. Still another advantage in serving a cold pâté (though hot pâtés are included in the book) is that the oven is free for other dishes. No juggling is necessary. As an additional aid to the cook, recipes for hot dishes carry a note on how to cook ahead—at which point to stop and how to reheat the dish successfully. Though pâtés and terrines are blessed with patience and will wait for days, improving all the time, the inevitable question arises: Can they be frozen? Really not. The texture will change and become a bit watery. If you want to freeze leftovers, by all means do; just recognize that the next time around the taste will not be quite the same.

Pâté de foie gras is expensive and worth it. But other than that glory of French cuisine, pâtés are surprisingly economical. Because the principal ingredient is combined with other products, the price tag is considerably lower than it would be if one served just beef, duck, crab, ham, or lamb. A Shrimp Terrine to serve eight is made for about $14, while any sort of shrimp dish for the same number would cost at least $10 more. A spectacular hot Veal and Ham Pâté wrapped in a pastry crust handsomely serves eight hungry diners for about $11, but any veal dish you might want to serve could easily pinch your budget for $30. Vegetable terrines dip as low as $3.50; lowly chicken livers are elevated to a creamy parfait for a mere $9. There is even at $6 a Lasagna Pâté that can be the delicious surprise of a dinner party. The inventive cook can shave still more cost by taking advantage of sales and special prices. Once certain principles are understood, pâtés may be varied at whim. If veal is beyond the pocketbook, substitute turkey breast; hazelnuts or walnuts can stand in for pistachios. No recipe in the book calls for truffles, but there is hardly a pâté that wouldn't benefit from the heady fragrance of a *fresh* one. Play up, play down, but do play and be imaginative with pâtés.

The myth persists that the making of pâtés and terrines is beyond most nonprofessional cooks. Yet few would be daunted at the thought of making meat loaf. Just remember that a pâté is nothing more than a French meat loaf that's had a couple of cocktails. In many cases one need do no more than season ground meats and bake them. That is precisely how popular Pâté de Campagne *(Country Pâté)* is produced. The only extra step is the wrapping of fat that helps moisten the pâté as it bakes. Though adding layers of solid garnishes into the ground meats rarely changes flavors, it does create patterns that are visually attractive. Here again the artistry of the cook can add to or delete from the ingredients in the recipes. Pâtés are very accommodating. This book begins with basic Meat Loaf Terrine and moves along to more elaborate varieties. In each section—meat, fish, vegetable—the progression from simple to show-stopper is followed. You will find that it takes no more time to prepare a pâté than most other main courses. Ungarnished terrines can be put together in as little as fifteen minutes, and the most complicated versions need no more than an hour. Most fall in between. The recipes may seem to run long, but that is because every detail is explained. I felt it better to give too much information than not enough.

Pâté offers a change of pace when served as the main course. Guests sit up and take notice because it is unexpected. It is time to stop thinking of cold main courses as strictly summertime fare. Oviously the menu must be designed to balance a cold main course with hot dishes or to surround a hot pâté with compatible foods. Since a slice of pâté by itself looks rather lonely on a plate, small accompanying garnishes have been created to replace the traditional, and banal, sour pickle. To help the reader prepare orchestrated meals, the book is presented as twenty-five menus, with extra pâté and terrine recipes to offer a wider choice. Please remember that these menus are not carved in stone or meant to be commandments. If you've had your fill of asparagus, try red pepper and snow peas from another menu, or substitute one of your own favorite recipes. However, an effort should be made to maintain the juxtaposition of hot and cold. Recipes within each menu are given in order of advance preparation, not by place in the meal. The recipes move from those done several days before through to those that least tolerate standing. Here again, I hope this helps the reader.

Now for the main controversy about pâtés and terrines. When do you call them pâtés and when do you call them terrines? Technically only meat wrapped in pastry should be called pâté. *Terrine*, from the French root *terre* (earth), means the loaf has been baked in a dish, classically one of earthenware. The circumflex over the *a* in pâté is the clue in defining a true pâté. It indicates the dropping of an earlier *s* from the original *paste* or pastry. It really is redundant to say pâté en croûte, or pastry in crust. Still, the French do so, and since they are the chief pâté makers of the world, why shouldn't we do the same? They serve Pâté de Campagne, even though it is always baked in a dish. And who offers Terrine de Foie Gras? Not Maxim's. To that restaurant it's pâté, despite its lacking a crust. I've also wondered if pâté (paste) may not at one time have referred to the pasty consistency of the ground meats. I like to go by the way the title sounds. Some word combinations are just better than others. You may unscramble them as you like. No matter what they are called, pâtés and terrines are wonderful eating. Enjoy!

CHAPTER TWO

The Techniques of Pâté Making

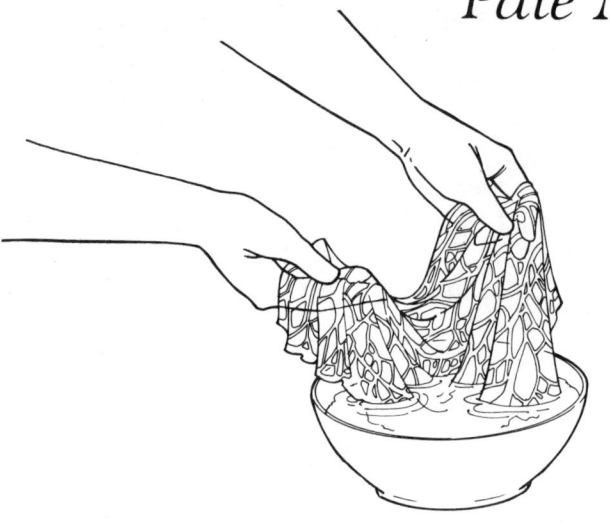

1. Caul is the fatty membrane from the stomach of a pig. It has a thick-and-thin texture that ranges from ribbons of fat to almost transparent sections. During the baking, caul melts and browns and leaves a lacy pattern on the terrine. It can be bought from specialty butchers fresh, dry-salted, or frozen. Always rinse caul; dry-salted caul should be soaked in several changes of water for a few hours.

2. When lining a terrine with caul, make certain it fits well into the bottom and against the sides. Scissors are the best implement for cutting caul. Overhanging caul should be pulled over the forcemeat; then more should be added to cover the entire surface. As the terrine bakes, the patches will meld together.

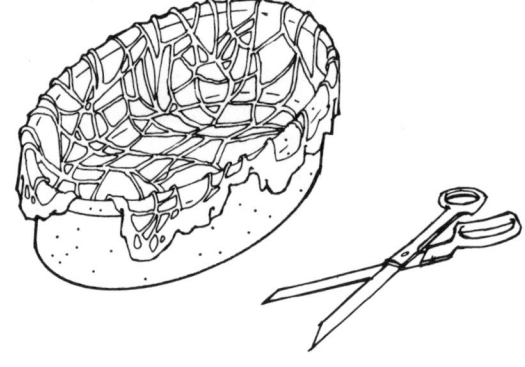

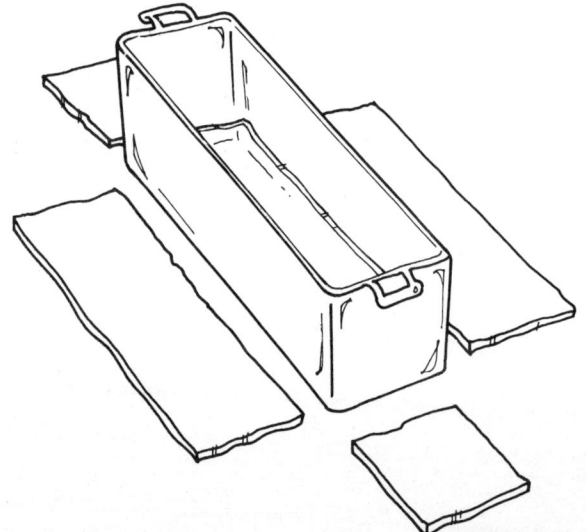

3. Thinly sliced pork fatback (bards) is the most widely used lining and covering for terrines and pâtés. It is solid white fat that remains white after baking. A strip is in place in the bottom of the mold, the pieces beside the terrine fit against the sides, and an additional strip is to be cut for the top. Always overlap the edges of all fatback pieces so they bake together. Fatback can also be fitted in across the terrine, as in illustration 9.

THE SECRETS OF CREATING SUCCESSFUL PÂTÉ · 7

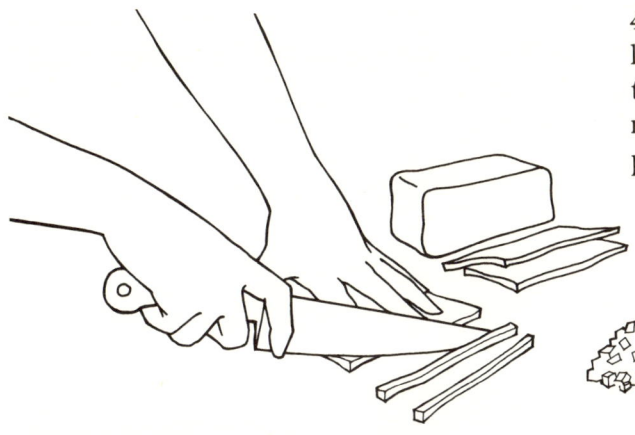

4. A piece of fatback can be cut into long strips (lardons) or cubed for adding to forcemeat. As the fatback bakes, it melts and moistens the interior of the pâté or terrine. It cuts best when cold.

5. Meat lardons are used to create decorative patterns inside the loaves. As you plan these interior garnishes, always keep in mind their color when they are baked. The ham strips, shown here, will remain pink, veal will range from very pale pink to beige, chicken will be white, and tongue will be red. Usually the lardons are marinated to perfume the pâté interior. Other flavorful and colorful additions, such as pistachio nuts, truffles, olives, and red pepper or pimiento strips, can be strewn between the lardons. The possibilities are limited only by your imagination.

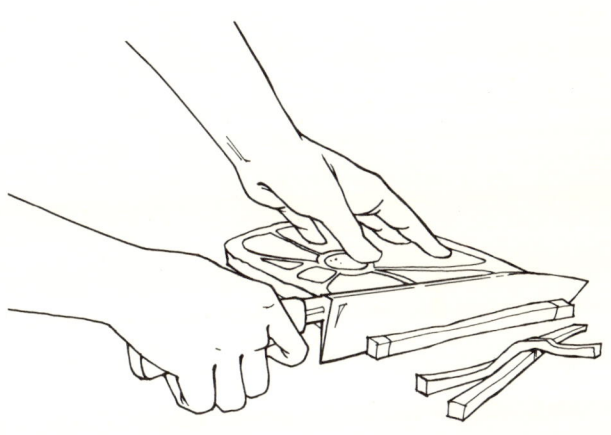

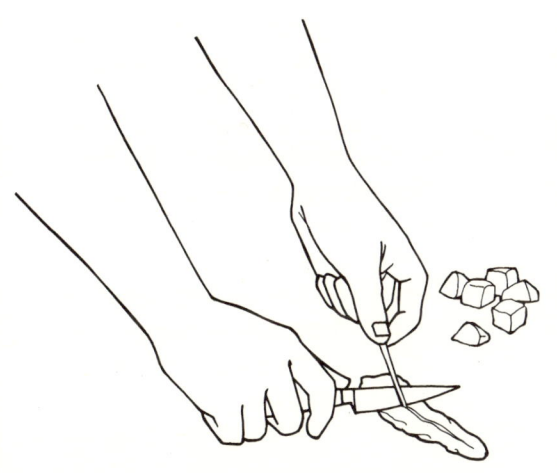

6. It is preferable to grind meats at home to ensure that all tough membranes and gristles have been cut away since they become hard and unchewable when baked. Meat chunks have been cut, and a chicken breast is being stripped of its tendon. A grinder produces the best texture for pâtés, but a food processor can readily be used by following a few rules. Do not chop too much meat at a time; fill the bowl only to the one-third level. Chop the meats first with the on/off switch to reduce the chunks to a more uniform size; then process them for a few seconds at a time until the right consistency has been achieved. *Do not overprocess.* There should be about twice as much lean meat as fat, including the fatty covering, but proportions vary from recipe to recipe.

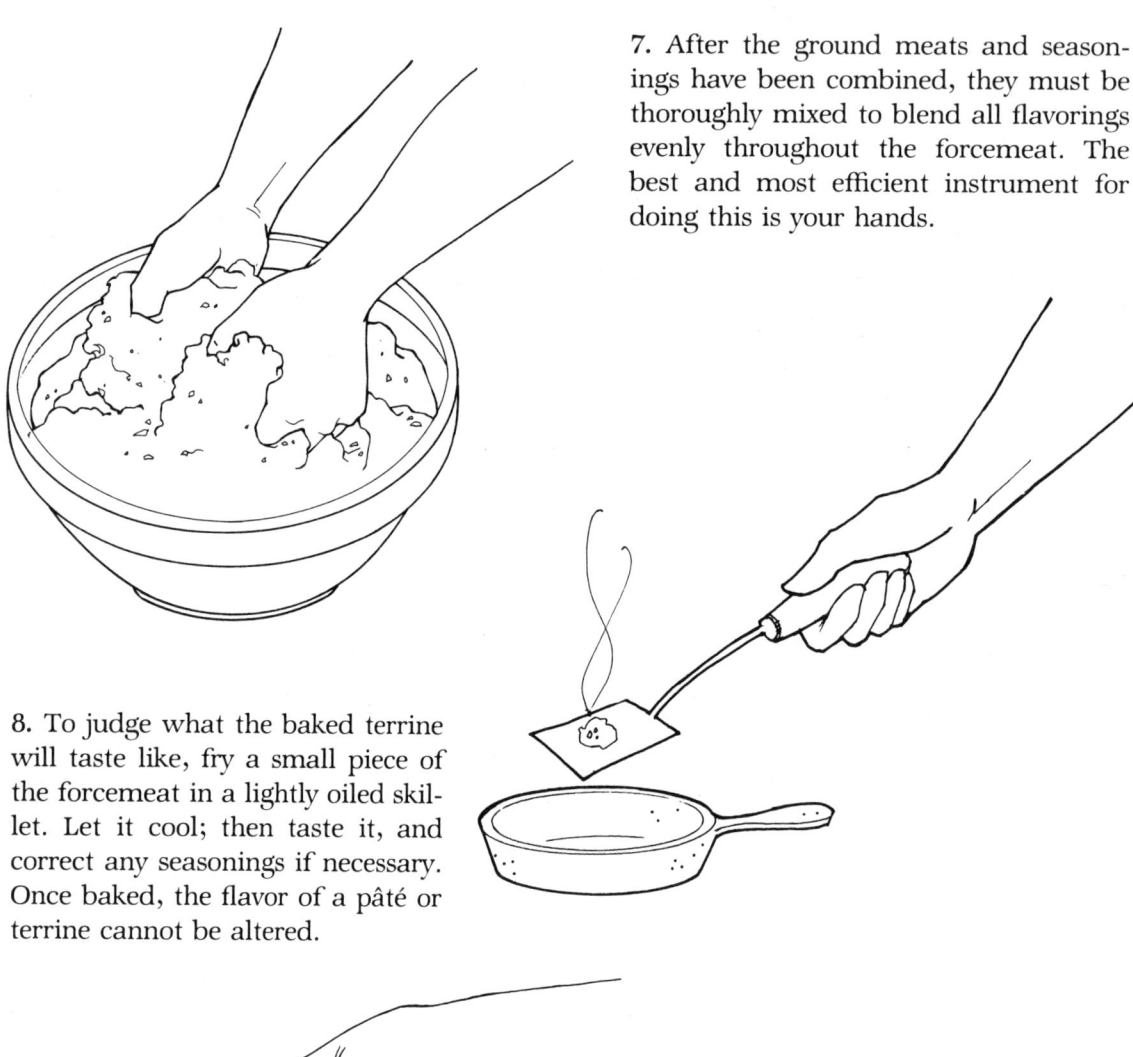

7. After the ground meats and seasonings have been combined, they must be thoroughly mixed to blend all flavorings evenly throughout the forcemeat. The best and most efficient instrument for doing this is your hands.

8. To judge what the baked terrine will taste like, fry a small piece of the forcemeat in a lightly oiled skillet. Let it cool; then taste it, and correct any seasonings if necessary. Once baked, the flavor of a pâté or terrine cannot be altered.

9. Alternating layers of forcemeat and lardons, plus pistachio nuts here, fill the terrine. When a layer of forcemeat is smoothed into the mold, lift it several inches and hit it on the counter. This sharp tapping settles the meat solidly into the mold. As lardons and garnishes are added, they should be lightly pressed into the forcemeat.

THE SECRETS OF CREATING SUCCESSFUL PÂTÉ · 9

10. Time was when chefs sealed the terrine lid to the dish with a strip of pastry. This seal ensures a minimum loss of juices. The small round hole in the lid permits steam to escape. Today most cooks use heavy-duty aluminum foil as a primary cover under the lid and eliminate the pastry. The foil must not hang down loosely into the water bath, where moisture would be trapped under the foil and would steam, rather than bake, the pâté. Roll up and fold the foil tightly against the dish. Once the lid is in place, poke a skewer through the hole to pierce the foil for a steam vent.

11. The sides of a properly baked terrine should not have a dry crust. This is prevented by putting the filled mold in a water bath. Use a roasting pan or gratin dish large enough to allow a free flow of water around the mold, and add hot water to the two-thirds level. To prevent any accidents, it is advisable to add the water once the pan is on the oven rack. As water evaporates during the baking, add more to maintain the level.

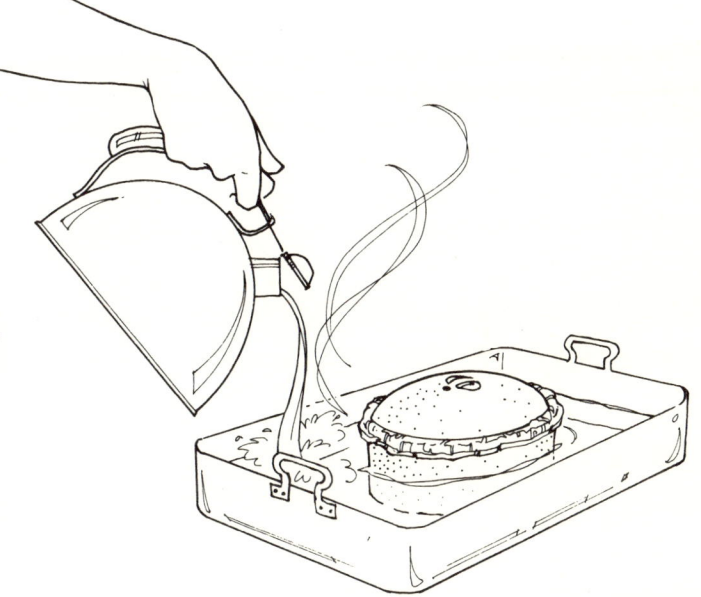

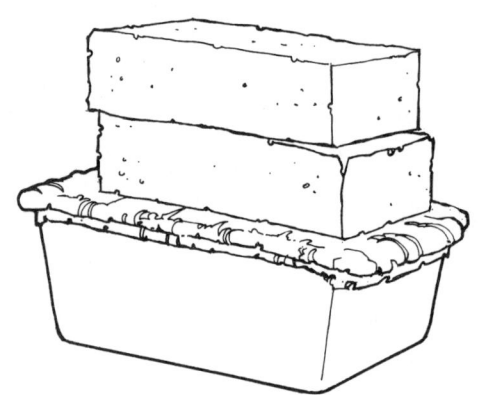 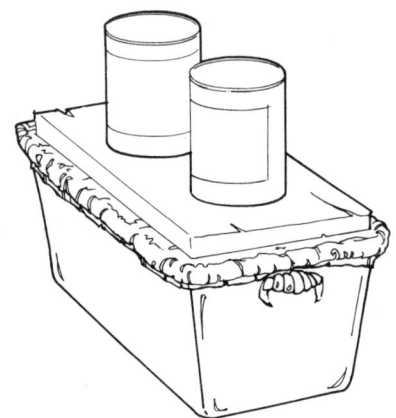

12. After a terrine has been baked, it should be weighted to produce a denser texture for easier slicing. Allow the terrine to stand for twenty to thirty minutes. When the terrine is removed from the oven, the retained heat in it continues to cook for a while, and the juices are still active. Once they have receded back into the meat, it can be weighted. Weighting too soon will drive the juices out of the meat. Weights should cover the surface of the meat as completely as possible and not rest on the edge of the dish. (A) Bricks can be used, (B) a piece of wood cut to fit the mold, plus cans or any heavy object, will serve, or (C) one can even use a smaller mold of the same shape filled with water. The meat loaf will have shrunk during the baking, giving off some fat and juices. These juices collect around the meat in the dish and are very savory. Before serving, spoon out or pour off the juices, and save them to flavor stews and quick meat sauces.

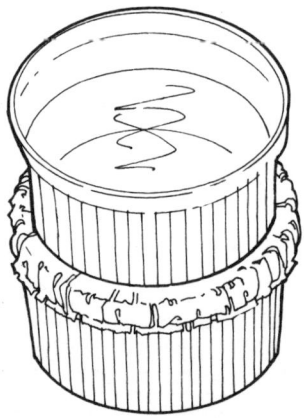

THE SECRETS OF CREATING SUCCESSFUL PÂTÉ · 11

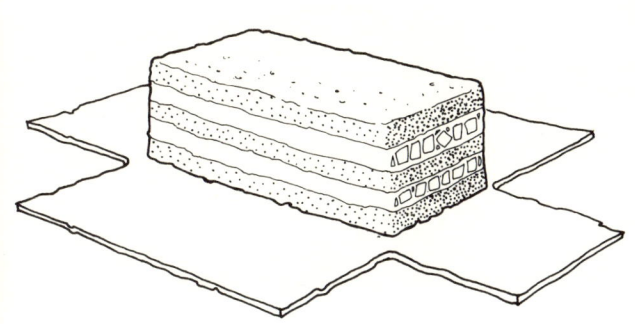

13. Any meat pâté or terrine can be wrapped in pastry for handsome effect. Here are layers of garnished forcemeat ready to be wrapped in pastry. Corners of pastry are cut away for neater folding and to eliminate excessively thick pastry at the ends. The pastry cutouts do not reach all the way to the loaf of meat; once folded, they could cause a bad seal. Leave a half inch of pastry at the four corners.

14. Pull one long side of pastry taut over the meats, and brush the edge in the center with beaten egg. Brush egg over the edge of the other long side, and pull it over and beyond the edge of the first side. Similarly handle the ends, always brushing with egg to seal seams.

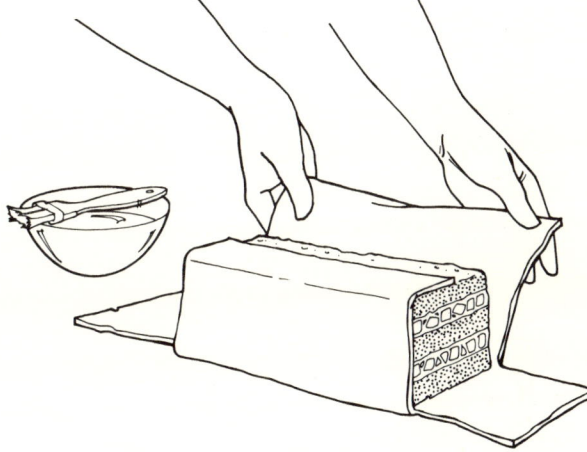

15. There are two ways to bake a pâté on a greased baking sheet. An extra sheet of pastry may be placed over the top to cover the center seam, and other pastry decorations may mask the side seams. Alternatively, the loaf may be turned over, upside down, to place all seams on the bottom. In either case roll pastry scraps between your palms to make a rope that can go around the pâté. Brush all around the bottom of the pâté with egg, and press the rope slightly under and against the base of the pâté. This strip gives extra support to the pâté, especially during the early baking stages, when the dough is still soft. Cut two small holes of pastry from the top, and fill them with rolled parchment paper chimneys. These chimneys allow steam and overflowing juices to go straight up rather than to dribble on the pastry. Paint the entire surface with beaten egg to produce a golden brown shiny crust.

16. Pâtés can also be baked in metal molds that are hinged for easy removal after baking. The molds should be generously buttered before the pastry goes in. They are available in both loaf and oval shapes.

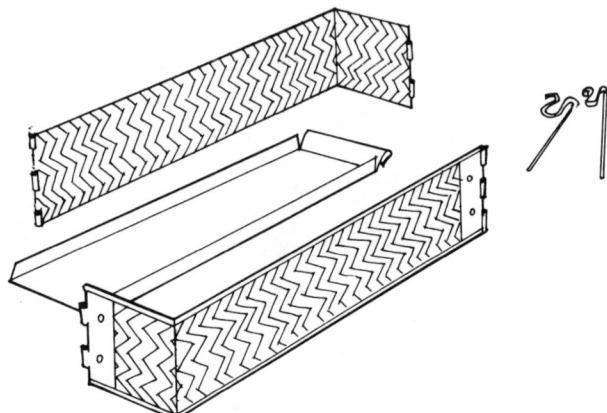

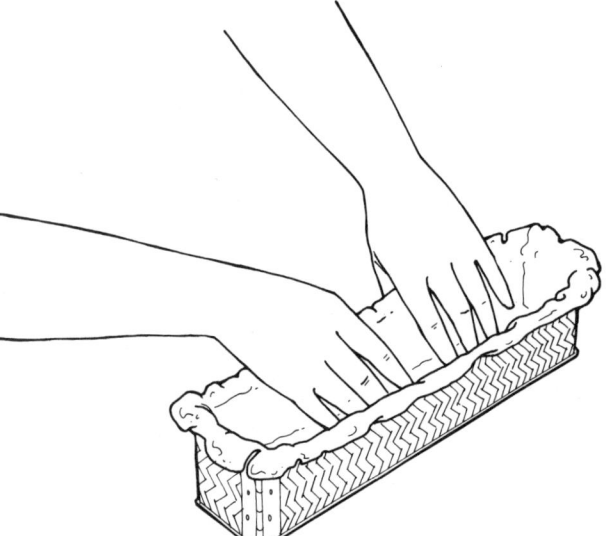

17. When lining the mold with pastry, make certain it fits flat against the bottom, against the sides, and well into the corners. The pastry will be imprinted with the design of the mold.

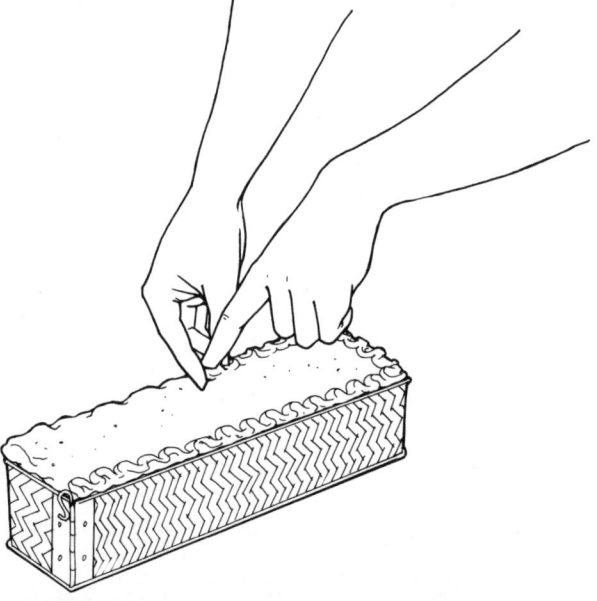

18. Before placing the pastry top over the forcemeat, use beaten egg to brush the edges of the lining and the top. After decorating the pâté, cut out a vent hole in the center, fill it with the parchment paper chimney, and brush the entire surface with beaten egg.

THE SECRETS OF CREATING SUCCESSFUL PÂTÉ · 13

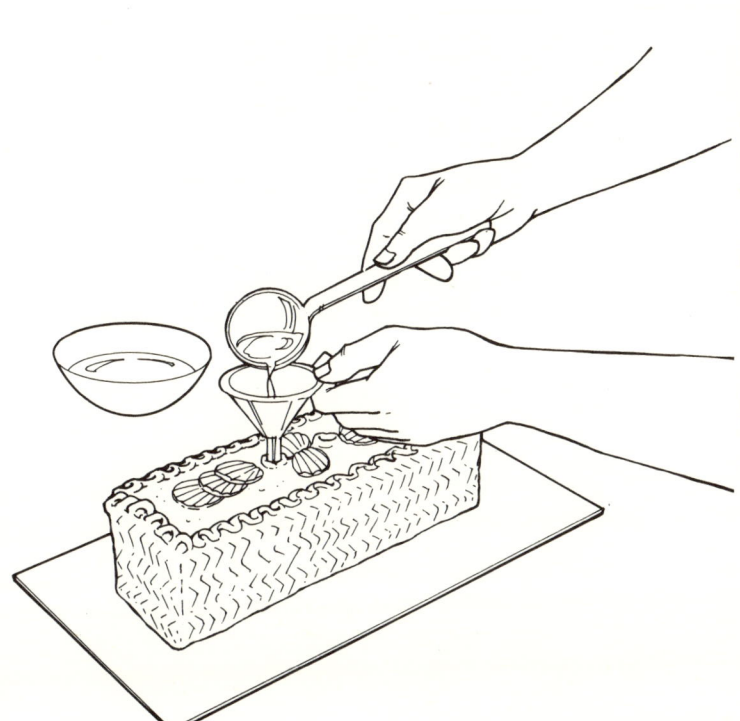

19. As the meat bakes, it shrinks and leaves spaces under the pastry. For more attractive serving slices, the space can be filled with aspic once the pâté has been thoroughly chilled. The day before serving, pour aspic through the vent holes. Do this several times, allowing a few minutes for the aspic to flow throughout the filling before adding more. If there are leaks in the pastry, patch them with softened butter, chill to harden the butter, then continue pouring in the aspic.

20. Almost all fish and most vegetable terrines are based on a mousse or mousseline. Originally these mixtures were laboriously pounded in a large marble mortar with a heavy pestle. Today the food processor makes beautiful mousselines if the few rules included in the recipes are followed. Of paramount importance is the chilling of all ingredients and the processor bowl and blade. Once the mousseline has been made, it should be tasted for seasonings before you proceed to fill the mold. Poach a small spoonful in a small amount of gently simmering water. Turn it over once during the poaching, and allow it to cool before tasting.

21. Cut two sheets of parchment or wax paper to fit the top and bottom of the mold. Lightly score the paper with the point of a small knife; then cut it out with scissors.

22. A well-buttered mold is fitted with a sheet of paper on the bottom, which in turn is buttered again. The first layer of mousseline is being spread in with particular attention to filling the corners. The layer should be smooth and even. Tap the mold on the counter after each mousseline layer addition, but do so lightly.

23. When garnishes are layered over mousseline, the next layer of mousseline must be carefully handled. To disturb the garnish arrangement as little as possible, it is best to work with several large scoops of mousseline which can be spread with short strokes rather than long, sweeping ones which might pull the strips out of place. Dipping the rubber spatula into cold water helps make smooth layers.

THE SECRETS OF CREATING SUCCESSFUL PÂTÉ · 15

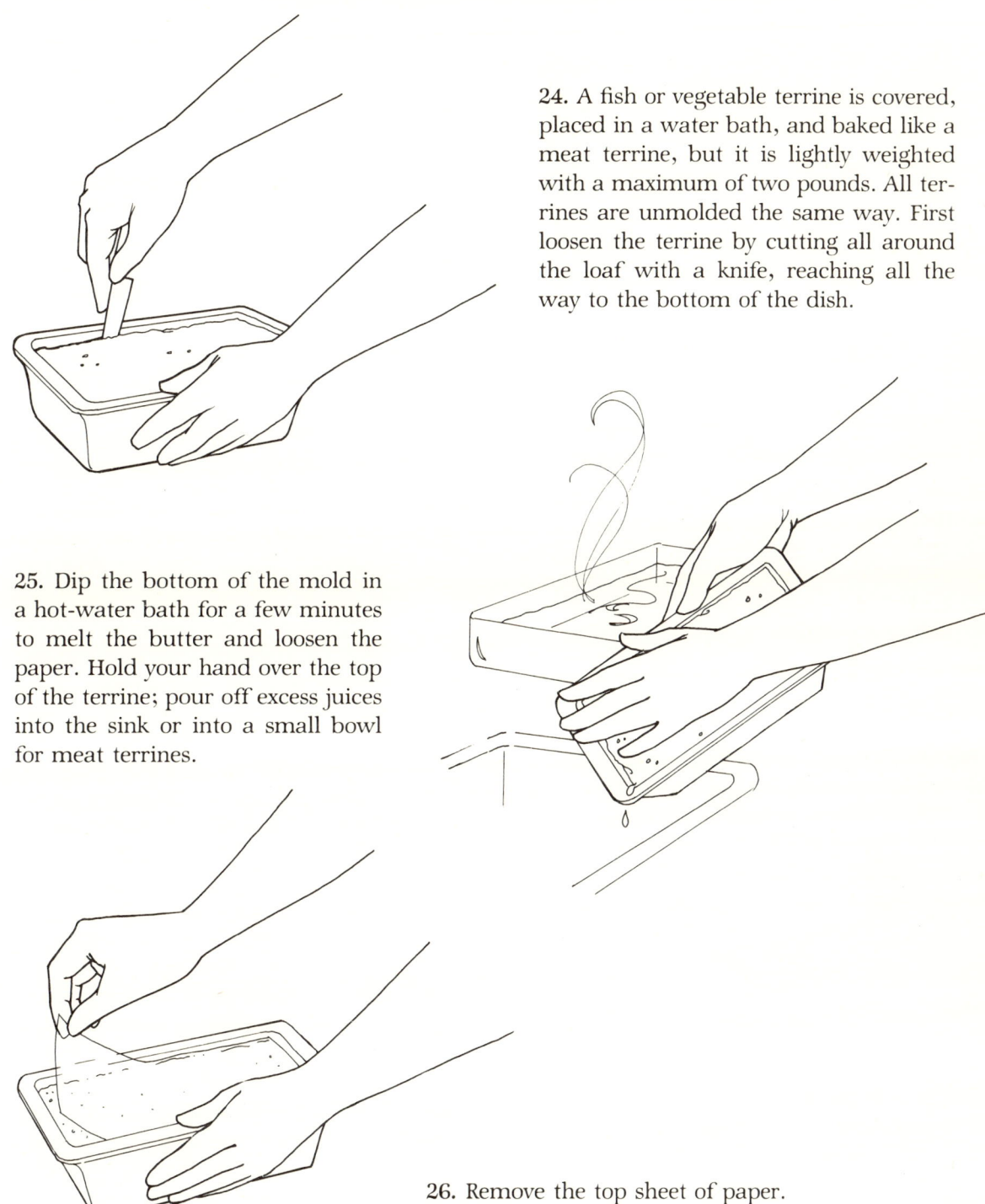

24. A fish or vegetable terrine is covered, placed in a water bath, and baked like a meat terrine, but it is lightly weighted with a maximum of two pounds. All terrines are unmolded the same way. First loosen the terrine by cutting all around the loaf with a knife, reaching all the way to the bottom of the dish.

25. Dip the bottom of the mold in a hot-water bath for a few minutes to melt the butter and loosen the paper. Hold your hand over the top of the terrine; pour off excess juices into the sink or into a small bowl for meat terrines.

26. Remove the top sheet of paper.

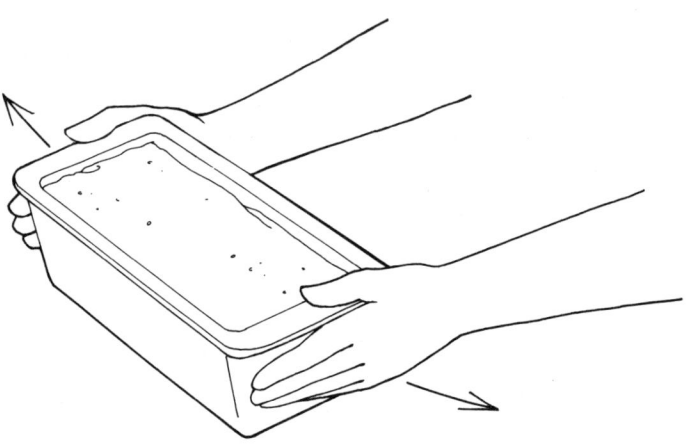

27. To loosen the terrine as much as possible in its mold, shake it back and forth a few times. The weight of the loaf will cause it to pull away from the mold. Do not shake it too vigorously since mousseline-based terrines are delicate.

28. Place a serving platter over the top of the mold, and reverse the two together. The terrine should fall into the platter. If not, let it stand for a few minutes; usually the law of gravity will work, and the terrine will come down. If even that fails, lift the edge of the mold, and slide a knife between the mold and the loaf to break the vacuum.

29. Peel the second piece of paper from the terrine, and garnish as you like, or if it is colorful enough, don't.

THE SECRETS OF CREATING SUCCESSFUL PÂTÉ

A Few Decorative Garnishes for Terrines

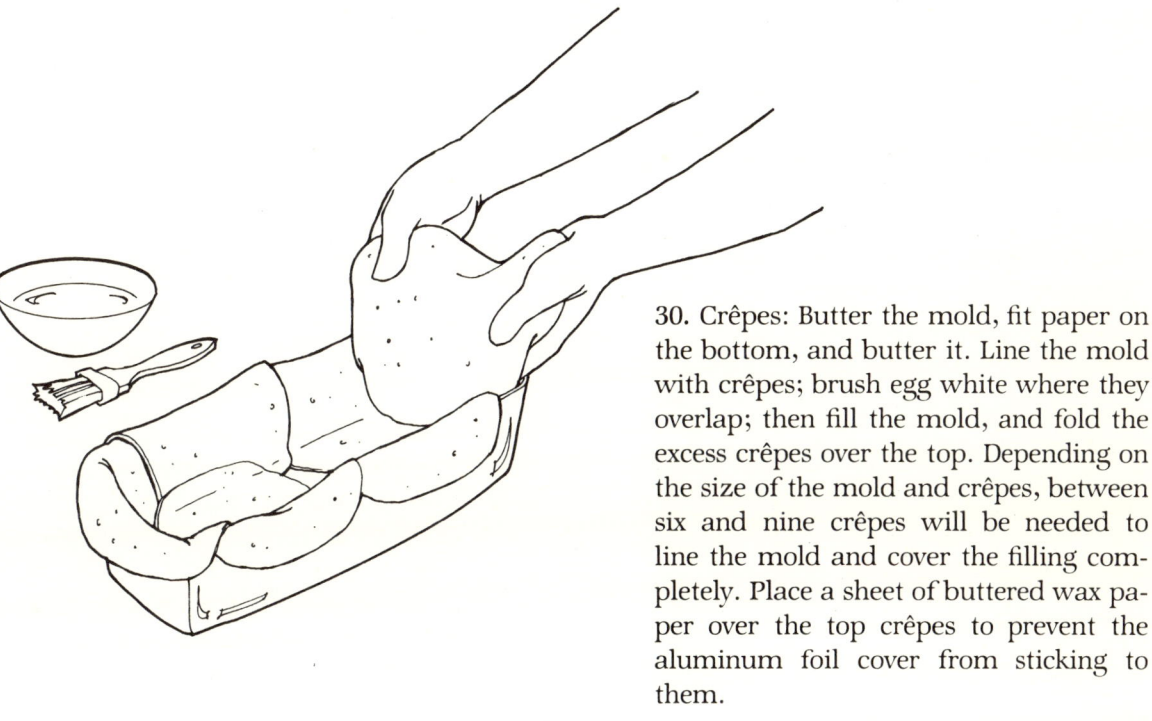

30. Crêpes: Butter the mold, fit paper on the bottom, and butter it. Line the mold with crêpes; brush egg white where they overlap; then fill the mold, and fold the excess crêpes over the top. Depending on the size of the mold and crêpes, between six and nine crêpes will be needed to line the mold and cover the filling completely. Place a sheet of buttered wax paper over the top crêpes to prevent the aluminum foil cover from sticking to them.

31. Spinach: Blanch large leaves of spinach; spread between towels to dry; then place the spinach over the unmolded terrine. A coating of aspic will help make the leaves shine.

32. Aspic: Chill aspic in a shallow dish; unmold it; cut it into slices; then chop and scatter the slices over and around the terrine. Cutouts may also be stamped from sliced aspic and arranged over the terrine. Before aspic completely sets, it can be brushed in layers for a glistening coating; chill to set each layer before adding the next. Herbs or sliced vegetables can be encased in the aspic. A brief blanching helps preserve the color of most greens and vegetables. Aspic takes on a bloom after two or three days and begins to deteriorate. Add aspic coatings or garnishes the day before serving.

33. Flowers: Flowers can be made with scored and sliced carrots that are boiled until crisply tender. Their leaves and stems are blanched chives or scallion greens cut into thin strips. A center dot of red pimiento may be added.

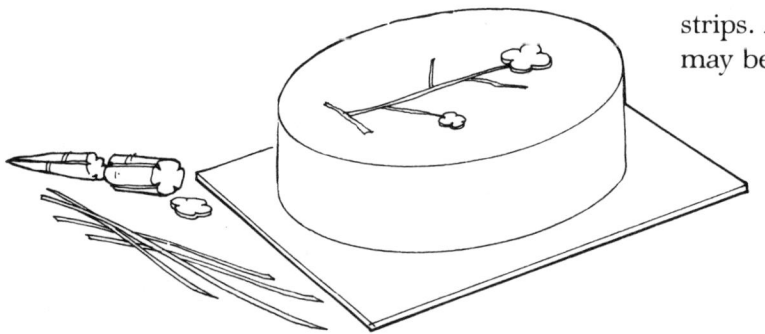

THE SECRETS OF CREATING SUCCESSFUL PÂTÉ · 19

34. Strips: Pâtés may be decorated in many fanciful ways with scraps of leftover dough. Strips are cut with a knife or pastry wheel; ropes are rolled between your palms. The illustrated decorations take a minimal amount of pastry. Elaborate designs might require more than just the leftover pastry. For safety's sake, prepare a little extra; what pastry is not used can be frozen.

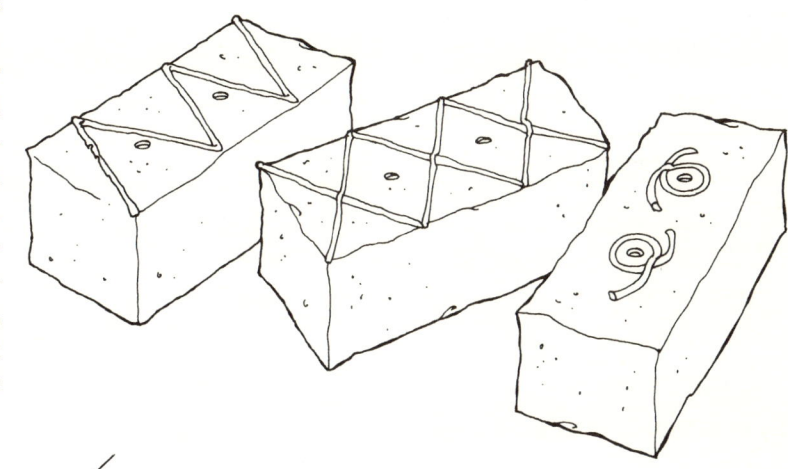

35. Cutouts: Circles, crescents, and leaves are cut from leftover pastry. Here the leaves are lightly scored with the tip of the knife to simulate their veins.

36. Scallops: Stamp pastry scalloped circles with a 1½- or 2-inch cookie cutter. Dip the back of a small chef's knife in flour; hold the wider section in place at the base of a scalloped round. Working from left to right, lift the knife up and down while moving across the circle to score the pastry with radiating lines. Always keep the hand at the base in place.

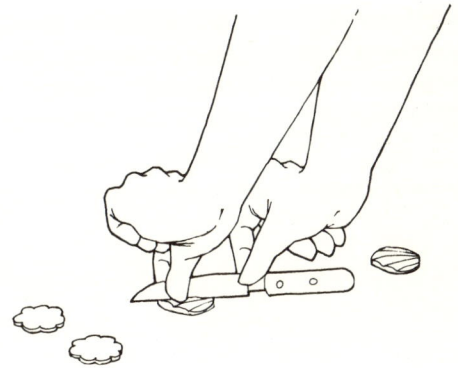

20 · PÂTÉ: THE NEW MAIN COURSE FOR THE '80s

The Variable Classic

There is no single correct dish for baking pâtés and terrines. Any baking dish can become a pâté or terrine mold—gratin dishes, glass loaf pans, soufflé dishes, pie pans, casseroles, even custard cups for individual servings.

CHAPTER THREE

Tips for Better Cooking

Lard or Butter Coating: A sleek topping for baked meat terrines can easily be achieved by pouring cooled melted lard or Clarified Butter (page 222) over the loaf. These fat toppings not only add a polished look, but preserve the terrine for as much as two weeks by sealing out air. Remove any bard or caul from the top of the terrine and wipe the surface. Slowly ladle the melted fat over the loaf, allowing it to seep all around it and to cover it by about ½-inch. Chill to set the lard or clarified butter, which will shrink slightly as it hardens. Add more melted fat to fill in any empty spaces and chill again. Refrigerate until needed.

Scales are vital in the kitchen of the pâté maker. Since the ideal proportions are twice as much lean meat as fat, including fatty coverings, only a scale ensures accuracy.

It is stated elsewhere, but bears repeating: Remove all membranes and gristles from meats before you grind them.

When chopping meat in a food processor, do not just turn on the switch and let it run. Use the on/off switch to chop the meat into small pieces. Continuous processing should be done only occasionally.

Thoroughly chill meats for grinding to minimize juice loss.

When dicing bacon, first freeze the slab for at least a half hour.

Pâtés must be covered with a coating of fat before baking. Choices are thin strips of fatback (bards), caul, or oil. I do not recommend bacon; for most pâtés its smoky flavor is too assertive.

Do as the professionals do, and wipe the edges of the pâté dish before baking. Once bits of meat have been baked onto the mold, they are hard to remove.

Use heavy-duty foil for covering baking molds.

Always taste hot stocks and sauces at a point where the liquid is bubbling. The bubbles push away floating fats so that the sample you get is clean and accurate in flavor.

If pressed for time and using canned chicken broth, improve its flavor by simmering it with a little onion, carrot, celery, parsley, and a pinch of thyme for about twenty minutes. A splash of white wine also helps.

Canned beef broth can similarly be improved in the way the chicken broth is above, but also add a small piece of bay leaf. Red or white wine can be used.

When using garlic, always remove the green sprout, with its bitter oils, from the center of the clove.

Several recipes call for one or two oil-packed anchovies. Transfer the remainder from the can to a small plastic container, and freeze it. Anchovies defrost quickly because of their oil and salt content.

Many cooks advise keeping on hand a pre-mixed combination of spices for seasoning pâtés. The French refer to this as *épices fines*. I much prefer to add herbs and spices individually, altering the proportions for different meats.

When substituting dried herbs for fresh, do so with some degree of caution. Most books instruct you to substitute one third the amount of dried for the fresh amount. You may find this too little since the strength of dried herbs varies from bottle to bottle and diminishes with shelf life. Often at least half the amount, if not more, is required. Beware of oregano, though; it becomes powerfully strong when dried.

When making fresh bread crumbs, simply rub the bread between the palms of your hands. No need to use a blender or food processor. Work over a sheet of wax paper or directly into the mixing bowl.

Egg whites keep indefinitely in the freezer. Store them in small jars or glasses (not plastic, which may have some fat clinging to it); then defrost as much or as little as you need. Two tablespoons equal one egg white.

Delicate, as well as acidic ingredients, can take on an unpleasant taste from iron or aluminum pots. For this reason a number of the recipes that follow will specify a nonreactive pot or pan, such as tin-lined copper, enameled, or stainless steel. Many new compound metal products now on the market are also suitable.

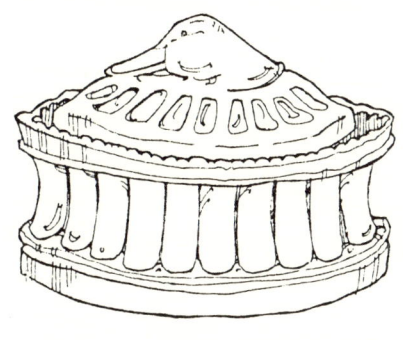

PART TWO

⇊

The Pâtés, Terrines, and Their Accompaniments

CHAPTER FOUR

The Menus and Recipes

The recipes in the twenty-five menus that follow are arranged in a different order than is usual. As mentioned earlier, the recipes within each menu are given in the order of advance preparation, but not by place in the meal. The recipes move from those that can or must be made several days before through to those that least tolerate standing.

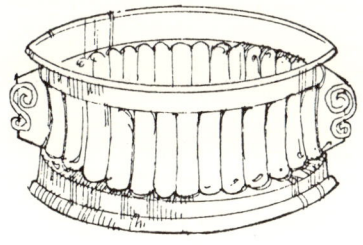

A Simple Dinner with International Flavors

SERVES 8

Le Tourin (Mild Onion Soup)

Meat Loaf Terrine

Red Rice Salad

Singapore String Beans

German Wine Pudding

This simple yet stylish menu would make a perfect Sunday midday meal or a dinner for friends who are interested in good, not fancy, food. A creamy hot onion soup is followed by the cold terrine with the rice salad. Flecks of red in the white rice add a bright note to the dish against the unadorned Meat Loaf Terrine. Green string beans come next as a separate course, but on the same plate. The meal ends on a soft note with a cool wine pudding. Even though this is a family-style meal, it has been planned to vary the colors of the dishes and follow hot with cold throughout. A chilled Beaujolais would be an ideal wine, as would a California rosé from either the Zinfandel or the Cabernet grape.

Meat Loaf Terrine

2½ pounds
calories per serving—371

As stated in Chapter One, if you can make a meat loaf, you can make a pâté. The recipes begin with this American classic to emphasize the point. As in all pâtés and terrines, the foundation is well-seasoned meat. The inclusion of layers of garnishes is pretty but not essential. In fact, France's beloved Pâté de Campagne is nothing but glorified meat loaf with a bit of alcohol usually thrown in. American cookbooks differ on whether meat loaf should be baked in a mold or not. For the purposes of this book the dish is necessary, as is the lid. The finished loaf will retain more moisture for being baked under wraps. Beef is often mixed with pork for meat loaf. If you elect to do that, do not add the oil to the meats.

Preheat oven to 350 degrees.

1. Use 2 teaspoons of the oil to grease a 6-cup loaf pan, approximately 9 × 5 × 3 inches. Put the meat in a mixing bowl. Add ¼ cup of the oil and all remaining ingredients except the eggs. Mix thoroughly with your hands; add the eggs, and mix again. Transfer the seasoned meat to the loaf pan, and pat to smooth the top. Smear the remaining teaspoon of oil over the top of the meat; cover, and bake for about 1 hour, or until a thermometer reaches 160 degrees.

2. To transform this meat loaf into a terrine, simply allow it to cool; then refrigerate it for 2 or 3 days. To achieve a better-cutting texture, place weights on it after it has cooled for 30 minutes.

⅓ cup oil
2 pounds ground beef
1 onion, chopped fine
⅓ cup parsley, chopped fine
2 garlic cloves, minced
½ cup bread crumbs
1⅓ cups Light Tomato Sauce (page 224), reduced by half
2 tablespoons prepared mustard
2 teaspoons Worcestershire sauce
salt and pepper
2 eggs beaten

↯↯↯

Le Tourin (Mild Onion Soup)

This is one version of a country soup from the Landes area in southwestern France. It is distinguished by a robust but still mild flavor. I have changed it by puréeing half the soup. This makes a creamier body and a more delicate appearance with just occasional strands of onions floating here and there. It definitely is not the country presentation.

1. Melt the fat in a large, heavy pot, and stir in the onions and garlic. Cover and simmer very slowly until completely soft and sweet, about 40 minutes. Stir from time to time, and do not allow the onions to brown.

2. Add the stock, water, salt, and pepper. Cover and simmer another 30 to 40 minutes. If you prefer, purée half the soup in a blender or food processor, and return it to the pot with the onion slices.

3. Just before serving, bring the Tourin back to a simmer. Beat together in a small bowl the egg and vinegar, remove the pot from the fire, and stir the egg into the hot soup, mixing vigorously to distribute the strands of cooked egg white.

4. Either ladle the soup into a soup tureen and serve it at the table, or fill individual soup bowls and garnish each with the optional toast slice. Serve at once.

Cooking Ahead: The basic Tourin can be prepared several days in advance and refrigerated. The egg-vinegar addition must be done at serving time.

- 2 tablespoons lard, olive oil, goose fat, or chicken fat
- 4 medium-large onions (about 1¾ pounds), sliced thin
- 6 garlic cloves, chopped fine
- 3 cups Chicken Stock (page 218)
- 6 cups water
- salt and pepper
- 1 egg
- 2 tablespoons vinegar

OPTIONAL:
- 8 slices French bread or other crusty loaf bread, toasted

Red Rice Salad

This rice salad is actually twice red—once from paprika and again from red pepper. It can also be served as a hot dish with many meats by substituting ¼ cup butter for the yogurt.

1 cup long-grain rice
2 cups hot water
¾ teaspoon paprika
¼ teaspoon rosemary
½ cup diced red pepper or pimiento
salt and pepper
¾ cup yogurt

1. Select a heavy pot with a tight-fitting lid, pour in enough oil to film the bottom generously, and place on medium heat. When the oil is hot, dump in the rice, and immediately begin stirring with a wooden spoon. Keep stirring until the translucent rice grains turn opaque white.

2. Add the water, paprika, rosemary, red pepper, salt, and pepper. When the water returns to the boil, place the pot on a flame deflector pad, turn the heat to low, cover the pot, and cook for 20 minutes without lifting the lid. (Once the water and seasonings have been added, the rice can also be cooked in a 350-degree oven for 20 minutes, again tightly covered.)

3. Remove the pot from the heat; let stand for 5 minutes; then fluff the rice with a fork. Do not stir with a spoon (this could cause lumps to form). Transfer rice to a bowl. Once it is cool, stir in the yogurt.

Cooking Ahead: The rice can be cooked 1 or 2 days in advance and refrigerated, but the yogurt should not be added until just before serving time.

German Wine Pudding

No need to worry about getting tipsy from wine pudding. As it cooks, alcohol burns off, alas, leaving just the flavor of the wine. Simple local wines are used in Germany, which means a wine that is fruity and slightly sweet. Imported Liebfraumilchs are suitable, as are California Chenin Blancs.

⅓ cup sugar
⅓ cup cornstarch
¾ cup milk
3 cups slightly sweet white wine
3 egg yolks

1. Put the sugar and cornstarch in a heavy nonreactive saucepot, and stir them together. Add the milk and wine while stirring with a wire whisk. Place the pot over very low heat, and slowly bring the liquid to the simmering point. Whisk often, but once it has begun to simmer, beat constantly until the sauce thickens. If there is any danger of cooking it too rapidly, place the pot on a heat-diffusing pad.

2. Put the egg yolks in a mixing bowl, and slowly pour the sauce over them while beating vigorously with the whisk. Return the sauce to the pot, and cook for 1 minute more, again whisking constantly. Do not allow it to boil.

3. Spoon the pudding into individual dessert dishes, preferably glass. Cover immediately with plastic wrap to prevent a crust from forming. Cool; then chill until ready to serve.

Singapore String Beans

A few Far Eastern spices turn ordinary string beans into a real palate cleanser. The heat of the chili peppers can be adjusted to your taste, but not so much that the dish loses all its fire.

1. Heat the oil in a large skillet; add the onions, garlic, lemon rind, and peppers; and sauté them for 2 to 3 minutes while stirring constantly.

2. Add the beans, and mix thoroughly to coat them with the aromatics and oil. Pour in the chicken stock, add the salt and sugar, cover, and cook for about 5 minutes, or until almost tender but not soft. A touch of crispness is essential to the character of this dish.

Cooking Ahead: Prepare the sauce, add the beans, and cook for only 2 or 3 minutes. Remove from the fire at once. The beans and their sauce can be refrigerated and then cooked until crisply tender just before serving.

¼ cup oil
½ cup chopped onions
1 garlic clove, minced
2 teaspoons grated lemon rind
½ teaspoon chopped jalapeño or dried chili peppers
1 pound string beans
¼ cup Chicken Stock (page 218)
1 teaspoon salt
pinch of sugar

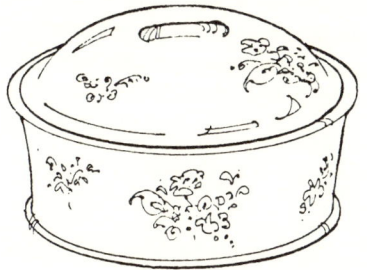

An Informal Gathering Featuring Hearty Food

SERVES 8 (pâté serves 12 to 15)

Steamed Soft-Shell Clams

Pâté de Campagne (Country Pâté)

Ginger-Baked Cranberries

Steamed Vegetable Pesto

Rosé Snow

This pâté is a large one, enough for twelve to fifteen main-course servings. All other recipes serve eight and could easily be doubled for a larger party. Since the pâté keeps so well, almost two weeks, one could also have two separate dinner parties. The menu has been tuned to the rustic style of the pâté, with Steamed Soft-Shell Clams first. The ginger-spiced cranberries stand up to the pungent pâté and provide an attractive deep red garnish on the plate. The medley of vegetables in pesto sauce, served as a separate hot course on the same plate, is surprisingly refreshing, despite the lusty sauce. Sparkling pink Rosé Snow is a treat anytime. For this menu a big, almost rugged wine, such as Zinfandel or a Côtes du Rhône, is needed.

Pâté de Campagne (Country Pâté)

5 pounds
calories per serving—471

This is standard restaurant, charcuterie, and home fare in France. It is as variable as meat loaf is here. Every cook has a special formula or ingredient that stamps it as her or his own. The meats are ground, mixed with lots of seasonings and some alcohol. Country Pâté begins to depart from meat loaf when it is enveloped in fat, in this case caul (see Chapter Two), though fatback bards (see Chapter Two) are sometimes used. Here the bards are used to create an attractive pattern on top.

Some recipes do not bake Country Pâté in a water bath; I prefer to. If it is baked without a bath, the edges of the terrine tend to become dry and crusty. I find the contrast between the dry top and moist sides desirable. Another departure is weighting the pâté. Since it's meant to be a rustic loaf, the coarser texture is acceptable. For better slicing, though, weighting, uneven though it is, becomes necessary.

Since Country Pâté keeps so well, almost two weeks, the recipe here is for a large one, providing lots of extra good eating.

1. Rinse the caul, and soak it in acidulated water (pg. 6). If salt pork is used, freeze it for about 15 minutes, cut into very thin slices, blanch for 2 minutes, and rinse under cold water.

2. Melt the butter in a skillet, and sauté the onion slowly until it is soft and translucent, about 10 minutes. Put all the ground meats into a large mixing bowl. Scrape in the sautéed onion, and add the alcohols and all other seasonings.

3. Tear the bread into pieces, rub them into crumbs, add to the meats, and mix well. Add the eggs, and mix again. Fry a spoonful of the mixture, taste for seasonings, and correct if necessary.

Preheat oven to 350 degrees.

4. Lift the caul out of the water, spread it on a towel, cover with another towel, and pat dry. Select a large 3-quart gratin dish, approximately 14×9×3 inches. Line the dish with the caul, letting all excess caul hang over the edges. Fill the dish with the forcemeat, mounding the center a little. Cut the fatback or salt pork into ½-inch-wide strips, and arrange them in a crisscross pattern over the meat. Place the bay leaves on top of the strips, pull up the extra caul, and stretch it over the

¼ pound caul
½ pound fatback or salt pork
¼ cup butter
1 large onion, chopped
2 pounds turkey breast, ground
2½ pounds fatty pork shoulder, ground
2 ounces cured prosciutto-style ham, ground
¼ cup brandy
⅓ cup whiskey
¼ teaspoon ginger
¼ teaspoon nutmeg
1 teaspoon sage
1 teaspoon thyme
½ teaspoon cayenne
¼ teaspoon allspice
5 or 6 garlic cloves, minced

forcemeat. Patch where necessary with extra pieces of caul. As the caul melts during the baking, any seams will disappear. Place in a water bath, and bake for about 1½ hours, or until a thermometer reaches 160 degrees.

4 slices white bread
3 eggs, beaten
2 bay leaves

5. Remove the pâté from the water bath, and allow it to cool for 30 minutes. Place aluminum foil over the surface, add a chopping board, and weight with cans or whatever. Because of the curved surface, you will not be able to weight the entire pâté. Cool and place the pâté in the refrigerator with the weights, if possible. Remove the weights after 6 hours or so, cover the pâté closely with foil or plastic wrap, and let it ripen for at least 4 days before serving.

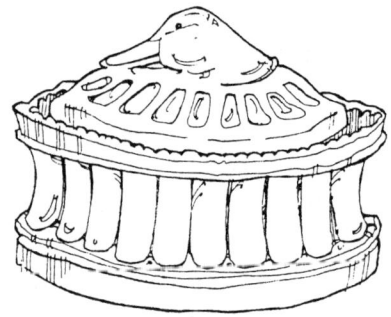

Ginger-Baked Cranberries

True, opening a can of cranberries is very fast. All you've given up for that convenience is the sharply crisp taste of fresh berries. Are four minutes too much to recapture it? That's all the time needed to put Ginger-Baked Cranberries together.

Makes about 2½ cups

Preheat oven to 375 degrees.

1. Rinse the berries, and place them in a single layer in a baking dish. Pick off any remaining woody stems. Sprinkle on the sugar, pour in the ginger ale, and mix all together with a spoon. Pat the berries back into a single layer, and tuck in the ginger slices. Cover the dish, and bake for about 20 minutes without stirring. Remove ginger slices, and chill.

2. To serve, spoon the berries into a bowl, and if desired, overlap several thin slices of oranges in the center.

4 cups (12 ounces) cranberries
¾ cup sugar
¾ cup ginger ale
4 or 5 thin ginger slices
OPTIONAL GARNISH:
orange slices

Rosé Snow

As pretty as rosé wine is in the glass, it is even more so as a frozen dessert when it takes on a rosy pink color that glistens with icy sparkles. Until recently I used French rosés. Now I find California's Zinfandel and Cabernet rosés eminently superior. These native wines have the color of a true rosé with no orange hue to it. I especially like the robust Zinfandel flavor, which gives character to a wine that too often these days has deteriorated to insipid pop.

To freeze sherbet in the freezer, most recipes specify ice cube trays. Since the object is to have a thin layer of the syrup so that it will freeze quickly, I find the broader surface of a cake pan better, and that is what is called for in the frozen ices in this book. Also, it is much easier to beat the slush in a round pan than an oblong tray. A real ice cream freezer, of course, is best of all.

1. In an uncovered 1-quart saucepot boil together the ½ cup sugar, ½ cup of the water, and salt for 3 minutes. Sprinkle the gelatin over the remaining ¼ cup water, and set aside to soften. Add the wine, nectar, lemon juice and softened gelatin to the hot syrup; stir to dissolve the gelatin. Cool for a few minutes; then taste for sweetness, add the extra tablespoon of sugar if needed, and stir to dissolve. Cool for 10 minutes, stir in the cassis, and let the mixture cool completely.

2. Pour the rosé syrup into an ice cream maker or into a 9-inch cake pan, and place it in the freezer. When ice crystals begin to form, beat with a wire whisk; then beat again one or two more times during the freezing process. Remove from the freezer about 15 minutes before serving.

½ cup plus optional 1 tablespoon sugar
¾ cup water
pinch of salt
1 tablespoon gelatin
1 bottle (3½ cups) slightly sweet rosé wine
½ cup fruit nectar—peach, apricot, mango, or papaya (not orange or apple)
1 tablespoon lemon juice
1 tablespoon crème de cassis

Steamed Vegetable Pesto

Food presented in puffed-up parchment paper is truly an impressive sight. It's fine for restaurants where a waiter transfers the cooked food from the package to a serving dish, a procedure not often done in private homes. Baking in aluminum foil is just as effective, if less showy, and that is the method recommended here. Since one doesn't eat from the foil either, it is suggested that the vegetable mélange be transferred to a serving bowl in the kitchen. By the way, one tends to call this a baking operation because of the dry oven heat. Since the vegetables actually steam inside the airtight package, that's what I call them. After all, it is steam that produces that parchment puff. Vary the vegetables as you like, always using those that cook in approximately the same length of time.

Preheat oven to 350 degrees.

1. Stir the pesto and chicken stock together until well blended. Cut the zucchini and celery into diagonal slices about ½ inch thick. Lay a large sheet of aluminum foil, about 20 inches long, on a baking sheet. With a spoon spread about half the pesto sauce on the center of the foil. Scatter the sliced vegetables and the tomatoes over the sauce, and dribble on the rest of the sauce.

⅓ cup Pesto (page 231)
½ cup Chicken Stock (page 218)
¾ pound zucchini
1½ celery ribs
16 cherry tomatoes

2. Carefully fold up the excess foil to make an airtight package, folding the seams over several times so they won't pull apart. Steam for about 30 minutes, or until the zucchini and celery are crisply tender. Transfer to a warm serving bowl, and spoon some of the juices from the package over the vegetables.

Cooking Ahead: The foil package can be made up several hours in advance, but the baking must be done just before serving. Put the baking sheet in the oven just before serving the main course. The steamed package can be held for 10 to 15 minutes in the oven with the heat turned off and the door slightly ajar.

Steamed Soft-Shell Clams

Few shellfish require as little preparation as clams. A quick scrub under running water is all the cook (or her five-year-old helper) need do; then a few minutes in the pot, and you are rewarded with one of America's great classic dishes: steamed clams. For this dish by all means buy soft-shell clams, also known as longnecks. They are much cheaper than hard-shell clams, remain luxuriously tender when properly cooked, and even come equipped with a little tail to accommodate easy finger eating.

1. Scrub the clams with a stiff brush under running water, and place them in a large pot. Discard any clams that remain open after tapping them. Sprinkle on the celery seed, and pour in the water. Place the pot on high heat, and as soon as the water comes to a boil, cover and steam it for about 4 or 5 minutes, or just until the shells open. Shake the pot once or twice during the cooking to turn the clams over and distribute them more evenly over the heat.

2. While the clams are cooking, preheat the clarified butter, allowing about ¼ cup per person. I like to add a little lemon juice to the butter, but it's strictly a matter of taste. If you prefer, lemon wedges may be passed at the table instead, thus leaving the decision up to the individual. For each diner you will need a deep bowl for the clams, one cup and saucer for the broth, and one small cup or custard cup on a saucer for the butter. Place a large bowl for shells in the center of the table.

3. With a perforated skimmer lift the clams out of the pot, and divide them among the bowls. Pour the clam broth from the pot into a warmed pitcher, leaving behind the sand that collects on the bottom. Pour the hot melted butter into the small cups, and take them and the clams to the table. Now pour the clam broth into their cups, again leaving behind the sand at the bottom. The sand falls to the bottom quickly, and the little bit of time spent serving the clams and butter is enough to clear the broth.

4 dozen (about 2½ pounds) soft-shell clams
¼ teaspoon celery seed
2 cups water
about 1 pound butter, clarified (page 222)
OPTIONAL:
1 lemon

4. To eat the clams, break off the shells and toss them into the discard bowl. Pull off the dark neck skin that covers the siphon (neck), and discard it. Hold the clam by the siphon, dip it in the clam broth to wash off any clinging sand, then into the butter, and finally pop it into an eager mouth. After the clams have been eaten, the broth makes a delicious drink, but again let it sit for a minute or so after the final clam rinsing, and do not drain the cup. Provide lots of paper napkins.

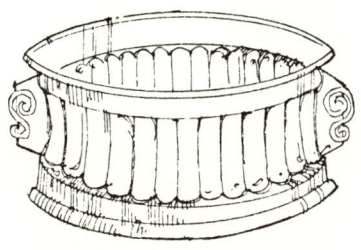

A Celebration of Delectable Delicacy

SERVES 8

Chou-fleur, Sauce Crevette
(Cauliflower with Shrimp Sauce)

Terrine Fine

Herbed Cucumbers

Peach Gratin

Subtlety is the hallmark of this menu. As robust as the Country Pâté in the previous menu is, this pale terrine is delicate. Yet the method of preparing them is precisely the same; only the mix of meats and seasonings has changed. The terrine is preceded by cauliflower bathed with a pale rosy shrimp sauce. Herb-flecked green-tinged cucumbers play nicely against the terrine and accent the green pistachios in the meat. A hot peach dessert completes the dinner, showing the only strong color of the menu. White wine, perhaps a California Chardonnay or a Mâcon-Villages, is the best choice here.

Terrine Fine

3 pounds
calories per serving—449

In French *fine* is pronounced "feen," which gives a nice alliteration to the title of an exceptionally subtle and complex terrine. The complexity is entirely limited to its flavor, not to preparation. In fact, for the cook this is a very simple terrine, nothing more than an intriguing combination of ground meats plus flavorings.

1. Trim the salt pork of any rind, rinse well, place in a pot, cover with cold water, and bring to a boil. Lower the heat, and simmer for 10 minutes; drain; rinse again. When it is cool, cut the pork into chunks.

2. Meanwhile, soak the sweetbreads in cold water for 15 minutes to remove excess blood. Change the water, if necessary, until it remains clear. Peel the membranes from the sweetbreads. Trim the pork shoulder, veal, and chicken livers of any gristle or membranes. Using a grinder or food processor, grind the meats separately in the order given in the ingredients list, beginning with the salt pork. After each processing, scrape the ground meat into a large mixing bowl. Finally, break the bread into pieces, and grind it into fine crumbs, adding it, too, to the mixing bowl.

3. To the meats add the shallots, brandy, sherry, thyme, allspice, mace, marjoram, coriander, salt, and pepper. Mix well to distribute all the flavorings, cover, and put aside for at least 4 hours at room temperature or overnight in the refrigerator.

Preheat oven to 350 degrees.

4. Beat the eggs and sour cream together; add to the meats, along with the pistachios; and again, mix well. Fry a small piece of the mixture, taste, and correct seasonings if necessary.

5. Oil a 1½-quart terrine or meat loaf pan, and pack the mixture into it, briskly tapping the mold on the counter several times. Cover with aluminum foil and lid, place in a water bath, and bake for about 1½ hours, or until a thermometer registers 160 degrees.

6. Lift the mold from the water bath, let it rest for 30 minutes, and weight it. When the mold is cool, refrigerate it overnight with the weights in place. Remove the weights, cover well, and refrigerate the terrine for 3 or 4 days before serving.

½ pound salt pork
½ pound sweetbreads
1 pound pork shoulder
½ pound veal
¼ pound chicken livers
1 slice white bread
2 tablespoons shallots, chopped
2 tablespoons brandy
2 tablespoons sherry
¼ teaspoon thyme
¼ teaspoon allspice
¼ teaspoon mace
¼ teaspoon marjoram
½ teaspoon ground coriander
2 teaspoons salt
½ teaspoon pepper
4 eggs
2 tablespoons sour cream
½ cup unsalted pistachios
1 teaspoon cooking oil

Herbed Cucumbers

For most of the year the long European-style cucumbers deliver more flesh and fewer seeds for the money than regular cucumbers. Either variety, though, marries well with a few herbs. Cutting the flesh with a melon ball scoop makes a prettier presentation, but alas, there is waste.

1. Bring at least 2 quarts of water to a boil, add a little salt, dump in the cucumbers, and cook for 3 to 4 minutes, or until the flesh turns slightly transparent and a sharp knife pierces a piece fairly easily. Do not overcook. Drain immediately, blanch in cold water, and drain well again.

2. About 30 minutes before serving, toss cucumbers with the tarragon, dill, salt, pepper, and oil. Transfer to a serving bowl, and garnish with the optional parsley sprigs.

Cooking Ahead: The cucumbers can be cooked a day in advance and refrigerated, but do not toss them with the seasonings. The cooked vegetable continues to exude water when left to stand, and this would dilute the dressing. When seasoning them at serving time, lift the cucumbers from the storage bowl to another bowl, thus leaving behind any collected liquid.

5 or 6 regular cucumbers or 1½ long cucumbers, enough for 4 cups of seedless ½-inch pieces
2 teaspoons tarragon
1 tablespoon dill
pepper
3 tablespoons oil
OPTIONAL:
a few parsley sprigs

Chou-fleur, Sauce Crevette
(Cauliflower with Shrimp Sauce)

Given the fanciful price of shrimp these days, one needs recipes that make much of a little bit. This recipe is an eminently successful one, for more than just its economy. The presentation of the mound of cauliflower covered with a rosy shrimp sauce immediately announces that this is something special. Another way to save money on the dish is to use rock shrimp, which are deliciously sweet. My supermarket has two-pound boxes of frozen rock shrimp for a third less than the price of a single pound of the regular crustacean, which is also usually frozen before the fishmonger defrosts it. Handle rock shrimp carefully; the shells are prickly, so cut them heedfully. The vein contains sand, pull it away, and rinse the shrimp well. The flesh cooks almost instantly, so don't let it linger in the pot. Cauliflower heads are not large enough to serve eight as a first course, so two medium heads are called for. If you will be only six at the table, one large head should do.

1. Bring a large quantity of water to a boil, and add the salt. Meanwhile, wash the cauliflowers, cut away all the green leaves, and cook until tender, about 7 minutes once the water has returned to a boil. Drain very well, but cover to keep warm.

2. Meanwhile, melt the butter in a heavy saucepot, stir in the flour, and cook together for 2 minutes. Slowly pour in the cream while stirring with a wire whisk. Add all remaining sauce ingredients except the shrimp. Taste for seasoning, and correct if necessary. Simmer the sauce for 5 minutes. Cut the shrimp into pieces about ¼ inch thick, reserving 4 whole ones for garnish, and add the pieces to the sauce just before serving.

3. Place the cauliflower heads in two serving bowls, spoon some of the hot shrimp sauce over the top, lightly sprinkle with paprika, and garnish with the reserved shrimp. Pour the rest of the sauce into a sauceboat, and pass separately. Provide two large spoons for serving.

Cooking Ahead: The sauce can be prepared a day in advance and refrigerated, but the shrimp should not be incorporated until serving time. If need be, the cauliflower can be cooked several hours in advance and kept tightly covered at room temperature. It can be reheated in boiling water for a few minutes or sprinkled with water, covered, and placed in a 375-degree oven for about 8 minutes.

1 teaspoon salt
2 medium heads cauliflower

SAUCE:
   3 tablespoons butter
   2 tablespoons flour
   2 cups cream
   2 teaspoons anchovy paste
   2 tablespoons tomato paste
   2 tablespoons sherry
juice of ½ lemon
⅛ teaspoon Tabasco
good pinch of freshly grated nutmeg
salt
   12 ounces cooked, deveined shrimp
paprika

Peach Gratin

Baked fruit desserts have at least one advantage over many others. Though fruit is superb when at its peak season and sweetness, less accommodating examples are infinitely helped by the addition of other flavorings that penetrate the flesh in the heat of the oven. Orange juice is added to the Caramel Sauce here because its citrusy aroma marries so well with peaches.

Preheat oven to 300 degrees.

1. Pour the Caramel Sauce into a small pot; add the orange juice, kirsch, and brown sugar; and bring to a simmer to blend all the ingredients and dissolve the sugar.

2. Bring a pot of water to a boil; two or three at a time, plunge the peaches in for a few seconds, longer if they are very firm. Remove with a skimmer, cool, and slip off the skins. Cut the peaches in half, remove the stones, and place the fruit halves, rounded sides up, in a baking dish that will hold them in one layer. Pour sauce over the peaches, and bake, uncovered, for about 15 minutes, basting one or two times.

3. Preheat the broiler, baste the fruit again, and broil for about 1 minute, or until the peaches are lightly caramelized.

Cooking Ahead: The gratin dish can be prepared in advance if the sauce is cooled and poured over the peaches and if each half is turned over one or two times to coat it completely with the sauce. The sugary caramel and the acidic orange juice will seal the fruit from contact with the air and prevent it from turning brown. Cover and refrigerate for 2 to 3 hours. Allow an extra 5 minutes' baking time if the dish is not brought back to room temperature before being baked.

1½ cups Caramel Sauce (page 233)
½ cup orange juice
2 tablespoons kirsch
¼ cup dark brown sugar
8 peaches

Dinner à la Française

SERVES 8

Onion Compote

Terrine de Foies de Volaille aux Épinards et Herbes
(Terrine of Chicken Livers with Spinach and Herbs)

Marinated Red Pepper Strips

Hot Banana Puffs

There is a nice progression of color and flavor change in this menu. Red tomatoes and green parsley lace the creamy sauce that holds tiny onions—a deliciously mild and unusual first course. The terrine brings a more emphatic flavor, as do the bright red pepper strips. We return to a soft note for dessert. One red wine, especially a Beaujolais-Villages or a light red from the Loire Valley, such as a Chinon or Bourgueil, can see the menu through.

Terrine de Foies de Volaille aux Épinards et Herbes (Chicken Liver Terrine with Spinach and Herbs)

3½ pounds
calories per serving—319

This recipe introduces layers into the terrine to reveal an attractive interior when sliced. Making the basic forcemeat is the same principle as for the preceding recipes. The flavor of this loaf is less robust than that of Country Pâté and hints at what subtleties can be incorporated in making pâtés and terrines. The forcemeat is flecked with the green of spinach and parsley, a compatible background for the spinach stripe and the nuggets of chicken livers.

1. Pick over the chicken livers, place in a small bowl, and sprinkle with salt, pepper, and allspice. Pour over just enough alcohols barely to cover the livers; cover and let stand for 3 hours or overnight.

Preheat oven to 375 degrees.

2. Wash and blanch spinach, or steam in a pressure cooker for 5 seconds. Drain, squeeze dry, and chop coarsely.

3. In a grinder or a food processor, grind the onion chunks, and scrape them into a large mixing bowl; add the garlic. Reserve 5 or 6 chicken livers; lift the rest out of the marinade; grind and add them to bowl. Next chop the ham, pork, parsley, and bread in that order, and add to bowl. Pour the marinade into a small skillet, reduce by half, and scrape into the bowl. Add all seasonings and half the chopped spinach. Mix well with your hands, and fry a teaspoonful of the mixture; let it cool, and taste for seasonings; correct if necessary. Add the egg, and mix again.

4. Oil an 8-cup pâté mold. Scoop in half the mixture, and pat it smoothly into the mold. Scatter the reserved chopped spinach over the forcemeat. Make another layer of a little less than half the remaining forcemeat, and scatter the reserved chicken livers over it. Finally scrape in the remaining forcemeat, and smooth the top. Tap the mold sharply a few times on the counter to settle the mass well into the mold. Oil the top, and

1 pound chicken livers
salt and pepper
¼ teaspoon allspice
Madeira and brandy
1 pound fresh spinach
1 medium onion, cut into chunks
2 garlic cloves, minced
¾ pound cured prosciutto-style ham
1¼ pounds fatty pork shoulder
1 cup parsley leaves
1 thin slice white bread
1 teaspoon tarragon
½ teaspoon allspice
½ teaspoon rosemary
good pinch of nutmeg
¼ teaspoon cayenne
1 egg, beaten
oil
bay leaves
OPTIONAL:
8 to 10 spinach leaves and beef aspic (page 222) for decoration

press a few bay leaves into the surface. Cover first with foil, then with a lid, poking a hole through the lid vent. Place the mold in a pan of water that reaches at least a depth of two-thirds of the mold. Bake for 1½ to 1¾ hours, or until the thermometer registers 160 degrees.

5. Remove the mold from the pan of water, and cool it for about 30 minutes. Place weights on top of the terrine, and cool completely. Refrigerate overnight with weights in place. Remove the weights the next day, cover the terrine closely, and refrigerate for 3 or 4 days before serving.

Optional Decoration

Brush on one or two layers of Madeira-flavored beef aspic after removing the bay leaves. Chill well between layers. Blanch the spinach leaves, dry well, and spread over the top of the pâté. Continue brushing with aspic, and chilling, until a nice shiny coating has been achieved (page 17).

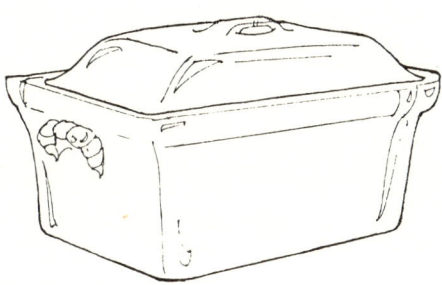

Marinated Red Pepper Strips

Even the slightest cooking seems to give red peppers a stronger flavor. That more assertive character is definitely what is needed here. Broiling peppers accomplishes two things: It softens the flesh, and it chars the skin. Once the skin is blackened, it peels off quite easily. Whenever cooking with red peppers, always take a few minutes to peel them since failing to do so toughens the skin, making them unpleasant to eat.

Makes 3 cups

1. Place the peppers in a baking dish, and broil until all surfaces are blackened. This charring can also be done over an open flame at the stove. Tongs are ideal for turning peppers since they can grasp the stems. Place the charred peppers in a paper bag, close, and put aside for at least 10 minutes to allow the steam time to soften the skins. With a small knife, peel off the skins; then pull out the stem, seeds, and membranes, and discard. Cut the peppers into strips about ¼ inch wide.

2. Put the stock, olive oil, 1 tablespoon of the basil, salt, and pepper in a pot, and bring to a boil. Add the pepper strips, cover, reduce the heat, and simmer for 5 minutes. Immediately remove the peppers and sauce to a bowl, cool, and chill.

3. Remove the bowl from the refrigerator at least 2 hours before serving time. With a slotted spoon, lift the peppers out of the sauce, and place them in a serving dish. Sprinkle with additional chopped basil, if desired.

Cooking Ahead: The red peppers should marinate in the sauce for at least 1 day; 2 days are better.

6 red peppers
½ cup Chicken Stock (page 218)
2 tablespoons olive oil
1 or 2 tablespoons chopped basil
salt and pepper

Onion Compote

This vegetable compote is best with tiny pearl onions. Though boiling onions, cut in half, can be substituted if need be, regular yellow onions cannot because they are too strong. Another substitution that cannot be made is canned tomatoes for fresh. The bright look of the compote depends on those definable pieces of red. When the only kind of tomato available is perfectly round and perfectly tasteless, use it nevertheless, but add a teaspoon of tomato paste to the sauce.

1. A few at a time, plunge the tomatoes into boiling water for a few seconds, remove, cool, and peel. Cut the tomatoes in half, and gently squeeze out the seeds and juice. Chop the flesh into ½-inch pieces, and put them in a saucepot that can hold all the ingredients.

2. Pour the onions into the boiling water, cook for 3 minutes, drain, and cool under cold running water. Cut off the root end, and gently squeeze from the stem end to pop the onion out of its skin. Since onions are not of uniform size and thus are not boiled to the same degree, some will need help with a paring knife to remove the skin. Add the onions to the pot.

3. Pour in the wine, and season the sauce with the garlic, mint, sugar, salt, and pepper. Bring the wine to a simmer, cover, and cook over low heat for about 15 minutes, or until the onions are soft when pierced with a small, sharp knife. Boiling onions will take about 5 minutes longer.

4. Add the sliced mushrooms, cover, and cook for 3 minutes. Pour in the cream, and simmer for 2 minutes, uncovered. Remove the pot from the heat, and stir in three-fourths of the chopped parsley.

5. Spoon the compote into consommé cups, small bowls, or regular cups, and sprinkle with the remaining parsley.

Cooking Ahead: Onion Compote can be prepared a day in advance without the final additions of mushrooms and cream. Reheat just before serving time, and finish the dish.

6 tomatoes (about 1½ pounds)
3 cups (about 12 ounces) pearl onions
¾ cup white wine
3 garlic cloves, minced
2 tablespoons chopped mint
½ teaspoon sugar
salt and pepper
¾ pound mushrooms, sliced
¾ cup light cream
1 cup chopped parsley leaves

Hot Banana Puffs

Puréed banana is only slightly puffed in this dessert. Still, like a temperamental soufflé, once baked, it cannot wait. Light Chocolate Sauce obligingly masks any wrinkles. The dessert is put together quickly, and the baking is fast, so prepare the puffs just before removing the main course dishes. Lacking proper-sized baking cups, use foil baking cups, serving one or two per person, depending on size.

Preheat oven to 375 degrees.

1. In a blender or, preferably, a food processor, purée the bananas, 2 tablespoons of the sugar, rum, cinnamon, and vanilla. Scrape into a mixing bowl.

2. Beat the egg whites to the foamy stage, add a large pinch of cream of tartar, and beat until very firm, gradually incorporating the remaining 2 tablespoons sugar. Scoop about one-third of the beaten whites over the banana purée, and fold in thoroughly with a wire whisk. Add the rest of the beaten whites, and delicately fold in with a rubber spatula until well mixed; but do not overwork and deflate the whites.

3. Completely fill ½-cup baking cups, and smooth the top. Bake for 10 to 12 minutes, or until nicely puffed and slightly firm to the touch. Serve at once with Light Chocolate Sauce.

Cooking Ahead: The bananas can be puréed, tightly covered, and refrigerated several hours in advance. The rest of the recipe must be done at serving time.

4 bananas
¼ cup sugar
3 tablespoons rum
¼ teaspoon cinnamon
2 teaspoons vanilla
3 egg whites
cream of tartar
Light Chocolate Sauce (page 232), at room temperature

↓↓↓

An Adventurous Medley

SERVES 8

Gratinéed Mussels with Saffron Sauce

Lasagna Pâté

Spaghetti Squash Salad

Apple Gratin

Here is a small United Nations of a menu, though this one works together harmoniously, unlike the real one. A sauce of Swedish inspiration covers the mussels steamed in the French manner; Italy donates the lasagna striping the pâté, as well as the flavorings for the spaghetti squash; and from America is an old-fashioned hot apple dessert. If we could discover where spaghetti squash had its real origins, there might be still another country to include. The main-course plate has remarkable eye appeal. The pâté contrasts pale green lasagna and pink meats and is accompanied by spaghetti squash of an intense orangy hue. The wine selection can come from Italy—Chianti Classico—or California—Barbera.

Lasagna Pâté

3¼ pounds
calories per serving—290

Not all attractive pâté patterns are made with meats, as a number of recipes in this book demonstrate. In this case, green spinach lasagna is used to stand out in relief against the rosy meats. The color of the forcemeat is attenuated by poultry and sour cream, while chopped pimiento and basil add the final fillip. This is a fast-preparation pâté since no marinating is called for. Do not feel locked into using the two lean meats indicated below. I've also used turkey and tongue, and chicken and chicken livers are just another possibility. Only the ground pork remains constant. Do try to use fresh pasta. I've tried packaged varieties and find they become somewhat tough, especially spinach pasta, which manufacturers usually make with whole-grain wheat. Packaged plain lasagna is better. If you must use boxed lasagna, don't fret. The final product will be good, just not as smooth in texture as fresh.

Preheat oven to 350 degrees.

1. Bring a large pot of water to a boil; add a little oil and salt and the lasagna. Add the pasta gradually to maintain the boiling point. Cook for about 3 minutes for fresh pasta, 15 minutes for packaged. Do not overcook; the lasagna must be *al dente* (to the tooth) or give a hint of resistance when bitten. Drain at once, and cool under cold running water. Stretch the lasagna on towels, and pat dry.

2. While the lasagna is cooking, put the pork, chicken, ham, and bread into the container of a food processor, and chop into pieces by using the on/off button. Add the mace, cayenne, salt, and pepper, and process until chopped into small pieces. In a small bowl heat together the sour cream with 1 egg, the brandy, and Madeira. With the motor running, add the cream mixture to the meats, and process until very smooth and like a thick purée. Add the basil and pimiento, and process very briefly, just enough to incorporate them into the forcemeat.

3. Generously oil a 6-cup loaf dish (about 8×5×3 inches). Place a piece of wax paper on the bottom, and oil it as well. Beat the remaining egg in a small bowl or cup, and keep it and a pastry brush handy on the counter. Make a layer of the lasagna, using one-third of the cooked amount. Brush the pasta

oil
salt
½ pound spinach lasagna
¾ pound fatty pork, cut into 1-inch pieces
½ pound chicken meat, preferably breast, cut into 1-inch pieces
½ pound lightly smoked ham, cut into 1-inch pieces
2 slices white bread, crusts removed, torn into pieces
½ teaspoon ground mace
cayenne
pepper
¾ cup sour cream
2 eggs
3 tablespoons brandy

with the beaten egg; then spoon in half the forcemeat, and brush it with the egg. Make another layer of lasagna, using about half the remaining amount; leave the nicest pieces for the top layer; patching doesn't matter in the center. Brush again with the egg, cover with the rest of the forcemeat, and brush with egg. Make the final layer of lasagna, and generously brush it with oil.

2 tablespoons Madeira or port
½ cup fresh basil, chopped
¼ cup (2 ounces) chopped pimiento

4. Cover the dish, place it in a water bath, and bake for about 50 minutes, or until a thermometer reaches 160 degrees. Remove the dish from the water bath; cool it for 30 minutes; then weight the pâté. When it is cool, refrigerate the pâté overnight with the weights in place. Remove the weights the next day, cover the pâté well, and refrigerate for at least 3 days before serving.

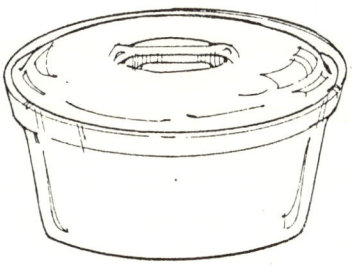

Spaghetti Squash Salad

This cold garnish is cooked exactly as for Cocktailed Spaghetti Squash (page 168). Here, however, the dish is served cold instead of hot and, before serving, is given a final moistening of olive oil and sprinkling of basil.

Cook the squash according to the directions on page 168, including mixing the squash strands with the reduced juice. Cool. Just before serving, toss with the olive oil and basil.

Cooking Ahead: The spaghetti squash can be prepared the day before and refrigerated. Remove from the refrigerator at least 2 hours before serving, and toss with oil and herbs about an hour before serving.

- 2- to 2½ pound spaghetti squash
- 2 cups vegetable cocktail juice
- Tabasco
- salt and pepper
- 3 tablespoons olive oil
- ¼ cup basil, chopped, or 2 tablespoons dried basil mixed with 2 tablespoons chopped parsley

↡↡↡

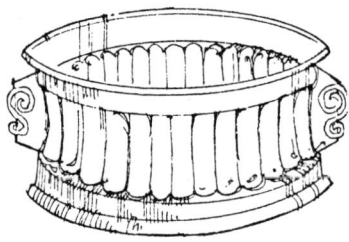

Gratinéed Mussels with Saffron Sauce

There is no end of ways to capitalize on the sweet flesh of mussels. This combination, with musky saffron flavor, is as appealing as it is unusual. If broiling space for all the mussel shells is a problem, scallop shells can be used for individual servings instead.

1. In a large pot combine the water, onion, parsley, carrot, salt, pepper, and lemon juice. Cover and bring to a boil; then simmer for 15 minutes.

2. Scrub the mussels, pulling off any beards that cling to them. If any mussels are open a little, tap them sharply on the counter; if they don't close, discard them. Also be suspicious of any unusually heavy specimens, which may be full of sand and no mussels. Slide the two halves between your fingers; they will come apart if there is no mussel inside. Rinse well under cold running water, and plunge briefly into a bowl of cold water while rubbing them against each other vigorously. Do not let them soak, or they will lose their sea-water juices.

3. Add the wine to the cooking broth, bring to a fast boil, and add the mussels. Cover tightly, keep on high heat, and shake the pot once or twice during cooking to mix up the mussels. (If the pot is too large or heavy to shake easily, just stir the mussels quickly with a large spoon.) As soon as the mussels have opened (about 5 minutes), they are cooked. Transfer the mussels to a bowl.

4. When it is cool enough to handle, pull off and discard one shell, leaving the mussel on the other shell. For better presentation, pull off the dark loose band of flesh around each mussel; this is optional but preferable.

5. Preheat the boiler. Spoon about ½ tablespoon of Örebro Saffron Sauce over each mussel, and place on a jelly roll pan. A baking sheet is not advisable since some juices may overflow from the mussels. Broil for about ½ minute, or just until the sauce is hot and bubbly. Use tongs to transfer the mussels to

1 cup water
1 small onion, chopped fine
4 or 5 parsley sprigs
½ carrot, diced
½ teaspoon salt
¼ teaspoon pepper
juice of ½ lemon
4 dozen mussels
1 cup white wine
1½ cups Örebro Saffron Sauce (page 225)

individual plates, and serve at once. Follow the same procedure if scallop shells are used.

Cooking Ahead: The mussels can be cooked 1 or 2 days in advance. Remove them completely from the shells, and place in a plastic container. Once the cooking broth is cool, decant it carefully to leave behind the sand at the bottom. Pour the broth over the mussels, cover tightly, and refrigerate. Reserve half the shells in a plastic bag, and refrigerate. The sauce must be made just before using.

Apple Gratin

Lemon rind is a wonderful flavoring agent for everything from cold soups to hot desserts. Have you ever noticed the oils that shoot into a martini when lemon peel is twisted over it? Watch what those oils do for apples.

Preheat oven to 325 degrees.

1. Chill beaters and a bowl for whipping the cream. Butter an 8-cup soufflé or similar baking dish. Peel the apples, quarter them, remove the cores, and slice thin.

2. With a swivel-bladed vegetable peeler, remove the rind from the lemon; chop it fine. Put one-third of the apples in the baking dish; then sprinkle them with one-third of the lemon peel, 2 teaspoons of the brown sugar, and 1 tablespoon of the liqueur. Repeat two more times.

3. Cover the dish closely with aluminum foil, and bake it for about 1¼ hours. The apples will be soft but still maintain their shape. Sprinkle 3 or 4 tablespoons of brown sugar over the top, enough to make a thin layer. The apples will have sunk into the dish, but it doesn't matter. Broil the sugar coating for 1 or 2 minutes or until it is hot and bubbly. Let it stand for 10 minutes before serving.

4. While the apples are baking, whip the cream, using the chilled bowl and beaters. Once the cream is thick, add the powdered sugar, and continue beating until it is very thick. Add the vanilla, and beat for another 10 seconds. Scoop the whipped cream into a serving bowl.

5. Spoon Apple Gratin onto serving dishes, and pass the whipped cream separately.

Cooking Ahead: The apples can be baked several hours in advance and kept at room temperature. The final gratinéeing should be done at serving time. Depending on the quality of the whipping cream, once beaten, it can stand from 30 minutes to several hours. Cream that has not been ultrapasteurized is more stable than that which has been and will not weep when standing. This cream can be bought in health food shops.

1 tablespoon butter
3 pounds (about 12 or 13) apples, preferably Stayman, York, or Rome Beauty
1 lemon
5 to 6 tablespoons brown sugar
3 tablespoons orange liqueur
1 cup heavy cream
1 tablespoon powdered sugar
1 teaspoon vanilla

⇊⇊⇊

Smoothly Sophisticated

SERVES 8

Snails on Toast

*Pâté de Ris de Veau aux Épinards
(Sweetbread Pâté with Spinach)*

Carrot-Pear Purée

Snow Peas with Red Peppers

Crown of Cognac Cream

In planning a menu around the Sweetbread Pâté, it seemed appropriate to give it some sophistication. Snails certainly do that, as does the molded cognac cream dessert. For the main-course plate, the pale green-flecked pâté is beautifully set off by the orange-colored purée. The hot snow peas and red peppers, served on the same dish, come next as a separate course. Nowhere in the menu is the basic color repeated, and there also is a pleasing taste rhythm from somewhat garlicky to mild to snappy and to a final note that is rich and suave. A white or light red wine could be served throughout. A California Chardonnay or a Burgundy would be excellent choices for white; cool Beaujolais for the red. If two wines are desired, the same whites could be served with the snails, and a small Bordeaux red for the rest of the meal.

Pâté de Ris de Veau aux Épinards
(Sweetbread Pâté with Spinach)

3 pounds
calories per serving—325

The delicacy of sweetbreads, in both flavor and texture, is the hallmark of this pâté. Brains, which are similar, could be substituted. The pâté forcemeat is flecked with spinach, providing the perfect framework for whole sweetbread morsels. If you would like to embellish the picture, buy some extra spinach and blanch it. Use the spinach leaves for wrapping the whole sweetbreads before layering them into the forcemeat.

1. Place the sweetbreads in a bowl, cover with cold water, add the lemon juice, and soak for 1 hour. Change the water one or two times, or until the water remains clear. Place the sweetbreads in a nonreactive pan, cover with fresh cold water, bring to a boil over medium heat, reduce the heat, and simmer gently for 5 minutes. Pour out the water; place the pan under cold running water until the sweetbreads are cool enough to handle. Peel off the outer membrane with your fingers, and trim off any dark spots. Reserve about one-third of the sweetbreads, and roll the remaining two-thirds in a towel. Place a chopping board over the sweetbreads, and weight them with cans or a heavy pot. The weighting helps firm the flesh of the sweetbreads, making them easier to slice. Leave the weights in place for at least 3 hours or overnight in the refrigerator.

Preheat oven to 350 degrees.

2. Clean and blanch the spinach, cool in cold water, and squeeze out all the liquid; if using defrosted frozen spinach, simply squeeze out the juice, and do not cook. Chop the spinach.

3. Cut the reserved unweighted sweetbreads into 1-inch pieces, place in the container of a food processor, add the ground veal and pork, and process until all the meats are thoroughly combined and very smooth. Transfer the meats to a large mixing bowl. Cut the fatback into 1-inch pieces, place in the food processor; add the onion, coriander, nutmeg, allspice, tarragon, cayenne, salt, and pepper; and process until chopped into coarse pieces. Beat the egg and cream together, and with the

1 pound sweetbreads
1 tablespoon lemon juice
1 pound fresh spinach or 10-ounce package frozen spinach, defrosted
1 pound lean veal, ground
¾ pound lean pork, ground
½ pound fatback
1 small onion, quartered
½ teaspoon ground coriander
½ teaspoon nutmeg
½ teaspoon allspice
1 teaspoon tarragon
⅓ teaspoon cayenne
salt
1 teaspoon pepper
1 egg
¼ cup heavy cream
2 tablespoons brandy
3 tablespoons port or Madeira
oil
1 bay leaf

motor running, add to the bowl. Process until very smooth. Scrape the fatback mixture into the bowl with the other meats.

4. Add the spinach plus the brandy and 2 tablespoons of the port to the meats. With your hands, mix all the meats and flavorings until well blended. Fry a small piece of the forcemeat, cool, taste, and correct if necessary.

5. Oil a 6-cup mold, scoop in one-half of the forcemeat, and pat into a smooth layer. Tap the mold sharply on the counter. Arrange one or two rows of the weighted sweetbreads down the center of the dish, and lightly press them into the forcemeat. Cover the sweetbreads with the remaining forcemeat and smooth the surface. Give the dish several sharp taps.

6. Oil the top layer, press in the bay leaf, and sprinkle the remaining tablespoon of port over the surface. Cover the dish, place in a water bath, and bake for about 1½ hours, or until a thermometer registers 160 degrees. Lift the mold from the water bath, let it rest for 30 minutes, and weight it. When the mold is cool, refrigerate it overnight with the weights in place. Remove the weights, cover well, and refrigerate for 3 or 4 days before serving.

↡↡↡

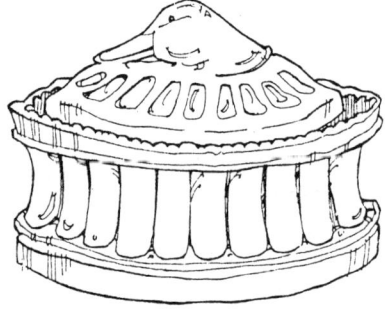

Carrot-Pear Purée

Purées serve a very special role at the table. They are the perfect answer when the menu does not really call for a vegetable, yet some sort of garnish is desirable. Often, as in this case, they can add a strong color note to the dinner plate, enlivening even a dull-looking pâté. The fact that they also are delicious makes them about indispensable. This is an especially intriguing version since the vivid orange color of the carrot disguises the fact that it embraces a flowery pear undertone.

I strongly suggest giving some thought to the presentation of this or any other purée. As good as they are to eat, since they have no form, they just don't look like much in a plain bowl. Try to select a particularly attractive and colorful bowl. Lacking one, you can line a simple bowl with vegetable leaves. I've used red cabbage leaves inside a white bowl to hold this orange-colored purée. These same leaves would also set off white purées to good advantage. Dark green lettuce leaves are another possibility.

Makes 3 cups

pinch of salt
½ teaspoon sugar
1½ pounds (about 6 or 8) carrots
½ cup heavy cream
¼ teaspoon ground coriander
2 medium (about 12 ounces; half the weight of the carrots) pears

1. So that the cooking and reheating can be done in the single utensil, select a 1- or 1½-quart enamel pot. Boil together 3 or 4 cups of water with the salt and sugar. Meanwhile, peel the carrots, and cut them into 1-inch pieces. Add the carrots to the boiling water, and cook until tender, 15 to 20 minutes depending on the age of the vegetable.

2. While the carrots are cooking, measure the cream and coriander directly into the blender. Just before the carrots have finished cooking, peel the pears, then quarter and core them.

3. Lift the carrots out of the water with a perforated skimmer, and transfer them to the blender. Add the pear quarters to the water, and boil them for 2 or 3 minutes, or until barely cooked at all (they should retain a bit of crispness). Lift the pears out with the skimmer, and add to the blender. Reserve the cooking water for the time being. Purée the carrots and pears until smooth. If the mixture seems a little thick, add some of the cooking water, a tablespoon at a time until the desired consistency is reached.

4. Pour out the remaining cooking water, and scrape the purée back into the pot. Reheat over low fire, for a few minutes; then cool.

Cooking Ahead: Carrot-Pear Purée can be made several days in advance, covered tightly, and refrigerated. Bring it back to room temperature before serving.

Crown of Cognac Cream

Because of its delicate flavor, this molded cognac cream is best served unadorned. Fresh sliced fruit, such as strawberries or peaches, could be spooned over the dessert, but that destroys the subtlety of the cream. For decorative purposes, the center can be filled with a bunch of grapes or whole strawberries, or if you are lucky enough to have a small bowl that fits the space, fill it with cookies. Great cognac is not necessary, but a good quality is.

1¼ cups milk
1⅓ tablespoons gelatin
2 egg yolks
6 tablespoons sugar
⅓ cup cognac
1 teaspoon vanilla
¾ cup heavy cream
oil

1. Chill a bowl and beaters for whipping the cream. Pour ½ cup of the milk into a small cup, sprinkle on the gelatin, and put aside to soften. Pour the remaining milk into a nonreactive pot, and bring to the boiling point.

2. Meanwhile, beat the egg yolks and sugar together in a mixing bowl until light and frothy. Pour the hot milk over the egg-sugar mixture while whisking vigorously. Return the hot milk mixture to the pot, place on a low fire, and cook while whisking constantly until the sauce thickens enough to coat a spoon. Remove the pot from the heat, add the gelatin, and stir until it dissolves. Add the cognac and vanilla. Cool the sauce; then refrigerate until it thickens to a syrupy consistency. Beat with a whisk from time to time.

3. Whip the cream, using the chilled bowl and beaters. Beat the thickened cognac sauce with the wire whisk, add about one-third of the whipped cream to it, and blend in thoroughly with the whisk. Add the remaining whipped cream, and lightly fold it into the cognac sauce with a rubber spatula.

4. Lightly oil a 6- or 7-cup ring mold, and spoon in the cognac cream. Refrigerate for at least 4 hours, or until the mixture has set.

5. To serve, dip the ring mold into hot water for a few seconds, then unmold it onto a chilled serving dish.

Cooking Ahead: Crown of Cognac Cream can be made a day in advance, well covered with plastic wrap, and refrigerated.

⇊⇊⇊

Snails on Toast

Tradition demands laboriously twisting snails back into their shells so that after being cooked they can be pulled out again—usually with great difficulty, not to mention butter splattering. Since few private kitchens are equipped with all the utensils necessary for correct serving of snails, I tried another route with these plump morsels; sautéed in garlic butter and served on toast which becomes deliciously soaked with the sauce.

1. Cream together the soft butter and seasonings. Refrigerate or freeze until needed.

2. Drain the snails, place in a sieve, and rinse under cold running water. Shake the sieve to remove excess water. Meanwhile heat about 3 tablespoons of the snail butter in a large, heavy skillet. When it is quite hot, add the snails, and using a wooden spoon, turn them over a few times. Add butter if the pan seems dry, and keep the flame moderately high. Cover the skillet, and simmer the snails for about ½ minute while placing the toast on individual plates. Place 5 snails on each slice of toast. (In all, the snails will cook no more than 2 minutes, ensuring their tenderness.)

3. Return the skillet to the fire, pour in the wine, and add 2 tablespoons of snail butter. Boil this sauce briskly for about ½ minute; then pour over each of the snail toasts. Garnish with sprigs of parsley.

Cooking Ahead: As mentioned in the recipe, the snail butter can be prepared well in advance and refrigerated or frozen. The snails can be rinsed early in the day and refrigerated. The brief sautéeing must be done at the last moment because reheating would toughen them. Toast can be rewarmed in the oven.

SNAIL BUTTER:
- ¼ pound butter, softened
- 1 shallot, chopped fine (about 1 tablespoon)
- 2 or 3 garlic cloves, chopped fine (about 2 teaspoons)
- 1 tablespoon lemon juice
- salt and pepper

8- or 9-ounce can (40) snails
8 slices white toast
½ cup white wine
8 parsley sprigs

Snow Peas with Red Peppers

For color reasons alone, this is an obvious combination. The pairing has another advantage—the textural play between the crunchy snow peas and limp peppers. When snow peas are unavailable, string beans can be substituted.

1. Peel the peppers according to the instructions in Step 1 for Marinated Red Pepper Strips (page 48). Cut them into strips ½ inch wide.	4 red peppers 3 cups Chicken Stock (page 218) 2 tablespoons olive oil salt and pepper ½ pound snow peas 1 tablespoon cornstarch

2. Put chicken stock, olive oil, salt, and pepper in a pot. Bring the stock to a boil, add the peppers, cover, reduce the heat, and simmer for 3 minutes. Add the snow peas, and cook for another 2 minutes. (String beans need longer cooking time, so put them in with the peppers.)

3. Mix enough water with the cornstarch to make a paste, and stir it into the bubbling sauce. Stir until the sauce thickens and turns from opaque to clear. Once it is clear, the cornstarch is cooked through. Serve at once.

Cooking Ahead: The red peppers can be peeled a day in advance, closely covered, and refrigerated. It is best to prepare the rest of the dish just before serving. Cornstarch should never be used in hot preparations until the dish is ready to be served. Its thickening properties break down when it is held.

A Robust Repast

SERVES 8

Greek Stuffed Tomatoes

Terrine de Foies de Volaille (Chicken Liver Terrine)

Bean Sprout Salad

Raspberry-Baked Peaches

This is a menu that could be served for an informal dinner party or, with your best china, at a fancier function. Without the first course, it would also make a splendid luncheon offering. Each component of the menu commands attention for itself, thanks to emphatic seasonings and attractive presentation. Texture, as much as color, was considered in planning these recipes. Lima beans contribute the necessary solidity against melting feta cheese; crunchy bean sprouts were selected because this particular terrine has a soft texture. The peaches are not overbaked so that they will retain a little bite. For an informal dinner or luncheon a Spanish Rioja would be ideal; when upgrading the meal, try a Saint-Émilion.

Terrine de Foies de Volaille
(Chicken Liver Terrine)

3½ pounds
calories per serving—268

Though low in price, chicken livers deliver a lot of flavor for the money, and this simple terrine capitalizes on that serendipity. If you find the terrine a little moist for your taste, add a half cup of dry bread crumbs. In this particular recipe I happen to prefer the softer quality.

1. Carefully pick over the chicken livers, and remove any green spots, clinging fat, or membranes. Put the livers in a small bowl, pour in the Madeira, and sprinkle with the allspice, thyme, salt, and pepper. With your hands, mix well to distribute the seasonings; then tuck the bay leaf among the livers. Cover and put the bowl aside to marinate for at least 3 hours or overnight in the refrigerator.

Preheat oven to 350 degrees.

2. Melt the butter in a skillet, add the onion, cover, and cook gently for about 10 minutes, or until the onion is soft and translucent. Do not allow it to brown. Scrape the onion into a large bowl.

3. Remove the bay leaf from the marinade, and reserve it. Lift about three-fourths of the livers out of the marinade, and chop into coarse pieces in the food processor by using the on/off switch; do not turn them into a purée. (If a food processor is not available, it is better to chop the livers by hand than to put them through a grinder.) Add the chopped livers to the onion in the bowl.

4. Put the pork, ham, and bread in the processor or through a grinder in the order given. Process until the meats are well chopped and fairly smooth. Add to the liver and onion.

5. Pour the marinade from the livers into a small skillet; boil briskly over high heat until only a layer of solids remains; cool, then scrape into the bowl. Add the garlic, brandy, eggs, salt, and pepper, and mix well with your hands. Fry a small piece, cool, taste, and correct seasonings if necessary.

1½ pounds chicken livers
½ cup Madeira or port
½ teaspoon allspice
½ teaspoon thyme
salt and pepper
1 bay leaf
¼ cup butter
1 onion, chopped coarse
1 pound fatty pork, cut into 1-inch pieces
¼ pound lightly smoked ham, cut into 1-inch pieces
4 slices white bread, torn into pieces
2 garlic cloves, minced
1 tablespoon brandy
2 eggs, lightly beaten
oil or fatback for terrine dish

6. Oil an 8-cup mold, or line it with fatback, allowing excess fatback to hang over the edges. Put half the forcemeat in the dish, and tap it sharply on the counter several times. Make a layer of the reserved chicken livers, and push them lightly into the forcemeat. Scoop in the rest of the forcemeat, smooth the top, and tap the mold sharply on the counter. Place the reserved bay leaf in the center, and pull the extra fatback over the top of the meat, or smear oil over the surface if fatback is not used. Cover with aluminum foil, put on the lid, and poke a small hole in the foil. Bake in a water bath for about 1½ hours, or until a thermometer registers 160 degrees.

7. Lift the mold from the water bath, let it rest for 30 minutes, and weight it. When the mold is cool, refrigerate it overnight with the weights in place. Remove the weights, cover well, and refrigerate for 4 or 5 days before serving.

Note: Since this is a rather rustic terrine, it does not lend itself to fancy decoration. If fatback is used, nothing further is necessary. If not, a thin coating of lard or clarified butter would do the trick.

Greek Stuffed Tomatoes

Contrary to the way most cooks cut tomatoes for stuffing, I turn the vegetable upside down and remove the cap from the bottom. This produces a pretty dome shape if the cap is meant to be replaced. But more important, the thicker, broader shoulders of the tomato top make a sturdy foundation for baking and for sitting upright.

1. Turn tomatoes upside down, and cut off about one-third, reserving these small pieces for another use. With the handle of a teaspoon, ease out the seeds and juice. Use a grapefruit knife or serrated spoon to scoop out the tomato pulp, and reserve. Lightly salt the tomato cavities, turn them cut side down, and drain for at least ½ hour.

Preheat oven to 350 degrees.

2. Chop the tomato flesh, and place it in a mixing bowl. Crumble the feta over the tomatoes; add the lima beans, scallions, basil, ¼ cup of the parsley, dill, very little salt (feta is salty), pepper, and 3 tablespoons of the olive oil. Mix lightly to blend the ingredients.

3. Fill the tomatoes, mounding the tops nicely, and place in a baking pan. Dribble the remaining 3 tablespoons of oil over the filled tomatoes, and bake for about 20 minutes, or until the tomato flesh has softened a bit. Do not overbake, or they will become mushy. Sprinkle each baked tomato with a little of the remaining chopped parsley.

Cooking Ahead: The tomatoes can be prepared and stuffed, but not sprinkled with olive oil, covered, and refrigerated several hours in advance. If the tomatoes are not brought back to room temperature before baking, allow an extra 7 to 10 minutes in the oven.

- 8 medium tomatoes
- salt
- ¼ pound feta cheese
- 1¼ cups (about ½ 10-ounce package of frozen lima beans) cooked baby lima beans
- 2 scallions, including greens, chopped
- 1 tablespoon chopped basil
- ½ cup chopped parsley
- 1 teaspoon dillweed
- pepper
- 6 tablespoons olive oil

Bean Sprout Salad

Thanks to the widespread popularity of Asian cooking in America, the shopper no longer has to go to specialty stores to find sprouts. Either soy or mungo sprouts will do.

1. While bringing 2 or 3 quarts of water to a boil, dump the sprouts into a colander, and rinse well under cold water, tossing several times. Pour on the boiling water, stopping once or twice to mix the sprouts with a wooden spoon so the boiling water reaches all of them. Rinse with cold water, and shaking the colander several times, allow to drain well.

2. Shake together the oil, paprika, curry, and vinegar in a small jar. Dump the sprouts into a bowl, shred the radishes, and add to the bowl. About 1 hour before serving, pour the dressing over the vegetables, and toss well; your hands are the best implement for this. Transfer to a serving bowl.

Cooking Ahead: The dressing can be prepared the day before. The sprouts can be blanched several hours in advance, tightly sealed in a plastic bag, and refrigerated. The radishes can be shredded 1 or 2 hours in advance, tightly sealed, and refrigerated.

1 pound bean sprouts
½ cup oil
2 teaspoons paprika
¼ teaspoon curry
2 tablespoons rice wine vinegar
4 ounces (about 1 cup) radishes

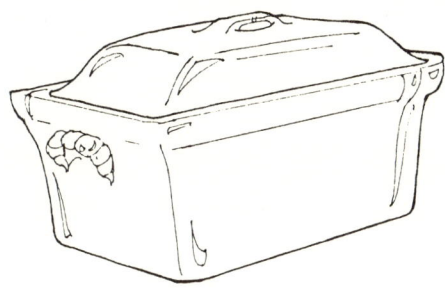

Raspberry-Baked Peaches

Today the Escoffier creation Pêches Melba is perhaps better known than the woman for whom it was named, famed Australian soprano Dame Nellie Melba. In her honor the great French chef put together the dessert, harmonious to both the palate and the eye—white vanilla ice cream, brilliantly yellow peaches, and deep red raspberry sauce. I find, though, that just the two fruits alone, especially when baked, produce a dessert equally worthy of dedication.

Preheat oven to 375 degrees.

1. In a blender purée the raspberries with the wine and kirsch; then force through a sieve to remove the seeds. There should be about 1½ cups of sauce.

2. Bring a pot of water to a boil; two or three at a time, plunge the peaches in for a few seconds, longer if they are very firm. Remove with a skimmer, cool, and slip off the skins. Cut the peaches in half, remove the stones, and place the fruit halves, rounded sides up, in a baking dish that will hold them in one layer. Pour the sauce over the peaches, and bake, uncovered, for about 10 minutes, basting one or two times.

3. Serve 2 halves per portion, spooning some of the raspberry sauce over them.

Cooking Ahead: Since the acidity in the raspberries and the alcohol will prevent the peach flesh from turning brown, the baking dish can be prepared as much as 2 or 3 hours ahead of time, if it is covered and kept refrigerated. Turn the peach halves in the sauce to coat all surfaces. Allow an extra 5 minutes baking time if the dish is not brought back to room temperature.

10-ounce package frozen sweetened raspberries, defrosted
½ cup white wine
2 tablespoons kirsch
8 peaches

Easy Elegance

SERVES 8

Mussels à la Townshend

Parfait de Foie de Volaille (Chicken Liver Parfait)

Pears in Red Wine

Zucchini Leaves

Fruit Velvet

Because of the richness of the Chicken Liver Parfait, everything else in the menu has been kept lean. Only the mussels have a sauce, and it is a very light one, containing just a bit of mayonnaise to mask the gray color of the mussel broth. Fruit is served twice, but in totally different degrees of sweetness. The Pears in Red Wine are sharply seasoned with raspberry vinegar, to garnish and provide a balance for the luxurious quality of the parfait. Hot Zucchini Leaves follow the main course, and the meal ends with ice-cold scoops of a satiny pink froth that is nothing but puréed fruit. This is an elegant meal that in no way gives away the fact that it is exceedingly easy to prepare. A Sancerre or California Sauvignon Blanc would be the wine to pour with the mussels. The parfait needs a big red, the likes of a Saint-Émilion or Barolo.

Parfait de Foie de Volaille
(Chicken Liver Parfait)

3 pounds
calories per serving—315

This is about as elegant as you can make chicken livers—a loaf of silken texture and unctuous richness. Still, it is child's play to make.

Even though the livers are sieved after puréeing, I strongly recommend spending the few minutes necessary to pick over them before marinating them. By doing this, you will assure the smoothest texture possible since it gives double insurance that not a single stray membrane will find its way into the terrine.

1. Pick over the chicken livers to remove any fat, green spots, or thick membranes. Drop the livers into the bowl as you go over them; then sprinkle them with the salt, pepper, allspice, thyme, and mace. Pour in the ¾ cup Madeira, and mix with your hands. Cover and put aside for about 2 hours.

2. Meanwhile, put beef stock and 1 tablespoon of the Madeira in a small pot, and sprinkle the gelatin over the liquids; put aside to soften. Place on medium heat, and while stirring, bring almost to the boiling point to dissolve the gelatin. Put aside at room temperature.

3. Melt 4 tablespoons of the butter in a large nonreactive skillet, add the shallots, reduce the heat to low, cover, and cook for 2 minutes. Do not allow the shallots to brown. Lift the chicken livers out of the marinade, add them to the skillet, turn the heat to medium, cover, and cook for 5 minutes, stirring several times. The livers should be slightly firm with almost all traces of pink gone. Lift the chicken livers and shallots out of the skillet with a slotted spoon, put them in a food processor, and purée. Pour the marinade into the skillet; boil briskly to reduce the liquid to a thick glaze, about 10 minutes; add to the livers; and process again.

4. Sieve the liver mixture through a nylon or stainless steel sieve. Rinse and wipe out the processor bowl, and pour in the liver purée. Add half the remaining butter, the dissolved gelatin, and the remaining 1 tablespoon of Madeira; process. Add the rest of the softened butter, and process until very smooth. Taste for salt and pepper; correct if necessary.

- 2 pounds chicken livers
- 1 teaspoon salt
- ½ teaspoon pepper
- 1 teaspoon allspice
- 1 teaspoon dried thyme
- 1 teaspoon mace
- ¾ cup plus 2 tablespoons Madeira or port
- 1 tablespoon Beef Stock (page 219)
- 1 teaspoon gelatin
- 1¼ pounds butter, softened
- 2 shallots, chopped coarse (about ¼ cup)

5. Oil a 6-cup loaf dish, spoon in the parfait mixture, and tap the dish sharply on the counter to smooth out the purée. Cut a piece of paper to fit the top, and place it directly over the parfait. Chill for at least 3 days before serving.

Note: Since chicken liver purées tend to darken on contact with the air, once the parfait is well chilled, I like to top it with a coating of about ¼ inch of melted lard (page 21). Not only does lard seal out all air, but it also offers a stark white contrast to the pink interior. Clarified Butter (page 222) could also be used.

↡↡↡

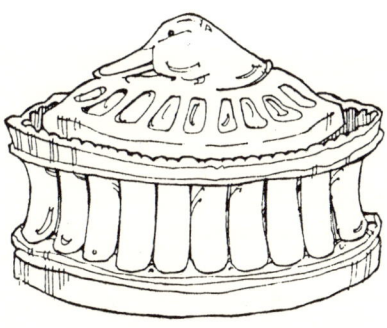

Mussels à la Townshend

While perusing the late Waverley Root's estimable tome *Food*, I learned that the lowly turnip had an early promoter in one Lord Townshend, who worked on improving the root—for livestock anyway. Though still not universally appreciated, the turnip is an admirable vegetable, and I believe more people would eat it if they gave it half a chance. I hope this presentation serves as an introduction for some converts.

1. In a large pot which can hold the mussels, put the onion, carrot, parsley, bay leaf, salt, pepper, celery if used, and the water. Bring to a boil, cover, and simmer briskly for 15 minutes. Meanwhile, scrub the mussels with a stiff brush, and pull off the beards. Discard any mussels that are open and will not close when sharply rapped. Also discard any that feel unusually heavy; they may be filled with nothing but sand. Add the wine to the cooking broth, bring to a boil again, and add all the mussels. Cover, bring to a boil over high heat, and cook until the mussel shells open, usually just a few minutes. After a minute or so of cooking, shake the pot vigorously to mix up the mussels, or turn them over with a long spoon. Cool; remove the mussels from their shells; strain and reserve the cooking liquid.

2. Prepare the turnips by cutting them in half from top to bottom, then cutting each half into ¼-inch slices. Cut across the slices to make ¼-inch strips. Bring a pot of water to a boil, add a little salt and the turnips, and cook for only 3 or 4 minutes or just until the turnips are crisply tender; do not overcook Drain at once, and cool under cold running water.

3. Roll the romaine leaves tightly, and cut across to make shreds. You will need about 6 cups of shredded lettuce.

4. Put 1½ cups of the mussel broth into a saucepot that can also hold the mussels and turnips, and bring to a simmer. Stir another 2 tablespoons of the mussel broth into the cornstarch to make a paste. While stirring, add this paste to the simmering broth; then flavor it with the liqueur, salt, and pepper. When the sauce has thickened, stir in mayonnaise, add the mussels and turnips to the sauce, and as soon as they are hot, remove the pot from the fire.

1 small onion, chopped
1 small carrot, sliced
6 parsley sprigs
½ bay leaf
salt and pepper
OPTIONAL: 4-inch piece celery rib
2 cups water
4 dozen mussels
1 cup white wine
1 pound turnips
romaine lettuce
1 tablespoon cornstarch
1 tablespoon anise-flavored liqueur (Pernod, Ouzo, Arak, etc.)
¼ cup Mayonnaise (page 226)

5. Pile the lettuce on warmed plates. Spoon the mussels and turnips over the shredded lettuce, and serve at once.

Cooking Ahead: Everything except the sauce can be prepared in advance. The mussels can be prepared the day before and kept in the refrigerator in their strained cooking broth. The turnips can also be cooked a day in advance, drained, and refrigerated in a tightly covered container. The lettuce can be shredded early in the day and refrigerated in a plastic bag. Bring all three elements back to room temperature before proceeding with the recipe.

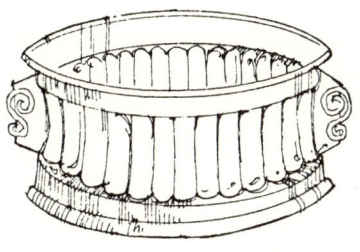

Pears in Red Wine

Farther on is a recipe for Pears in Red Wine with Broccoli Purée served as a hot vegetable. With minor adjustments in the seasoning of the poaching liquid, the fruit becomes a very tasty cold garnish.

1. Prepare the wine sauce and poach the pears according to Steps 1 and 2 on page 189 for Pears in Red Wine with Broccoli Purée, but cut the pears once more lengthwise to produce quarters.

2. Cool and chill the pears in the syrup, turning them occasionally for darker color throughout.

Cooking Ahead: See page 189.

⅓ cup raspberry vinegar
½ cup fresh basil leaves or 2½ tablespoons dried basil
salt and pepper
4 Anjou, Bartlett, or Bosc pears
3 cups red wine

Zucchini Leaves

All one sees is the green zucchini with a red pepper or pimiento stripe embedded in the center. The unexpected taste is that of the onions hiding beneath.

Preheat oven to 375 degrees.

1. Heat ¼ cup of the oil in a skillet; add the onions; cover; and stirring occasionally, sauté for 5 minutes. Add the oregano, recover, and sauté for about another 5 minutes, or until the onions are soft. Stir in the bread crumbs, and cook for 1 minute, stirring constantly. Remove from the heat, and add the parsley.

2. Cut each zucchini in half lengthwise; then slice from the root end to within 1 inch of the stem end. Slice the pepper or pimientos into ¼-inch strips. Place a zucchini half on a chopping board or flat dish, spread it open, and stuff with some of the sautéed onion mixture. Place pepper strips over the stuffing; slide a spatula under the zucchini with its stuffing; and pressing the zucchini together slightly, transfer to an oiled baking dish.

3. Dribble the rest of the olive oil over the zucchini, cover, and bake for about 25 minutes, or until the zucchini are soft when pierced with a small knife. Serve at once.

⅓ cup olive oil
1 cup sliced onions
½ teaspoon oregano
½ cup bread crumbs
¼ cup parsley leaves, chopped
4 medium zucchini
1 red pepper or 3 pimientos

Cooking Ahead: Zucchini Leaves cannot be baked in advance or their flesh will collapse and be unattractive, even though the flavor remains the same. However, a few hours in advance the zucchini can be completely prepared, covered, and held at room temperature until ready for baking. If prepared in the morning, refrigerate the dish.

Fruit Velvet

The joy of this dessert is its utter simplicity, even though it looks and tastes devilishly rich. In fact, it is nothing but pure fruit and fruit juice whizzed together until thick, creamy, and voluminous.

1. Rinse and hull the berries, and place them in a plastic bag or box. Peel the bananas, cut them into 1-inch chunks, and immediately roll tightly in plastic wrap. Place the fruits in the freezer to freeze solid.

2. At serving time, place the frozen fruits in the container of a food processor, pour on the juice, and process with the metal blade. The fruits will be first chopped into small bits, then become amalgamated into a creamy pink mass. Serve at once, preferably in chilled wine glasses or glass bowls.

2 cups strawberries or other seasonal fruit
2 medium bananas
½ cup orange (or other fruit) juice

Duck Dinner with a Stylish Difference
SERVES 10

Scallops with Parmesan

Terrine de Canard à l'Orange
(Orange-Flavored Duck Terrine)

Lettuce Cushions

Baked Pears with Caramel Sauce

Duck pâté or terrine as the main course dictates a stylish menu, a term that should not be read as complicated. Every recipe surrounding the terrine is unfussy and preserves the purity of the basic ingredient. Scallops are broiled under a sheer veil of Parmesan cheese for the first course; to accompany the terrine, lettuce is cooked and shaped into cool green mounds speckled with sesame seeds; and the dinner closes with plain baked pears served hot under a drizzle of cold caramel sauce. Here is another example of how elegant a hot-cold-hot menu can be. This is a two-wine dinner: Muscadet, Chablis, or a dry California Chenin Blanc with the scallops and a Saint-Émilion or Chianti Classico with the terrine and dessert.

Terrine de Canard à l'Orange
(Orange-Flavored Duck Terrine)

4 pounds
calories per serving—258

Duck terrine is one of the most popular classic French dishes. It is garnished with everything from green peppercorns to apricots, prunes, and even figs. My own predilection is for orange flavor; perhaps it's the influence of that combination in so many hot preparations. Whatever, I find the acidic juice marries well with the rich meats. However, the juice must be fresh. If you take the time to bone a duck, it seems false economy of time to pour from a bottle rather than to squeeze one orange. If you like, the duck breasts can be ground into the forcemeat rather than kept whole. This gives a stronger duck flavor to the forcemeat, but the slices aren't as attractive.

1. Remove all the duck meat from the carcass. The best way to proceed is to remove first the legs with the thighs, then the wings. Cut through the meat along one side of the breastbone. To free the meat, work your knife against the bone while pulling the flesh with your hand. Carefully remove the skin. Reserve the breast pieces, and cut all remaining duck meat into pieces. From all portions of the meat, cut or pull away all gristle, skin, and tendons. Cut the breast meat into ½-inch strips.

2. Put the breast meat in a small bowl. Chop all the meats in the food processor, beginning with the duck pieces, as follows: Process the duck only briefly so that it is chopped into coarse pieces; transfer to a large bowl. Process the veal and pork until they are quite smooth, and add to the chopped duck meat. Next, process the fatback, duck liver, and shallot together until very smooth, and add to the other meats. Pour the orange juice over the chopped meats. Pour ¼ cup each of the brandy, Madeira, and orange liqueur over the chopped meats and 1 tablespoon of each over the duck breasts. Season the mixed meats with ¼ teaspoon allspice, ¼ teaspoon thyme, ¼ teaspoon sage, ⅛ teaspoon nutmeg, 2 teaspoons salt, and pepper. Season the breasts with only a pinch each of allspice, nutmeg, salt, and pepper. Mix the meats well with your hands to blend all the seasonings into the meats; break the bay leaf in half, and tuck it into the mixed meats. Turn the breast meat in the alcohols to coat each strip. Cover both bowls, and put aside for at least 3 hours or overnight in the refrigerator.

5-pound duck
½ pound boneless veal, cut into 1-inch pieces
½ pound lean pork, cut into 1-inch pieces
¾ pound fatback, cut into 1-inch pieces
1 duck liver
1 shallot, chopped coarse
½ cup fresh orange juice
⅓ cup brandy
⅓ cup Madeira or port
⅓ cup orange liqueur, preferably Grand Marnier
¼ teaspoon allspice
¼ teaspoon thyme
¼ teaspoon sage
⅛ teaspoon nutmeg
2 teaspoons salt
pepper
1 bay leaf

3. If using the pistachio nuts, cover them with boiling water, and let stand for about 1 minute. Drain, and as soon as you can handle them, slip off the skins.

Preheat oven to 325 degrees.

4. Remove the bay leaf pieces from the mixed meats, and reserve. Break the bread into pieces, and crumble them into the mixing bowl by rubbing them between the palms of your hands. Add the pistachio nuts and the eggs, and mix all very well with your hands. Fry a small piece of the forcemeat, cool, taste, and correct the seasonings if necessary.

5. Oil an 8-cup mold, or line it with fatback, allowing excess fatback to hang over the edges. Put half the forcemeat in the dish, and tap it sharply on the counter several times. Make a layer of the strips of duck meat, and push them lightly into the forcemeat. Scoop in the rest of the forcemeat, smooth the top, and tap the mold sharply on the counter. Place the 2 bay leaf pieces on the meat, and pull the extra fatback over the top of the meats; patch with other pieces, if necessary. If not using the fatback, smear oil over the surface of the meats. Cover with aluminum foil, put on the mold cover, and poke a small hole in it. Bake in a water bath for about 1¼ hours, or until a thermometer registers 160 degrees.

6. Lift the mold from the water bath, let it rest for 30 minutes, and weight it. When the mold is cool, refrigerate it overnight with the weights in place. Remove the weights, cover well, and refrigerate for 4 or 5 days before serving.

Note: The terrine can be served with no further decoration, but several elaborations could be considered. Once the fatback has been removed and the surface wiped dry, a well-flavored aspic (page 222) made with the duck carcass could be poured over the terrine in the mold. Or score an orange, cut into thin slices, and then cut each slice in half; these slices can be overlapped down the center of the terrine or arranged in several V formations with, perhaps, a sprig of parsley at the meeting point. Melted lard is another possibility (page 21); not only does the lard provide a satin-smooth coating, but it also prolongs the staying power of the terrine by at least a week.

1 slice white bread, crusts removed
2 eggs, beaten
oil or fatback for terrine dish

OPTIONAL:
½ cup pistachio nuts

Lettuce Cushions

This is really a salad of sorts, but with cooked instead of crisp lettuce. Small handfuls of the soft lettuce are formed into mounds and sprinkled with toasted sesame seeds. The whole thing could be tossed together in a bowl and served as is, but in dining, aesthetics also plays an important role.

1. Add the onions to a large pot of water, bring to a boil, and plunge in the lettuce. Cook for about 5 minutes, or until the center ribs are soft. Drain at once, cool under running water, and drain well again. Squeeze all the water out of the lettuce, a handful at a time, and chop into coarse pieces. Put the lettuce in a mixing bowl.

2. In a small jar shake together the mustard, horseradish, oil, vermouth, and salt. Pour the sesame seeds into a small, heavy skillet, and toast them over medium heat, stirring constantly. Toast only to a dark golden color, a matter of a minute or so.

3. Pour the dressing over the lettuce, and toss well. Sprinkle in half the sesame seeds, and toss again. About a half cupful at a time, pat the lettuce into 10 small mounds between your palms. Place the mounds on a serving platter, and sprinkle them with the remaining seeds.

Cooking Ahead: The lettuce, dressing, and sesame seeds all can be prepared a day or so in advance but not mixed. Just before serving, lift the lettuce from the storage bowl to leave behind any water, and continue with the recipe.

2 onions, quartered
3 pounds leafy lettuce, preferably escarole
1½ tablespoons mustard
½ teaspoon horseradish
½ cup oil
¼ cup vermouth
salt
¼ cup sesame seeds

Baked Pears with Caramel Sauce

Simple desserts are often the best. At the end of a satisfying meal all that is desired is a refreshing taste to linger on the palate. This hot-and-cold dessert fits the bill. The pears are baked with no adulterating flavorings, just a little water, thus preserving their intensely pure flavor to contrast with tangy Caramel Sauce. Since they are served hot, the pears should go into the oven about a half hour before serving time, but if need be, once baked, they can be held for fifteen minutes with the oven turned off.

Preheat oven to 350 degrees.

1. Peel the pears, and remove a slice from the bottom so that they will stand up. To keep the flesh white, drop the peeled pears into cold acidulated water.

2. Place the pears on a baking dish that will hold them snugly, pour in about ¼ inch of water, cover tightly with aluminum foil, and place in the oven. The pears will be tender in 20 to 30 minutes, depending on their degree of ripeness. Test with a small, sharp knife.

3. Serve the hot pears on individual dishes, and pass Caramel Sauce separately.

Cooking Ahead: If the pears are to wait for more than 1 hour before baking, keep them in the bowl of acidulated water in the refrigerator.

10 pears, preferably Bartlett
2 cups Caramel Sauce (page 233)

Scallops with Parmesan

This dish is simplicity itself, despite two caveats. Fresh scallops are absolutely necessary. First of all, so few ingredients are used that each must be impeccable; there are no masking flavors to disguise off notes. Secondly, frozen scallops exude far too much juice and would completely ruin the final effect of the crisply gratinéed dish. It follows, of course, that the Parmesan cheese must also be fresh, not sprinkled from a box or jar. Remember, attention to these small details pays off at the table.

1. Select either 10 small gratin dishes or large scallop shells, or a single large gratin dish that can hold the scallops in a single layer. Butter the dish, and arrange the scallops in one layer. Preheat the broiler.

2. Sprinkle over the scallops the wine, pepper, cheese, and melted butter. Place under the broiler, and gratiné for 1 or 2 minutes, or just until the surface is lightly browned.

Cooking Ahead: The scallops may be placed in their dishes several hours in advance, covered, and refrigerated. The seasoning and broiling must be done at the last minute.

- 2 pounds bay scallops or sea scallops, cut in half crosswise
- ⅓ cup white wine
- pepper
- ½ cup very fine-grated Parmesan cheese
- 3 tablespoons butter, melted

⇊⇊⇊

A Menu Full of Piquant Pleasures
SERVES 8

Gingered Shrimp on Leeks

Terrine d'Agneau aux Herbes de Provence
(Lamb Terrine with Provençal Herbs)

Stuffed Eggs with Capers

Pear Gratin

Ginger, leeks, Provençal herbs, and capers can add up to some pretty formidable flavorings—if used with a heavy hand. This menu balances seasonings to allow only one dish, the redolent lamb terrine, to be decidedly emphatic. The stuffed eggs served with the terrine contain just enough capers to add piquancy and visual interest, but not so much to compete with the main dish. The eggs are best arranged in pairs on lettuce leaves to facilitate transfer to the dinner plate. The preceding course starts the meal stylishly, presenting pink shrimp on a bed of creamy green and white leeks. The ginger slices used to flavor the shrimp are first sautéed to draw out their oils, then discarded, leaving no fiery pieces to bite into. Dinner ends on a refreshing, not-too-sweet note with a hot Pear Gratin topped with a crunchy crumb topping. An Alsatian Sylvaner or Riesling would complement the shrimp dish perfectly. For the Provençal-inspired lamb terrine one could remain in that part of France with a lively Côtes du Rhône, or cross the border into Italy for a young Chianti Classico.

Terrine d'Agneau aux Herbes de Provence (Lamb Terrine with Provençal Herbs)

3½ pounds, about $14
calories per serving—410

The hills of Provence are fragrant with pungent herbs of many kinds, the best known being rosemary, thyme, sage, and savory. This combination, with a bay leaf or two added, is often sold prepackaged, certainly costing more than the total of the individual components. Lamb also is a great Provençal specialty, and the marriage of this meat with the native herbs is a happy union indeed. Black olives, still another product of this bountiful region, stud the terrine.

Preheat oven to 350 degrees.

1. Sauté the onion in ⅓ cup of the olive oil until soft and translucent, about 10 minutes; add the garlic, and simmer for 1 minute more. Scrape them into a large mixing bowl.

2. Add to the bowl the lamb, pork, brandy, thyme, rosemary, sage, salt, pepper, and cayenne, and knead together with your hands to mix all the ingredients and flavorings. Add the bread crumbs, and work them in; then add the eggs, and mix in very well. Scatter the olives over the meats, and blend in. Fry a small spoonful of the terrine mixture, cool, taste for seasonings, and correct if necessary.

3. Cut the fatback into lardons about ½ inch square and 6 inches long. Oil an 8-cup terrine mold; scoop in about one-third of the forcemeat; tap the mold well on the counter; then lay in strips of half the fatback, lightly pressing them into the forcemeat. Repeat with another layer of forcemeat, of lardons, and a final layer of forcemeat. Tap the mold sharply on the counter several times. Smear the remaining tablespoon of olive oil over the surface, and place the bay leaf in the center.

4. Cover with aluminum foil; put the lid in place; then poke a small hole in the foil. Place the mold in a water bath, and bake for about 1½ hours, or until a thermometer registers 160 degrees.

- 6 tablespoons olive oil
- 1 large onion, chopped coarse
- 3 garlic cloves, minced
- 2 pounds lamb, ground
- ¾ pound fatty pork, ground
- ⅓ cup brandy
- 1½ teaspoons thyme
- 1¼ teaspoons rosemary
- 1½ teaspoons sage
- 1 tablespoon salt
- ½ teaspoon pepper
- large pinch of cayenne
- ½ cup bread crumbs
- 3 eggs, beaten
- ½ cup black olives, preferably oil-cured, rinsed and sliced
- ¼ pound fatback
- oil
- 1 bay leaf

5. Lift the mold from the water bath; let it rest for 30 minutes; then weight it. When it is cool, refrigerate the mold overnight with the weights in place. Remove the weights, cover the terrine well, and refrigerate it for 4 or 5 days before serving.

Note: Halved black olives make the obvious decorating scheme for this terrine. They can be arranged in a circular patten in the center, somewhat resembling the petals of a flower; a spot of red pimiento in the center brightens the effect. There are at least two ways to use the black olive halves in stripe formations: 1 lengthwise down the center or 3 or 4 diagonally across the top. Small sprigs of rosemary would add even more to the Provençal theme.

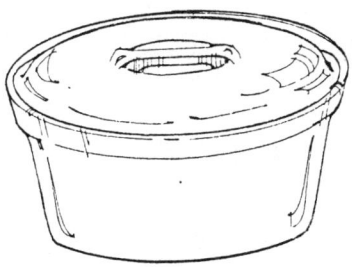

Gingered Shrimp on Leeks

Fresh ginger used to be an exotic flavoring in home kitchens. Thanks to the nationwide interest in Asian cooking, this is no longer true. Now even supermarkets carry the knobby root. I like to use it unexpectedly, in combinations that balance ginger's tang with soft, creamy notes. This is one such pairing. Since you can rarely buy just the amount you need, it's always there for sudden inspiration. It has been written that fresh ginger can be frozen for long storage. Forget it; it turns to mush. Far better to put a piece of plastic wrap over the cut end, and refrigerate it in the vegetable bin. It should keep for at least six weeks.

1. Prepare the leeks by trimming off the root ends and cutting off the green tops to about 1 inch above the white part. Make a cross cut into the light green tops to spread open the leaves that trap sand. Rinse very well under running water to wash away all sand and grit; then slice thin, and place in a large non-reactive pan.

2. Pour in the cream and 1 cup of the wine, sprinkle with salt and pepper, cover, and cook for 15 minutes. Remove the cover, and stirring occasionally, simmer briskly for about 10 minutes, or until almost all the liquid has evaporated.

3. While the leeks are cooking, plunge the tomato into boiling water and slip off the skin. Cut the tomato in half; squeeze out the seeds and juice; then chop the flesh into coarse pieces. Stir the tomato into the leeks at the end of their cooking time; then allow to simmer for 1 minute more.

4. To prepare the shrimp, boil together for 10 minutes in a covered pot the water, the remaining ½ cup wine, lemon juice, 4 slices of the ginger, celery seed, salt, and pepper. Add the shrimp, reduce the heat, cover, and cook for only 1 or 2 minutes more, or until they have barely turned pink. Do not overcook at this stage since the shrimp will be cooked again. Drain at once, and peel as soon as they are cool enough to handle.

5. At serving time, heat the oil in a large sauté pan with the remaining 3 slices of ginger. Turn the ginger several times to extract as much of its flavor as possible, about 2 minutes; then

2 bunches (about 1 pound, trimmed) leeks
1½ cups heavy cream
1½ cups white wine
salt and pepper
1 large tomato
1½ cups water
juice of 1 lemon
7 fresh ginger slices
¼ teaspoon celery seed
¾ pound shrimp
3 tablespoons oil

discard. Add the shrimp, and fry over high heat for only ½ minute, turning constantly with a spatula.

6. Divide the hot leeks among 8 warmed salad-sized plates, and top with the lightly browned shrimp.

Cooking Ahead: Simmer the uncovered leeks for only 5 minutes, leaving a visible layer of liquid in the pan; refrigerate. Finish the other 5 minutes of cooking and the tomato addition at serving time. The shrimp can be cooked and peeled the day before, tightly covered, and refrigerated but must be fried at the last minute.

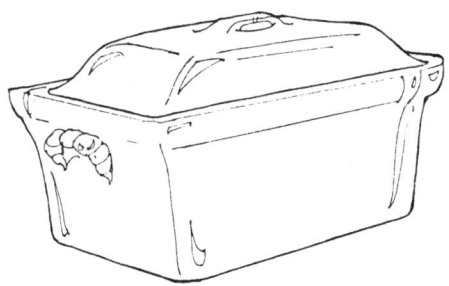

Stuffed Eggs with Capers

Buffet-table stuffed eggs tend to be very rich and filling. Since these are meant to be a garnish and accompany the terrine, yogurt replaces the usual mayonnaise. A bit of pesto and capers do wonders for adding zip. When cutting hard-boiled eggs in half, always wipe the knife with a paper towel between eggs. Bits of egg yolk cling to the knife and would be transferred to the whites of the next egg if not removed.

1. Cut the eggs in half lengthwise. With a teaspoon, scoop the egg yolks into a small mixing bowl, and mash them with a fork. Add 6 tablespoons of the yogurt, pesto, capers, salt, and pepper, and mix all the ingredients together very well until a stiff paste is formed. If it is too thick, add an extra tablespoon of yogurt.

2. Spoon the paste back into the egg-white shells, mounding the center. Garnish each half with a parsley sprig, if used, and place pairs together on lettuce leaves.

Cooking Ahead: Everything except stuffing the paste into the shells can be done a day or two in advance. Tightly cover the shells and stuffing separately, and refrigerate.

8 hard-boiled eggs
6 or 7 tablespoons yogurt
1½ tablespoons Pesto (page 231)
2 teaspoons capers, rinsed and drained
salt and pepper
OPTIONAL:
parsley sprigs and lettuce

↓↓↓

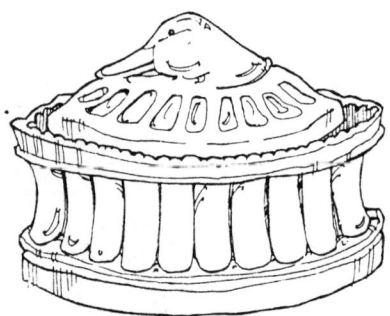

Pear Gratin

Because of the natural sweetness of pears and the sweetened graham cracker crumbs, little extra sugar is indicated in this recipe. If using end-of-season fruit, you may want to add an extra half tablespoon.

Preheat oven to 400 degrees.

1. Pour the graham cracker crumbs into a small bowl, and add the nutmeg and brown sugar. Stir the crumbs and flavorings to mix well; if the sugar is a little lumpy, use your fingers to break the lumps into the crumbs.

2. Pour ¼ cup of the cream into a 12-inch pie or gratin dish. Rotate the dish so that the cream covers the entire bottom. Peel the pears, dropping them into acidulated water to keep from darkening. Cut each pear in half lengthwise, then again in half lengthwise. Remove the cores, and cut one more time in half lengthwise, making 8 slices from each pear. Arrange the pears in the pie dish in a single, tightly packed layer.

3. With a spoon sprinkle the crumbs over the pears, completely covering them. Pour the remaining cream into the bowl, add the vanilla, and stir; then carefully pour the cream over the crumbs to moisten all surfaces. Bake for about 15 minutes, or until the top is brown and bubbly and the pears are soft when pierced with a knife. Remove from the oven, and rest the gratin for about 10 minutes before serving.

Cooking Ahead: The dish can be prepared with the pears and crumbs a few hours before baking. Tightly cover the dish, and keep in a cool spot, but not the refrigerator. Pour on the cream just before baking.

¾ cup graham cracker crumbs
¼ teaspoon nutmeg
1½ tablespoons brown sugar
1 cup light or heavy cream
1½ pounds (about 5) pears
1½ teaspoons vanilla

Sumptuous Springtime Dining

SERVES 8

Sautéed Scallops

Tongue and Ham Pâté

Turnip Purée

Hot Asparagus with Herbed Vinaigrette

Poppy Seed Flan

Asparagus places this menu in the spring or early summer. But the other dishes are too good to be limited by the season. Spaghetti Squash and Peas (page 127), Singapore String Beans (page 31), or Zucchini Leaves (page 77) could be stand-ins. The hot green vegetable is just the right color note to follow the pink-to-red pâté with its white purée garnish. It is best to put the scallops into small dishes that have some depth, like gratin dishes, so that the winy sauce can be enjoyed with a spoon. Pour a dry Riesling with the scallops, and go on to a Burgundy or California Pinot Noir for the rest of the meal.

Tongue and Ham Pâté

3 pounds
calories per serving—364

I think tongue is a much neglected meat in American cooking. Yet it is one of the easiest of all variety meats to prepare. It can be braised, stewed, jellied, baked, or just boiled with a few aromatics. Only a pound of tongue meat is needed for this pâté, so if you do not have a shop that sells it ready to eat, cook one and have the leftovers to enjoy in sandwiches and salads or grilled with a mustard coating.

1. Cut half the tongue and all the ham into ¼-inch strips about 5 or 6 inches long. Keeping them separate, place the meats in a shallow dish, and sprinkle with the bitters, thyme, ½ teaspoon each of allspice and coriander, plus a good grinding of pepper. Pour on ¼ cup each of the alcohols. Turn the meats with your hands to coat all the strips, tuck in the bay leaf, cover, and put aside to marinate for at least 3 hours or overnight in the refrigerator.

Preheat oven to 350 degrees.

2. Chop the onion into coarse pieces, and slowly fry them in 3 tablespoons of the oil until soft, about 10 minutes. Chop the garlic, add it to the onion for the last minute of frying; scrape them into a large mixing bowl. Melt the butter in the skillet, and pour it over the onions. Reserve the bay leaf, and drain the marinade from the meat dish into the skillet, boil briskly to reduce to about 3 tablespoons, and scrape into the bowl.

3. If using a food processor, chop the bread into fine crumbs first; if using a grinder, grind the bread last. Pour the crumbs into the mixing bowl; then grind the pork and the remaining ½ pound of tongue, and add to the bowl. Rinse the peppercorns very well under running water, drain thoroughly, and sprinkle over the meats with the remaining tablespoon each of Madeira and brandy, ¼ teaspoon each allspice and coriander, pepper, and a little salt; remember, the ham and tongue are already salty. With your hands, mix all the ingredients together very well, add the egg, and mix again. Fry a small piece of this stuffing in a little oil, cool, and taste for seasonings; correct if necessary.

1 pound cooked smoked tongue*
½ pound lightly smoked ham
1 tablespoon aromatic bitters
1 teaspoon thyme
¾ teaspoon allspice
¾ teaspoon ground coriander
pepper
⅓ cup Madeira or port
⅓ cup brandy
1 bay leaf
1 large onion
¼ cup oil
2 garlic cloves
2 tablespoons butter
2 slices white bread, torn into pieces
1¼ pounds fatty pork
1 tablespoon brine-packed green peppercorns
salt
1 egg, beaten
oil

4. Lightly oil an 8-cup pâté mold. Layer in one-third of the stuffing, place half the meat strips over the stuffing, alternating between the tongue and ham, and press them lightly into the forcemeat. Cover the strips with another third of the stuffing, and repeat a layer of the strips; this time begin with ham if you began with tongue on the lower arrangement. Use the final third of the stuffing for the top layer, and smooth the ground meats. Tap the mold sharply on the counter several times, press the bay leaf from the marinade into the center, and smear the remaining tablespoon of oil over the surface. Cover the mold with foil and a lid, pierce a hole through the foil with a skewer, place the dish in a water bath, and bake it for about 1¾ hours, or to 160 degrees on a thermometer.

5. Remove the mold from the water bath, cool it for 20 minutes, place weights on top, and allow to cool to room temperature. Refrigerate with the weights, but remove them after 12 hours. Refrigerate the pâté for an additional 2 days at least; 3 or 4 days are better.

OPTIONAL: Aspic
3 cups tongue or mild Beef Stock (page 219)
1 egg white
1½ tablespoons gelatin
¼ cup white wine
⅓ cup chopped parsley

Optional Aspic Garnish

The day before serving the pâté, clarify the stock with the egg white according to the directions on page 221. Soften the gelatin in the wine; add to the stock to dissolve; cool to the syrupy stage; then fold in the parsley. Drain any juices from the pâté, wipe the top of the pâté and the edges of the mold with a paper towel, and spoon the aspic over the pâté. It is best to spoon in one layer of aspic, chill to firm, then repeat two or three times. Serve the pâté from the mold.

---

* How to Cook Tongue

Put the tongue in a large pot, and cover with cold water. Bring to a boil, and simmer for 15 minutes. Discard water, rinse out the pot, replace the tongue in the pot, and again cover with cold water. Add one onion quartered and 1 whole onion studded with the cloves to the water, along with garlic, carrots, bay leaves, parsley, and peppercorns. Bring the water to a boil, reduce the heat, partially cover, and simmer for about 1½ hours, or until the flesh is tender when pierced with a small, sharp knife. Remove the tongue, and cool until it can be handled; then skin it. A slightly warm tongue will peel more easily than a cold one. Cut away the fatty section at the base of the tongue. Before discarding the cooking stock, read directions for Optional Aspic Garnish.

1 approximately 3-pound smoked tongue (beef tongues rarely come smaller than 3 pounds)
2 large onions
2 cloves
2 garlic cloves
2 carrots, cut into chunks
2 bay leaves
5 or 6 parsley sprigs
1 tablespoon peppercorns

Turnip Purée

It might look like mashed potatoes, and indeed, there are a few in there, but the sparkle comes from turnips. Potatoes are included only to add solidity to the purée. It's the lively turnip flavor, aided by a bit of horseradish, that is counted on to be a counterpoint against the pâté. For presentation suggestions please see the end of the introductory note for Carrot-Pear Purée (page 61).

Makes 4 cups

1½ pounds turnips
¾ pound potatoes
salt
1 tablespoon horseradish
¾ cup yogurt
pepper

1. Bring a large quantity of water to a boil while peeling and quartering the turnips and potatoes. Lightly salt the water, add the vegetables, and cook them for 15 to 20 minutes, or until soft. Drain them well, and transfer to a food processor or blender.

2. Add the horseradish, yogurt, salt, and pepper, and process until smooth. Serve at room temperature.

Cooking Ahead: Turnip purée can be prepared 1 or 2 days in advance.

⇊⇊

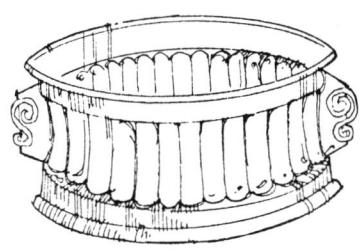

Poppy Seed Flan

Except for a sprinkle on some bread rolls, Americans rarely are served crunchy poppy seed. In fact, it is so little used that poppy seeds are most commonly sold by spice companies to be used for garnishing. Larger, more economical amounts can be found at ethnic and health food stores. The Hungarians and Slavs lavishly use the nutty seed as a filling in all sorts of sweet rolls and strudels. This flan comes from no particular cuisine, just a desire to create something that might introduce some readers to the exceptional qualities of this harmless seed which does come from the opium poppy.

¾ cup poppy seeds
3½ tablespoons sugar
1¾ cups milk
½ teaspoon grated orange rind
¼ cup semolina or cream of wheat
⅓ cup light cream
3 eggs
2½ teaspoons vanilla
butter
1½ cups sour cream
1½ tablespoons flour

OPTIONAL GARNISH:
1 teaspoon poppy seeds or candied orange peel

1. Put the poppy seeds and 2 tablespoons of the sugar in a medium-sized mixing bowl. Bring ¾ cup of the milk to the boiling point, pour over the poppy seeds, cover, and let stand for 1 hour.

Preheat oven to 350 degrees.

2. Use the same milk pot to boil the remaining 1 cup milk with the orange rind; reduce the heat, and stir in the semolina. Turn the heat to low, and stirring occasionally, cook for several minutes, or until very thick. Add the semolina to the poppy seed, and beat with a wooden spoon to blend the two mixtures thoroughly. Add the cream, 1 beaten egg, and 1½ teaspoons of the vanilla, and beat well.

3. Butter a deep 9-inch pie dish that can go to the table. Whisk the sour cream and flour together in a mixing bowl, add the remaining 1½ tablespoons sugar, the remaining 1 teaspoon vanilla, and 2 beaten eggs; beat until very well blended. Pour about one-third of the sour cream mixture into the pie dish, and rotate the dish with your hands to spread the cream into an even layer. Carefully ladle the poppy seed filling over the cream, trying not to disturb the cream. Slowly pour the remaining sour cream sauce over the filling, making certain the filling is completely covered.

4. Bake for about 40 minutes, or until a small, sharp knife plunged in the center comes out clean. Parts of the cream topping will bubble up and the outer edges will turn a nice brown. The puffiness disappears almost immediately when the dish is taken from the oven. Cool. The flan can be served as is or garnished with a few poppy seeds, candied orange peel, or a mixture of the two. Cut into wedges.

Cooking Ahead: Poppy Seed Flan can be baked the day before and kept in a cool spot or the refrigerator.

Hot Asparagus with Herbed Vinaigrette

Once the woody stems have been snapped off, there are two ways to prepare asparagus stalks. The traditional cook peels them, usually with a swivel-bladed vegetable peeler, and cooks them whole. The cook looking for speed with no compromise of flavor, chooses the Chinese method—long, thin, diagonal slices—which requires no peeling. Herbed vinaigrette dresses either version with great style.

1. Put the asparagus slices or whole stalks in a large flat skillet that can hold them in a single layer or with a minimum amount of overlapping. Sprinkle lightly with salt, and pour in enough water to reach a depth of ¼ inch. Cover the skillet.

2. Turn on the heat to high, and once the water has reached a boil, cook for about 2 minutes. The asparagus should be barely tender and still somewhat crisp. Drain at once.

3. While the asparagus is cooking, shake all remaining ingredients together in a jar. If the asparagus is sliced, put in a large serving bowl, pour on the dressing, and toss. For whole stalks, transfer the asparagus to a towel-lined platter, spoon a little sauce over the tips, and pass the rest separately.

Cooking Ahead: The vinaigrette can be prepared the day before and kept tightly covered. The asparagus can be peeled or sliced in advance and kept refrigerated in a plastic bag. The brief cooking must be done at the last minute.

- 1½ to 1¾ pounds asparagus, sliced or whole
- salt
- ½ cup oil
- 1 tablespoon wine vinegar
- 1 tablespoon lemon juice
- ½ teaspoon tarragon
- 1 teaspoon chives, snipped into small pieces
- ½ teaspoon basil, chopped, or ¼ teaspoon dried basil
- 2 teaspoons parsley leaves, chopped

Sautéed Scallops

Scallops must be cooked at the last minute, but since their sojourn in the frying pan is very brief, serving them does not impose any great strain on the cook. These scallops will be ready for the table in less than five minutes.

1. Use 1 or 2 skillets, whichever is necessary to keep the scallops in a single layer without crowding. Melt the butter, add the shallots, cover, and cook over medium heat for about 10 seconds. Add the scallops, turn up the heat, and fry them quickly while turning the scallops with a spatula. They should not fry for more than ½ minute if the pan is large enough. Sprinkle lightly with salt and pepper.

2. With a slotted spoon remove the scallops to a warm bowl, cover, and keep warm. Pour the wine into the skillet, add the parsley, and reduce over high heat until the juices are syrupy; this will take about 1 minute. Scrape the reduced juices and wine over the scallops, and mix to distribute them. Spoon the scallops into small heated dishes or scallop shells.

4 tablespoons butter
2 shallots, minced
1½ pounds bay scallops
½ cup white wine
2 tablespoons chopped parsley
salt and pepper

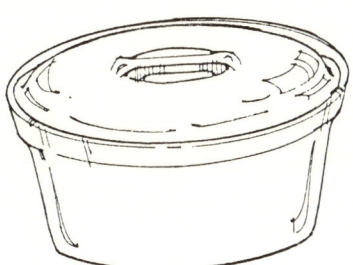

A Surprise Party of Unexpected Pleasures

SERVES 8

Champignons Balzac
(Fried Stuffed Mushroom Caps)

Ham and Ricotta Terrine

Zesty Radish Slices

Vegetable Ragout

Coconut Sherbet

Here is a menu bound to introduce guests to a number of new dishes. If you call the first course Champignons Balzac, few will guess that they are plain old mushrooms in a different guise. Serve the deep-fried morsels on a salad-sized plate with knife and fork. The filling in the pâté is another innovation—bright yellow corn kernels embedded in white ricotta. The pâté is paired with cooked marinated radish slices laced with green lettuce shreds. The second hot dish—Vegetable Ragout in red wine sauce—is served as a separate course. The main-course plate could be used, or switch to small, deep dishes that allow enjoying the sauce with a spoon. A seemingly rich and creamy Coconut Sherbet closes the meal, but this popular flavor is actually frozen into a skimmed milk base. Plain cookies would be nice with dessert. This is a menu that would welcome a cool Beaujolais, young Côtes du Rhône, or a California rosé from the Cabernet or Zinfandel grape.

Ham and Ricotta Terrine

3 pounds
calories per serving—295

A white stripe of corn-studded ricotta inlaid in a meat terrine is rather unexpected. This unusual filling provides a pleasant creaminess against the coarser meats. It's also showy enough to eliminate any need for further decoration. The resting time before weighting this terrine is slightly longer than most to allow the ricotta filling time to firm a little before weights are added.

Preheat oven to 350 degrees.

1. Put the corn in a sieve to drain. Using either a grinder or food processor, grind the pork and the ham, and put them in a mixing bowl. Trim the root ends of the scallions, cut the white and green tops into 1-inch pieces, and place them in the food processor with the parsley. Process only until they are chopped into coarse pieces; then add to the meats. Season the forcemeat with the tarragon, wine, brandy, pepper, and very little salt at this point since the ham is already salted. Sprinkle in the bread crumbs, add 1 lightly beaten egg, and mix well with your hands. Fry a small piece of the forcemeat, cool, taste for seasonings, and correct if necessary.

2. In a small bowl beat together the ricotta, the remaining 3 eggs, coriander, flour, salt, and pepper. Stir in the drained corn.

3. Oil an 8-cup loaf dish, and spoon in three-fourths of the forcemeat. Tap the dish sharply on the counter several times. With a tablespoon scoop out the center to a depth of about 1 inch, leaving about a 1-inch perimeter all around. This trough will contain the filling without allowing it to touch the edges of the dish. Spoon the ricotta-corn filling into the hollow.

4. Take handfuls of the remaining forcemeat, and press it between your hands to form flat patties. Wetting your hands helps keep the meat from sticking to your hands. Place the patties over the top of the ricotta filling and around the edges. It will not be smooth. Moisten a rubber spatula with cold water, and sweep it back and forth across the meat to smooth the surface. Keep wetting the spatula as needed. Smear a tablespoon

1 cup corn kernels
1 pound fatty pork, cut into 1-inch pieces
1 pound lightly smoked ham, cut into 1-inch pieces
3 scallions
1 cup parsley leaves
½ teaspoon tarragon
¼ cup white wine
¼ cup brandy
pepper and salt
⅓ cup bread crumbs
4 eggs
1 cup ricotta
¼ teaspoon ground coriander
1 tablespoon flour
oil

of oil over the top of the forcemeat, cover with aluminum foil, put on the mold cover, and poke a small hole in the foil. Place in a water bath. Bake for about 1½ hours, or until a thermometer registers 160 degrees.

5. Lift the mold from the water bath, let it rest for 45 minutes, and weight it. When the mold is cool, refrigerate it overnight, with the weights in place. Remove the weights, cover well, and refrigerate the mold for 2 or 3 days before serving.

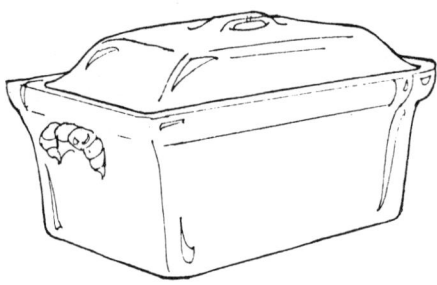

Coconut Sherbet

This is a rare instance when I recommend a canned product instead of fresh. In fact, of the three forms of coconut I tried, fresh coconut produced the mildest flavor, almost too mild to satisfy. Coconut milk is the key ingredient in this frozen dessert. Spanish and Asian specialty shops carry it in cans—a very thick coconut sediment decanted from the milk. Second best in flavor are the desiccated unsweetened coconut shreds available at most health food stores. Cream of coconut, found in supermarkets for piña colada mixing, will not work. Besides being cloyingly sweet, it contains vegetable gums and stabilizers that inhibit proper freezing. Instructions are given for making coconut milk if the canned product is unavailable.

Makes 1 quart

1. Pour the sugar and water into a pot, stir for a minute or so, and put aside for about 15 minutes. Place the pot on medium heat, stir several times, cover, and bring to a boil. Remove cover, and boil for 5 minutes. Pour the syrup into a bowl, and let it cool.

2. To the syrup add the coconut milk, skimmed milk, and egg white, and blend with a rotary beater for about 1 minute. Stir in the coconut flakes. Pour the mixture into an ice cream maker or two 9-inch cake pans, and place in the freezer. As ice crystals begin to form, beat the mixture in the pan, reducing almost to the liquid stage. Refreeze, and repeat the beating a few more times. The more often you beat the sherbet, the smoother it will be.

1 cup sugar
¾ cup water
2 cups coconut milk
1 cup skimmed milk
1 egg white, lightly beaten
½ cup sweetened coconut flakes

Coconut Milk

To make coconut milk from grated fresh or desiccated coconut, pour three cups of boiling water over two cups of coconut, cover, and let stand until lukewarm. Line a sieve with cheesecloth or a kitchen towel and pour in the coconut and liquid. Squeeze to extract as much of the liquid as possible. Discard the coconut. To prepare fresh coconut for the sherbet filling, stir about two tablespoons of syrup into one half cup of coconut and allow it to steep for about fifteen minutes.

Zesty Radish Slices

In these menus radishes come out of the salad bowl twice to be cooked and served as a garnish. Spiced Radishes (page 153) are kept whole. Here they are sliced, and the color of the two presentations is markedly different. When the radish is cooked whole, just the pink skin is visible; when it is sliced, the outer pink gives way to a thin circle of red and finally the white interior. Nature is a wonderful colorist indeed.

Makes about 6 cups

1. In a mixing bowl that can hold the radishes, make a dressing by whisking together the vermouth, oil, mustard, shallots, lime juice, tarragon, salt, and pepper.

2. Bring a large quantity of water to a boil while preparing the radishes. Discard the tops and tails, and slice the radishes about ⅛ inch thick. Add salt to the water with the radishes, and cook for 3 or 4 minutes, or until they are crisply tender. Drain well at once, shaking the colander sharply to drive off as much water as possible.

3. Immediately dump the radishes into the bowl with the dressing, and toss quickly to coat all the slices. Cover, and put aside for at least 1 hour, mixing occasionally.

4. Just before serving, roll up the lettuce leaves tightly, and cut them across into shreds. Toss the lettuce with the radishes just before serving.

Cooking Ahead: The radishes can be completely prepared the day before and refrigerated, but bring them back to room temperature before tossing with the lettuce and serving. The lettuce can be shredded several hours in advance and refrigerated in a tightly sealed plastic bag. An interesting change comes over the radish slices after a day or so: The pink-red-white coloration blends into a uniform pink.

½ cup vermouth
½ cup oil
1 tablespoon mustard
¼ cup shallots, chopped fine
juice of 1 lime
2 teaspoons tarragon, crumbled
salt and pepper
5 cups (4 6-ounce packages) radishes
3 or 4 romaine lettuce leaves

Vegetable Ragout

This unexpected little vegetable dish never fails to be greeted with surprised looks, quickly followed by satisfied smiles once it has been tasted. If there is some sauce left over, make that a beginning for a small supper: Replenish the turnips and mushrooms, and add new potatoes, carrots, and perhaps boiling onions.

1. Slowly heat the oil in a heavy saucepot while peeling and cutting the onion into thin slices. Cut the celery in half lengthwise, then across into ½-inch slices. Add the vegetables to the pot, stir to coat them with oil, cover, and simmer for 5 minutes over medium heat. Meanwhile, cut the ham into thin strips about 1 inch long and ⅛ inch wide, add them to the pot, and stirring often, cook for 5 minutes, uncovered.

2. Sprinkle on the flour, and stir into the ham and vegetables, scraping the bottom to keep the flour from burning. Add the wine, stock, tomato paste, and Madeira. Bruise the garlic cloves lightly, and pierce with toothpicks; depending on size, 2 or 3 cloves can be put on a pick. Make a bouquet garni of the parsley, thyme, tarragon, and bay leaf; add to the pot with the garlic. Sprinkle in the salt and pepper, cover partially, and cook for 30 minutes. From time to time skim off any scum that rises to the surface. Remove the bouquet garni, pressing it between two spoons to extract the liquid it holds. Lift out the garlic picks with a skimmer, and discard.

3. Add the turnips, and cook for about 10 minutes, or until tender when pierced with a small, sharp knife. Add the mushrooms, and cook for another 2 minutes.

Cooking Ahead: Prepare the sauce through Step 2, remove the bouquet garni and garlic, cool, and refrigerate. If desired, the thin layer of congealed fat on top of the sauce can be removed before you proceed with the recipe. At serving time, reheat the sauce and cook the turnips and mushrooms. If absolutely necessary, cook the turnips and mushrooms earlier in the day, but not the day before.

¼ cup olive oil
1 onion
1 celery rib
¼ pound cured prosciutto-style ham
2½ tablespoons flour
3 cups red wine
2 cups Beef Stock (page 219)
2 tablespoons tomato paste
2 tablespoons Madeira
6 garlic cloves, unpeeled
8 parsley sprigs
1 sprig fresh or ½ teaspoon thyme
1 sprig fresh or ½ teaspoon tarragon
1 bay leaf
½ teaspoon salt
½ teaspoon pepper
1¼ pounds turnips, peeled, quartered, and cut in half crosswise
½ pound mushrooms, whole if small, halved if large

Champignons Balzac
(Fried Stuffed Mushroom Caps)

When does a mushroom cap not look like a mushroom cap? When it is stuffed, paired with another, breaded, and fried. Rarely does a guest figure out what it is until the first bite. Although the crab stuffing is my favorite, other flaked, cooked fish could be substituted. Fried Parsley (see below) is a perfect accompaniment for the mushrooms but is not obligatory.

1. In a small, covered pan cook the shallots and green pepper until tender in just enough clam juice to cover. Scrape them into a bowl, and add crab meat, cheese, lemon juice, and bread crumbs. Season well with salt and pepper, adding a little clam juice if the mixture seems too dry.

2. Fill 2 similar-sized mushroom caps with the filling, press together, and scrape off any excess. Dip the stuffed cap in flour, and coat well; pay particular attention to the center seam. Dip first into the egg, then into bread crumbs. Coat the mushrooms well, place on a rack, and chill for at least 1 hour. If properly coated, the mushrooms will not separate during the frying, but if you worry, run a toothpick through the caps, and remove it before serving.

3. At serving time, in a large frying pan heat 1 inch of oil to medium-hot. Fry the mushrooms carefully, turning so that all sides will be a nice golden brown. Serve hot with the Green Sauce and lemon wedges.

Cooking Ahead: The coated mushrooms can remain in the refrigerator for as much as 5 or 6 hours. They cannot be fried in advance.

- 2 shallots, chopped fine
- ⅓ cup green pepper, chopped fine
- ½ to 1 cup clam juice
- 1½ cups crab meat
- ½ cup grated, mild Cheddar cheese
- juice of 1 lemon
- ⅔ cup bread crumbs plus bread crumbs for coating
- salt and pepper
- 32 large mushroom caps
- flour
- 1 egg, beaten
- oil
- Green Sauce (page 228)
- lemon wedges

Fried Parsley

1. Wash 1 bunch of very fresh parsley leaves, and dry thoroughly, really thoroughly. If any moisture clings to the leaves, it will splatter like Vesuvius in the hot oil. If in doubt, spread the leaves on a baking sheet, and place in a 175-degree oven for a few minutes.

2. Heat frying oil in a deep pan to 375 degrees. Put parsley leaves in a fine-meshed wire basket, and plunge into hot oil for no more than 5 seconds. Remove the basket, and drain parsley on paper towels. Sprinkle with salt, and serve immediately. Lacking a deep-fry basket, toss handfuls of parsley into a pan of hot oil, quickly remove them with a broad skimmer, and drain on absorbent paper.

⇊⇊⇊

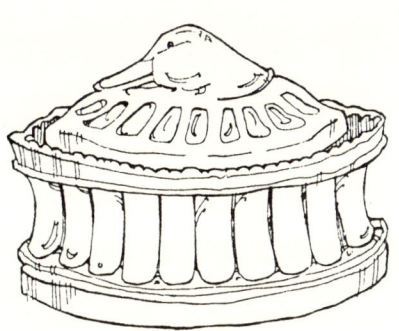

A Salute to Summer

SERVES 8

Fettucine Orvieto

Chicken in Lemon Aspic

Beet Relish

Steam-Baked Zucchini

Pecan Chiffon Custard

Jellied presentations are generally regarded as strictly summertime fare. Indeed, because of their glistening cool looks, they are especially inviting when the temperature soars. But there is no need to be so limited. Simply by bracketing the cold main course with hot dishes, you open many more months of the calendar to these delicious, easy-to-do terrines. The hot pasta beginning plate certainly says cool weather; for warm-weather menus try Double Mushrooms on Puffy Fried Noodles (page 140), Hot Asparagus with Herbed Vinaigrette (page 98), or Mushroom Flan (page 155). The Steam-Baked Zucchini are served on the main-course plate, each guest garnishing it as he likes. As for the terrine plate, you will find that the strong color of the beet relish is an emphatic presence next to the lemony aspic. Velvety smooth Pecan Chiffon Custard is a treat anytime. Whatever the month, rosé is the wine for this meal—a good Tavel or a Cabernet rosé from California.

Chicken in Lemon Aspic

4 pounds
calories per serving—226

Jellied meats and poultry open up another realm of terrine making. The flesh is first cooked in a well-flavored stock, cut into pieces, and encased in a shimmering aspic. Sometimes vegetables accompany the meat, sometimes not; much depends on the rest of the meal. When selecting a dish for the mold, pick one that fits a serving platter when turned upside down. A fairly deep, round bowl gives the best effect when the aspic is turned out, but a loaf dish is a good alternative.

Preheat oven to 350 degrees.

1. Heat the oil in a heavy casserole that can go into the oven, and add the sliced vegetables, slices of 1 lemon, and the garlic. Cover and simmer very slowly for about 20 minutes, or until the vegetables are quite limp but not at all browned. Sprinkle on a little salt and pepper.

2. With a slotted spoon, remove two-thirds of the vegetables, spreading the remainder evenly in the bottom of the pot. On this place a layer of chicken pieces, using half the quantity of chicken. Spread on half the remaining sautéed vegetables, and season with salt, pepper, ½ teaspoon of the fennel seeds, and slices of 1 lemon. Add the pimiento strips. Repeat again with the rest of the chicken and the remaining vegetables, condiments, and lemon slices.

3. Mix the vermouth, white wine, vinegar, and pimiento juice, and pour over the chicken. Then pour on enough chicken stock to raise the level of the liquid so that it almost completely covers the ingredients. Use as much liquid as possible to produce a good bit of aspic.

4. Bring the liquid to a slow simmer on top of the stove; place a piece of greased paper or aluminum foil over the chicken and vegetables. Cover with a lid, and bake for about 2 hours, depending on the quality of the chicken. Remove from the oven, uncover, and cool.

5. Place the chicken pieces in a colander over a deep dish to gather the liquid as it drips. Do the same with the cooked vegetables. Combine this drained stock with the rest of the cooking

½ cup oil
2 onions, sliced thin
3 celery stalks, sliced thin
4 large carrots, sliced thin
3 lemons, sliced thin and seeded
6 to 8 garlic cloves
salt and pepper
3- to 4-pound stewing chicken, cut into pieces
1 teaspoon fennel seeds
4-ounce jar pimiento, sliced into strips, juice reserved
½ cup dry vermouth
1 cup white wine
2 tablespoons wine vinegar
1 to 1½ cups Chicken Stock (page 218)
¼ pound string beans
1 to 2 tablespoons gelatin

stock. Cool and chill it so that the fat rises to the top and congeals; lift off the fat, and discard. Taste the aspic for salt. Remove the meat from the bones, discarding the skin and bones. Separate the meat into pieces.

6. Meanwhile, cook the beans until tender. To facilitate cutting later, they should not be too crisp, but not overcooked and mushy. It should take about 5 or 6 minutes. Drain and cool the beans at once under cold running water.

7. Depending on the jellied consistency of the stock (the bones of the chicken will have increased the gelantinous quality of the stock), add the necessary amount of gelatin. If the stock is slightly jellied, add only 1 tablespoon of gelatin for each pint. Use a little more rather than less gelatin since there will be some dilution of the aspic from the moisture that remains in the chicken and vegetables. Soften the gelatin in a little water, and then heat it thoroughly in the stock until it dissolves. Cool.

8. Ladle a thin layer of aspic into the mold, and chill to set. Decorate the mold with a circle of carrot slices in the middle and a red pimiento center. Arrange string beans in spoke fashion, radiating from the carrots. Any remaining string beans can be cut into short lengths and added to the cooked vegetables. Carefully ladle in enough of the syrupy aspic just to cover the vegetables; chill until firm.

9. Put layers of chicken meat in the mold, alternating with layers of the cooked vegetables. Press very lightly with the palms of your hands; then pour in enough aspic to cover the ingredients. Chill for at least 1 day; 2 days are better. Extra aspic can be chilled to set, then chopped to decorate the platter.

10. At serving time, quickly dip the mold into hot water, and unmold onto a serving platter. To slice, use a very sharp knife with a sawing motion.

Note: If a loaf dish mold is used, one possible decoration is a row of string beans arranged in Vs with carrot slices placed on alternating sides of the arms of the Vs.

Beet Relish

This is a colorful deep rosy purée. It is also an accompaniment that commands a lot of attention on the palate as well as on the plate. Thanks to the tang of horseradish and tartness of sour cream, it goes particularly well with all jellied terrines as well as with pastry-covered meat pâtés.

Makes about 1½ cups

Place all ingredients in the container of a blender or food processor, and process until smooth.

Cooking Ahead: Beet Relish can be made as much as 4 or 5 days in advance.

1½ cups (about 1 1-pound can) sliced beets, well drained
6 tablespoons sour cream
3 tablespoons horseradish
pepper

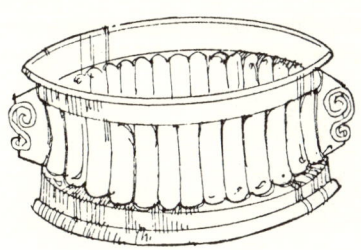

Fettucine Orvieto

Serving a small portion of pasta as a first course is very much in the Italian tradition in which it is most often used as a prelude to other enjoyments. Imported dry mushrooms are important to the sauce. Italian, French, Polish, even Hungarian will do, but not the Asian varieties. Grated cheese does not accompany this fettucine since the meat is already salted and strong in flavor, as are the mushrooms.

2 tablespoons dry imported mushrooms
1½ tablespoons butter
6 ounces smoked meat—tongue, ham, turkey breast
1 garlic clove, chopped fine
2 cups Chicken Stock (page 218)
pepper
2 eggs
2 tablespoons heavy cream
1 tablespoon oil
1 pound green fettucine
2 tablespoons parsley

1. In a small bowl cover the mushrooms with boiling water and allow to soak for 10 minutes. Drain well and save the water for other stocks and sauces. While the butter is melting, cut the meat into julienne strips. Then cook meat for 1 or 2 minutes over medium heat while stirring. Once the strips are lightly browned, add the mushrooms and garlic, and stir for a few seconds. Pour in chicken stock, grind in the pepper, cover, reduce the heat, and simmer for 10 minutes. Beat the eggs and cream together in a small bowl; pour in a ladleful of the hot stock while whisking vigorously. Return the diluted eggs to the pot, turn heat to very low, and cook about ½ minute, stirring continuously. There will be about 3 cups of sauce.

2. Bring a large quantity of water to a boil; add the oil and the fettucine. Keep the flame high, and add the pasta gradually to bring the water back to the boiling point quickly. Fresh pasta should be ready as soon as the water boils again; for dry fettucine a few minutes' cooking will be needed to cook until just *al dente*. Drain at once, shaking the colander vigorously to extrude all possible water.

3. Transfer the cooked pasta to a large mixing bowl, pour in the sauce, and toss together very well. Place on warmed plates, and sprinkle with a little parsley. Serve at once.

Cooking Ahead: The sauce improves if made the day before without the final egg-cream liaison. Just before serving, bring the sauce to a simmer, and add the beaten eggs and cream. The pasta must be cooked just before serving.

Pecan Chiffon Custard

Except for southern pecan pie and pralines, pecans are not used to their full potential in dessert making. Perhaps this recipe will help expand a few repertoires. If need be, walnuts could be substituted, but the final effect will not be quite so luscious.

1. Pour the water into a small cup, sprinkle the gelatin over it, and put aside to soften the gelatin. To grind the nuts in a food processor, use the on/off switch to prevent overprocessing the nuts and making them oily. If using a blender, grind in small batches.

2. Pour the milk into a heavy saucepan; add the cinnamon, sugar, and honey; and bring to the boiling point. Meanwhile, separate the eggs, putting the yolks and the whites in separate medium-sized bowls. Beat the yolks with a wire whisk; then slowly pour in about half the hot flavored milk, whisking vigorously all the time. If you wish, all the milk can be poured in. Return the egg yolk-milk mixture to the pot, and stirring constantly, cook it until the custard thickens enough to coat a spoon.

3. Scrape in the softened gelatin, and stir until it dissolves. Add the pecans, and cook for 1 minute more. Scrape the custard back into the mixing bowl; stir for a few minutes; then add the vanilla. Put aside to cool and thicken, about 1 hour; the thickening can be hastened by chilling the custard in the refrigerator after the mixture has cooled.

4. Beat the egg whites until quite firm, adding a little cream of tartar if a copper bowl is not used. Fold about one-third of the beaten whites into the nut custard, and incorporate them thoroughly with the whisk. Give the beaten whites a few more beatings with the whisk, scrape them over the custard, and lightly fold them in with a rubber spatula. Refrigerate for about 40 minutes.

5. Beat the cream until very stiff, fold it into the custard, and scoop it into a 6-cup serving dish or into 8 individual cups or dishes.

2 tablespoons water
½ tablespoon gelatin
1 cup pecans, ground
¾ cup milk
⅛ teaspoon cinnamon
¼ cup dark brown sugar, packed firm
2 tablespoons honey
3 eggs
1 tablespoon vanilla
cream of tartar
½ cup whipping cream

OPTIONAL GARNISH:
1 egg white, 16 pecan halves, sugar

6. To prepare the optional pecan garnish, preheat the oven to 350 degrees, lightly beat the egg white with a fork, place a pecan half on the fork, and lower into the white. Transfer the egg-coated nut to a baking sheet by pushing it off the fork with another fork. Sprinkle the coated nuts with a little sugar; then bake them for about 5 minutes, or until the coating has browned lightly. Remove at once from the baking sheet. Store in a cool spot in an airtight container. If serving from a large mold, place the nuts around the outer edge and a few nuts in the center; for individual dishes make Vs with 2 halves.

Steam-Baked Zucchini

This method of cooking zucchini isn't as much baking as it is steaming the squash in its own juice. The resulting sweet flavor far surpasses regular steaming, in which the vegetable juices fall into the steaming water below and are lost. This is the purest of the pure ways of cooking, and the most delicious.

Preheat oven to 350 degrees.

1. Cut off root and stem ends, and place the zucchini on a large sheet of aluminum foil. Seal the edges of the foil, and make an airtight package. Place the foil package on a baking sheet, and bake it for about 20 minutes, or until the zucchini are soft.

2. Serve the steamed zucchini whole; each guest splits it in half lengthwise and seasons it to his taste.

Cooking Ahead: The zucchini can be prepared in the aluminum foil package but cannot be baked until serving time. Since there is nothing to do, really, it should not worry the cook.

8 medium or 16 small zucchini, the smaller the better
seasonings: salt and pepper, melted butter, chopped chives, lemon wedges, Pesto (page 231)

Come by After the Theater

SERVES 10 to 12

Shredded Lettuce Soup
Goat Cheese Pâté
Marinated Onion Rings
Caramelized Pineapple

If served for an after-theater supper or weekend brunch, the rich Goat Cheese Pâté will easily serve twelve. Marinated Onion Rings provide the perfect sharp balancing note; Beet Relish (page 111) would be a good substitute for non-onion eaters. The meat begins with a very light but exotically flavored soup and ends with hot pineapple slices caramelized in a sauce that smacks of butterscotch. A light Zinfandel or Rioja would stand up to the pâté beautifully.

Goat Cheese Pâté

4 pounds
calories per serving—377

If pâté can be filled with meat, fish, and even vegetables, why not cheese, especially when the results are so devastatingly good? In several respects this pâté is a cousin to the Italian Crostata di Ricotta, which is made sweet or savory. Because of its richness, small portions of the pâté are in order. For this reason I've given two presentations, one traditional, the other more expeditious. I find the classic deep, round shape baked in a soufflé dish much prettier. But since today's dinner guest may prefer a thinner wedge, the recipe has also been worked out in a shallower version. Don't be tempted to serve this as a hot pâté. The soft cheese won't cut. On the other hand, if aspic is not used, any leftover slices can be *gently* warmed in the oven, just enough to remove the chill.

Preheat oven to 350 degrees.

1. Melt 6 tablespoons of the butter in a 1½-quart saucepot, add the garlic, and cook for ½ minute while stirring. Add the flour to make a very thick roux, and cook for ½ minute. Add the milk gradually while stirring with a wooden spoon; the sauce will be very thick. Add the cream, yogurt, nutmeg, kirsch, Tabasco, salt, and pepper. Remove the pot from the fire, add the Gruyère, and stir well. Let the sauce cool while slicing the ham into ¼-inch strips. Add the egg yolks to the cheese sauce and beat well for a few seconds.

2. Use the remaining 2 teaspoons of butter to grease a 7-inch soufflé dish or similar deep dish with a 5-cup capacity. Fold two 20-inch sheets of heavy-duty aluminum foil into four lengthwise folds, and place them in the dish in a crisscross fashion; this sling will help in removing the baked pâté from the deep dish. Roll out three-fourths of pastry into a 14-inch circle about ¼ inch thick. Fit the dough into the dish, pressing it against the sides and into the corners. With floured scissors cut away excess pastry, leaving a ½-inch edge, and add the trimmings to the reserved pastry.

3. Spoon one-fourth of the cheese sauce into the dish, and smooth it into an even layer. Slice half the goat cheese, and place it over the first layer. If properly moist, the goat cheese will crumble easily; that is why it is best to cut one slice, slide it off the knife directly into the dish, then continue with the next. Cover with another layer of one-fourth of the sauce, a

6 tablespoons plus 2 teaspoons butter
½ garlic clove, chopped fine
1 cup flour
1 cup milk
⅓ cup heavy cream
½ cup yogurt
⅛ teaspoon nutmeg
1 tablespoon kirsch
few drops Tabasco
½ teaspoon salt
½ teaspoon pepper
½ pound Gruyère, Emmenthaler, or fontina cheese, grated
¼-pound about ¼ inch-thick slice lightly smoked ham
2 egg yolks
2 pounds Pastry (page 217)
6 ounces goat cheese, preferably Montrachet or similar moist cheese

layer of the ham strips, another fourth of the sauce, a goat cheese layer, and a final topping of the cheese sauce.

4. Roll out the reserved pastry into a circle about 8 inches in diameter; brush water over the pastry edge in the dish and around the edge of the top circle. Reverse the top circle as it is placed in the dish so that the two wet edges meet. Fold over the edge of the bottom layer of pastry into the dish, and press it firmly against the top layer. Flute the edge, and run your finger around the rim of pastry so that none of it is over the edge of the dish, where it would bake and stick, making removal difficult. Cut a ½-inch hole in the center of the pastry, and fit a small parchment paper chimney into it. The top can be decorated with cutouts of leftover pastry. Brush the pastry with beaten egg, and bake for about 1 hour, or until the filling reaches a temperature of 140 degrees. Cool to room temperature.

5. With your hands, rotate the pâté slightly to make certain it is loose in the dish; then use the foil sling to lift it out onto a serving platter. Chill.

6. There will be space between the pâté filling and the pastry top which can be filled with syrupy chicken aspic. Add the aspic only after the pâté has been throughly chilled, and chill it again to set the aspic. At serving time, place a small bouquet of parsley in the center hole, and cut the pâté into wedges.

Alternate Version

1. Prepare the sauce as above, but after cutting the ham into strips, cut it into pieces about ½ inch long. Butter an 11-inch quiche pan or pie-pan, line it with three-fourths of the pastry, and spoon in half the cheese sauce.

2. Slice the goat cheese, and arrange the slices in concentric circles, starting about ½ inch from the edge. Scatter the ham pieces among the cheese slices; then cover with the remaining cheese sauce.

3. Roll out the rest of the pastry, and cover the filling; seal the edges as above. Because of the width of the pan, make 3 vent holes. Bake at 350 degrees for about 40 minutes, or until the filling reaches a temperature of 140 degrees. Cool to room temperature, remove from pan, place on platter, and chill.

1 egg, beaten
Optional: 1 cup chicken aspic (page 222)

⇊⇊⇊

Marinated Onion Rings

Blanching not only softens onion rings but also takes away the bite of the onion.

1. In a bowl that can hold the onions, beat together the oil, vinegar, orange juice, Tabasco, and salt.

2. Drop the onions into a pot of boiling water. Once the water has returned to a boil, cook for 10 seconds. Drain well.

3. Dump the onions into the bowl, toss well to coat all surfaces with the marinade, cover, and put aside for at least 3 hours. Lift the onions out of the marinade when serving.

Cooking Ahead: These onions will keep for several weeks in the refrigerator.

3 tablespoons olive oil
3 tablespoons rice wine vinegar
2 tablespoons orange juice
few drops of Tabasco
½ teaspoon salt
2 pounds onions, sliced thin

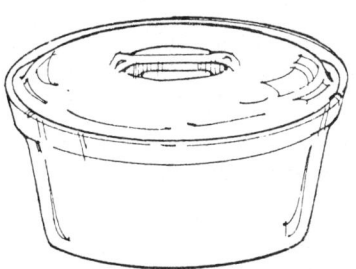

Shredded Lettuce Soup

The much disdained iceberg lettuce does have a few attributes. Crispness is definitely one of them. It is this quality that is called for in this slightly spicy soup.

1. Pour chicken stock into a pot. Make a thin paste of the curry with a little water, and add it to the stock, along with the ginger, soy sauce, and Tabasco. Cover and simmer soup for 15 minutes.

2. Meanwhile, shred the lettuce by cutting it first into wedges, then across to produce thin strips. There should be about 8 cups of shredded lettuce. Distribute it among 10 soup bowls.

3. When the soup is ready to be served, remove it from the fire, and add the sesame seed oil. Discard the ginger slices, and ladle the hot soup over the lettuce. Serve at once.

Cooking Ahead: The soup will be even better if cooked a day in advance and its flavor is allowed to deepen. Add the sesame seed oil only after reheating. The lettuce can be cut early in the day, kept in a plastic bag in the refrigerator, and removed about 2 hours before serving time so it will lose its chill.

8 cups Chicken Stock (page 218)
1½ teaspoons curry
6 thin slices fresh ginger
3 tablespoons soy sauce
⅛ teaspoon Tabasco or more to taste
1 iceberg lettuce
2 teaspoons sesame seed oil

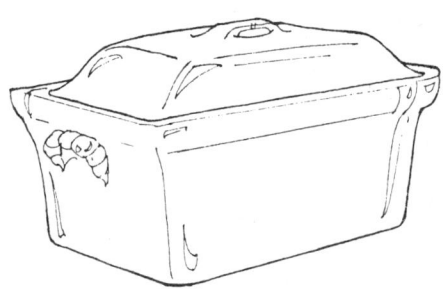

Caramelized Pineapple

Even though pineapple slices are coated with sugar in this hot dessert, the underlying tartness of the fruit maintains a refreshing balance.

1. Melt the butter in a large nonreactive skillet. Sprinkle ½ tablespoon of the brown sugar over each pineapple slice. When the butter is hot and foamy, put in the slices, sugared sides down. Fry for about 3 minutes, or until the bottoms are lightly browned. Sprinkle another ½ tablespoon brown sugar over each slice, turn, and fry the second side until it, too, is nicely browned. Remove the pineapple slices to a platter, keeping them in a single layer.	10 tablespoons butter ¾ cup dark brown sugar 10 slices pineapple, preferably fresh; if canned, unsweetened 1½ cups heavy cream 3 tablespoons kirsch

2. Pour the cream and kirsch into the skillet, and simmer while scraping in the caramelized sugar from the bottom of the skillet. The sauce should be thick and syrupy in about 1 minute. Return the pineapple slices to the sauce, and turn them several times to warm all surfaces. Serve on warm plates.

Cooking Ahead: The pineapple slices can be fried and the sauce can be made in the morning. Keep the pineapple covered in a single layer on a platter. Leave the sauce in a covered skillet; do not refrigerate. At serving time, reheat the sauce slowly, adding a tablespoon of water if it seems too thick. Once the sauce is bubbling, add the pineapple to reheat.

Come for a Celebration

SERVES 8

Crevettes au Pernod (Shrimp with Pernod)

Pâté Chaud de Veau et Jambon en Croûte
(Hot Veal and Ham Pâté in Crust)

Spaghetti Squash and Peas

Honeydew Balls in Strawberry Sauce

Pastry-wrapped pâtés are real show-stoppers. But they are not just looks; a lot of good eating is within. This veal and ham pâté is a particularly elegant one which could be a rather untraditional centerpiece for Christmas dinner. Since the first-course shrimp are meant to be eaten with fingers, they could be served during the cocktail hour, meaning one less plate service at the table. If sauce is offered with the pâté, the hot spaghetti squash is best served separately, following the pâté, but on the same plate. Dessert is a colorful and refreshing double fruit combination. When the shrimp are served at the table instead of with cocktails, pour a white Bordeaux, then go on to a small red Bordeaux for the rest of the meal.

Pâté Chaud de Veau et Jambon en Croûte
(Hot Veal and Ham Pâté in Crust)

4 pounds
calories per serving—270

Real pâtés, those wrapped in pastry, are extravagant-looking. No question of it, they take more time to put together. I have found, though, that the most time is spent on the decorating, which could be minimized without much artistic loss. Page 19 offers some decorative suggestions. For this menu the pâté is served hot, but it could also be served cold. In the latter case add a minced garlic clove, and increase all the seasonings. Once chilled, aspic can be poured through the chimney hole to fill in any spaces (page 13). Preparing a pâté in pastry is illustrated on page 11.

1. Cut the veal and ham into long, thin strips, no more than ½ inch wide. Remove all nerves and membranes, and place the meats in separate bowls. Scatter the shallots over both meats. Sprinkle the veal with salt and pepper; sprinkle the ham with ¼ teaspoon of the allspice and pepper. Pour enough white wine and brandy over the veal to macerate it; use white wine and brandy, plus Madeira, for the ham. Do not use so much alcohol that the meat swims in the liquid. Mix the meats with your hands to coat all strips with the seasonings. Cover, and put aside for at least 3 hours or overnight in the refrigerator. Mix occasionally.

2. Grind the pork two or three times, or process it in a food processor until fairly smooth. Put the pork in a mixing bowl, and add the remaining ¼ teaspoon allspice, the thyme, salt, and pepper. Pour in the unabsorbed alcohols from the marinating bowls, plus a little extra brandy and Madeira. Mix the pork very well; add the bread crumbs; mix again. Finally, add 1 beaten egg, and mix thoroughly. Fry a small piece of the forcemeat, cool slightly, taste for seasonings, and correct if necessary.

3. On a well-floured pastry board roll out Pastry into a rectangle approximately 18 × 12 inches. It should be twice as thick as for a tart. Cut off the edges of the dough to make the rectangle even; reserve the dough. In the center form the pâté into a rectangle approximately 11 × 4 inches.

1½ pounds Pastry (page 217)
½ pound 1-inch-thick veal scallop
½ pound 1-inch-thick lightly smoked ham
2 shallots, chopped fine
salt and pepper
½ teaspoon allspice
white wine
brandy
Madeira
1¼ pounds pork with some fat
½ teaspoon thyme
¼ cup bread crumbs
2 eggs
parsley sprigs
enough butter to coat a baking sheet
OPTIONAL:
⅓ cup pistachio nuts
Orbec Sauce (page 223)

4. First, spread about one-fourth of the forcemeat into that rectangular shape. When you work with the forcemeat, it is best to keep your fingers wet. Next, place half the meat strips over the pork, alternating the veal and ham slices. Pistachio nuts can be tucked between the rows. Do not stretch the meat slices, but keep them quite loose since the meat shrinks a little during the baking and would leave holes if stretched to fit. Now take half the remaining forcemeat, and pat it over the meat strips. This layer of forcemeat and the last will be a little thicker than the first since the pâté will be reversed and the heavier layers should be on the bottom. Repeat with the remaining meat strips and finally with the last of the forcemeat. As you are building the pâté, keep patting in the sides to keep them straight and firm.

5. To form the crust shell, cut away squares of pastry from the four corners, but do not cut as far as the meats; reserve the extra dough. Brush some of the remaining beaten egg over all the pastry, lift one of the long sides, and pull it up over the pâté; do not stretch the pastry. Brush with egg the strip of pastry over the top of the meat. Lift the opposite long side of pastry, and pull it over the first layer of pastry. Next, cover the ends of the pâté, always brushing with the egg. Heavily butter a baking sheet, and carefully slide a large spatula under the pâté to make certain that at no point is it sticking to the board. Lift the pâté and reverse it onto the baking sheet. (Note: This pastry covering and an alternative method that does not require reversing the pâté are discussed on page 11.)

Preheat oven to 450 degrees.

6. Take a small bit of the reserved dough, and roll it between the palms of your hands to form a rope almost ½ inch wide. Paint the bottom of the pâté crust with egg, and tuck one pastry rope against it; push it in slightly so that it forms a foundation for the pâté. If the rope is made in several lengths, brush the overlapping ends with egg. Roll out the remaining dough, and use it to decorate the crust, always brushing with egg. Paint the entire surface of the pâté with egg, and wipe away any egg that may have dropped onto the baking sheet and from around the bottom of the pastry rope.

THE PÂTÉS, TERRINES, AND THEIR ACCOMPANIMENTS · 125

7. Make two vent holes in the top of the crust, insert parchment paper chimneys, and place in the oven. When the crust whitens a little, about 15 minutes, indicating that it has begun to bake, reduce the heat to 375 degrees, and bake for about 1 to 1¼ hours, or until a thermometer registers 160 degrees. The juices visible in the paper chimneys should be clear. If the crust becomes too brown during the baking, cover it with aluminum foil. Remove the pâté from the oven, and let it rest for about 30 minutes before slicing. Tuck parsley sprigs into the chimney holes. Reheat sauce, and pass separately.

Cooking Ahead: The pâté can be formed and refrigerated a day before baking. It can also be baked, cooled, wrapped in aluminum foil, and refrigerated. To reheat, bring the pâté to room temperature, and bake it in the foil at 325 degrees for 30 to 40 minutes, or 130 degrees on the thermometer.

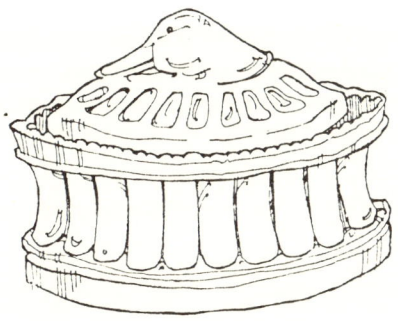

Crevettes au Pernod (Shrimp with Pernod)

The anise-flavored alcohol in this shrimp broth adds a bitingly refreshing note to the shellfish. This is a convivial dish that would provide perfect summertime enjoyment as a main course or star as a first course anytime an unusual beginning is called for. Once the diners have finished peeling the shrimp, they would welcome that Japanese nicety—a hot, wet washcloth. This first course could also be served during the cocktail hour. When available, crayfish may be used instead of shrimp.

1. Add the onion to the water in a 3-quart pot along with the bay leaves, rosemary, Tabasco, and peppercorns. Squeeze in the juice of the lemon, and toss the shells in as well. Bring the water to a boil, cover, and simmer for 10 minutes.

2. Add the liqueur and shrimp, cover, and simmer gently for about 2 minutes, or just until the shrimp begin to turn a bright pink. Remove from the heat immediately. It is important to undercook the shrimp slightly at this point since they will continue to cook in the hot broth. Put aside the pot, still covered, to cool to room temperature; then refrigerate. The shrimp should marinate for at least 1 day before being served.

3. To serve, place the shrimp in a bowl with some of the cooking broth spooned over them. Have another bowl ready for the discarded shells, and provide plenty of paper napkins.

Cooking Ahead: Although Shrimp with Pernod need at least 1 day of marinating time, they would only improve if given 2 or 3 days in the broth.

- 1 onion, chopped coarse
- 3 cups water
- 2 bay leaves
- 1 tablespoon rosemary, preferably fresh
- ½ teaspoon Tabasco
- 3 tablespoons crushed peppercorns
- 1 lemon
- ½ cup anise-flavored liqueur (Pernod, Ouzo, Arak, etc.)
- 2 pounds shrimp in their shells

Spaghetti Squash and Peas

Like most squashes, the spaghetti variety has a mild flavor, making it a perfect foil for more assertive seasonings. The squash can be baked or can be punctured with a few holes and boiled. I prefer to cut it in half and braise it in a seasoned broth to enable it to absorb flavor during the cooking. The only problem with this method is that the tough squash requires a large, sharp knife and a sturdy arm.

2 pound spaghetti squash
8 scallions, white and green, cut into ½-inch pieces
3 basil sprigs or 1½ tablespoons dried basil
salt and pepper
⅓ cup butter
½ to 1 garlic clove, sliced
10-ounce package frozen peas

1. Use a cleaver or a large, sturdy knife to split the squash in half lengthwise. Lay the edge of the knife or cleaver on the squash, and hit the knife with a wooden mallet or hammer to force it through the tough skin. Use a large spoon to scoop out the seeds and fibers inside the squash.

2. Scatter the scallion pieces in a large skillet or pot that can hold the squash halves side by side. Tuck a basil sprig inside each squash half and sprinkle with salt, pepper, and dried basil, if the latter is used. Place the squash in a skillet, cut sides down, and pour in water to a depth of about ½ inch. Bring the water to a boil, cover the skillet, and simmer for 20 to 25 minutes, or until a knife cuts through the skin fairly easily. Do not overcook, or the squash will become mushy and not produce spaghetti strands. Put the squash aside to cool. Remove the scallions with a skimmer, and place them in a 1½-quart pot.

3. While the squash is cooking, melt the butter with the garlic slices. Do not allow the garlic to brown. When the butter is melted, cover and put aside. If you like a stronger garlic flavor, as I do, leave the garlic slices in the butter for the time being.

4. Put the peas in the water used for cooking the squash and scallions, and cook them for just a few minutes. Transfer them with a skimmer to the pot containing the scallions. Pull out the spaghetti squash strands with a fork, and add them to the pot.

5. Sprinkle in about ¼ cup of the cooking water, stir to moisten the vegetables, cover, and reheat over low heat. Chop the remaining basil sprig. Just before serving, reheat the butter, remove the garlic slices, and pour the butter over the vegetables.

Toss to mix well, transfer to a serving bowl, and sprinkle with the chopped or dried basil.

Cooking Ahead: All three vegetables can be cooked the day before and refrigerated separately, adding the ¼ cup cooking water to the peas. Finish the reheating and butter addition just before serving.

↓↓↓

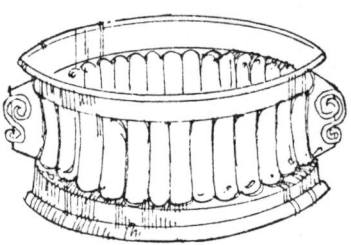

Honeydew Balls in Strawberry Sauce

Honeydew melons have not only a flavor that hints of honey but also a crisp texture that is especially refreshing at the end of a meal. Cut into balls, the pale green fruit is bathed in red strawberry sauce at the last minute, adding a contrasting color and a slight tartness to tickle the palate.

1. Place the strawberries in the blender, add ¼ cup sugar, the fruit nectar, mint leaves, lemon juice, and 1 tablespoon of the kirsch. Process until the berries are completely puréed. Taste, and add sugar if necessary, but remember to keep the sauce on the tart side.

2. Cut the melon in half, scoop out the seeds and membranes, and cut the flesh with a melon baller. Put the melon balls in a deep bowl, sprinkle them with 2 or 3 tablespoons of kirsch, and mix with your hands to bring all the fruit into contact with the alcohol. Cover the bowl tightly, and refrigerate for 1 hour. Mix the melon once or twice.

3. Just before serving, drain the kirsch and juice from the melon balls, pour the strawberry sauce over them, and mix thoroughly; here again, your hands are the best instrument. Transfer to a serving bowl, and place the mint sprig in the center if it is used.

Cooking Ahead: The sauce can be made 1 or 2 days in advance. The melon balls can be made in the morning and, if need be, even the day before. Always keep them tightly covered in the refrigerator. Do not mix the sauce and melon together until just before serving.

---

1 pint strawberries or 10-ounce package frozen strawberries, unsweetened
about ¼ sugar
¼ cup apricot or peach nectar
¼ cup fresh mint leaves
juice of ½ lemon
¼ cup kirsch
6-pound honeydew melon

OPTIONAL:
mint sprig garnish

A Warming Supper After the Game

SERVES 8

Artichoke Sunburst

Tourtière (Hot Canadian Meat Pie)

Tomatoes with Green Sauce

Poached Pears with Pear Custard

Tourtière is another pastry-wrapped pâté but quite unlike the preceding one. This Canadian specialty is baked in a pie dish, rather than in a loaf shape. It has more of a homespun look, and the flavor is as good as any home cooking you've had. The filling of the pie is brown, so to brighten the plate, tomatoes and a light green sauce go beside it. The Artichoke Sunburst is a dramatic-looking first course that can be served at the table or with cocktails. Pure pear flavor is the hallmark of the cool dessert in which pears do double duty as fruit and sauce. Particularly well suited to the menu would be Côtes du Rhône red or a California Petite-Sirah.

Tourtière (Hot Canadian Meat Pie)

3½ pounds
calories per serving—296

Though little is heard of Canadian cuisine, this hot meat pie is one exception. Tourtière (literally, pie dish) was brought below the border at the turn of the century, when Québecois settled to work in New England mill towns. As with any traditional dish, there are infinite variations. Some cooks use only diced meats, others only ground, and then there are those who compromise and use a combination. I prefer the latter since it gives the pie a more interesting texture. Potatoes, diced or mashed, are often added. This French Canadian specialty is indeed a pâté; only its shape is different. It is also good cold.

1. In a large, heavy skillet melt the butter, and simmer the onions and garlic for 5 minutes, covered; do not allow them to brown. Add the tomatoes with their juice, squashing the pulp as you do; cover; and cook for another 2 minutes.

2. Add the pork, and fry it while breaking up lumps with a fork. Fry until all traces of pink have disappeared from the meat. Add the beef, beef stock, wine, allspice, cloves, nutmeg, salt, pepper, and bay leaves. Reduce heat, cover, and simmer for 30 minutes.

3. Remove cover, turn up the heat, and cook until almost all liquid has disappeared; discard the bay leaves. Stir in just enough bread crumbs to bind the meats. Taste for seasonings, correct if necessary, and cool to room temperature.

Preheat oven to 425 degrees.

4. Line a deep 10-inch pie dish with pastry, spoon in the filling, and cover with pastry. Crimp the pie edges, and decorate the top, if you like, with leftover pastry scraps. Cut a 1-inch hole in the center, and fit it with a parchment paper chimney. Brush the entire surface with the beaten egg.

5. Bake for 15 minutes, reduce the heat to 350 degrees, brush the pastry again with more egg, and bake for another 20 to 25 minutes, or until a thermometer registers 150 degrees. Rest the pie for 15 minutes before cutting into wedges.

Cooking Ahead: Tourtière can be baked a day or two in advance and refrigerated. Bring back to room temperature, pour in about ¼ cup mixed beef stock and wine (or just stock) through the chimney, and reheat in a 350-degree oven for about 45 minutes, or until a thermometer reaches 140 degrees.

3 tablespoons butter or oil
2 onions, chopped fine
4 garlic cloves, minced
14-ounce can plum tomatoes
¾ pound blade shoulder pork, ground
¾ pound beef, cut into ¼-inch pieces
½ cup Beef Stock (page 219)
½ cup white wine or additional Beef Stock
¼ teaspoon allspice
⅛ teaspoon ground cloves
⅛ teaspoon nutmeg
salt and pepper
2 bay leaves
¼ to ½ cup bread crumbs
1 pound Pastry (page 217)
1 egg, beaten

↡↡↡

Artichoke Sunburst

This centerpiece first course may be served during the cocktail hour. A single artichoke is separated into petals, each holding a dollop of light green sauce. Possibilities for the filling are limited only by your imagination. Some suggestions might be cold scrambled eggs mixed with chopped tomatoes or Pesto (page 231), red pepper strips, shrimp with a dab of Pink Horseradish Sauce, even small squares of tofu and a few drops of sesame seed oil. The heart of the vegetable is turned into a receptacle for dipping sauce for crab claws. Have ready paper napkins and small dishes for the discarded artichoke leaves.

1. Snap off the artichoke stem, cut the sharp leaf points with scissors, and cook the artichoke in a pot of boiling salted water with the lemon slices. Test for doneness by piercing the bottom of the heart with a small, sharp knife; it should cut easily. The cooking time will vary between 20 and 30 minutes. Lift the artichoke out of the water, drain upside down, cool, and refrigerate.

2. Select a large round platter. Break off 1 artichoke leaf at a time, and arrange on the platter in concentric circles, allowing room to place the crab claws between them. As you reach the center core, the leaves will become too soft to use in this presentation. Twist off this center cone, and with a teaspoon, scrape out and discard the fuzzy choke covering the heart. Place the heart in the center of the platter.

3. Fill the artichoke heart with Pink Horseradish Sauce, tuck crab claws between the artichoke leaves, and spoon a little of the Niçoise Mayonnaise onto each leaf. Guests eat the sauce while scraping the flesh of the artichoke leaf between their teeth.

Cooking Ahead: The artichoke can be cooked 1 or 2 days in advance and refrigerated in a plastic bag. The sauce can also be done several days in advance and refrigerated. The arranging of the platter should not be done more than ½ hour before serving since it might begin to look a bit dry.

1 artichoke
salt
1 or 2 lemon slices
about 2 dozen crab claws
1 cup Pink Horseradish Sauce (page 229)
½ cup Niçoise Mayonnaise (page 227)

Poached Pears with Pear Custard

This custard is unlike others in that it begins not with a creamy base, but with puréed pears. The purée is then enriched with custard ingredients. A tiny bit of cinnamon is added to set the sauce apart from the flavor of the pure fruit itself.

1. Select a pan or skillet that will hold in a single layer 8 pears cut in half. Pour in the nectar or juice, sugar, and liqueur; bring to a boil; cover; reduce heat; and simmer slowly while peeling the pears.

2. Select 8 of the nicest-looking pears, peel them, cut in half lengthwise, remove seeds and core, and drop into acidulated water. Slip the pears into the syrup, re-cover, and cook until the fruit sections are soft but not overcooked. Remember, once removed from the syrup, the hot pears will continue to soften a little. They should be ready in 5 to 8 minutes, depending on their ripeness. Lift the pears out of the syrup with a skimmer, and place them in a large bowl that will not crowd them. Cool; then chill.

3. Meanwhile, peel the remaining pears, cut into quarters, and core them. Bring the syrup back to a boil, add these pears, re-cover, and simmer until they are quite soft. Lift the pears out of the syrup with a skimmer, and put them in the container of a blender or food processor. Reserve the cooking syrup.

4. Purée the pears; there should be about 1½ cups of purée. Scrape the purée into a saucepot, put on medium heat, and bring to the boiling point. In a bowl beat together the eggs, cream, cinnamon, and 1 tablespoon of the cooking syrup; beat all together very well. While constantly whisking, pour the egg-cream mixture into the purée, reduce the heat, and cook for about 1 minute more, or until the custard thickens. Do not let the custard come to a boil. Remove from the heat, cool for 1 minute, add the butter, and stir until the butter melts. Cool; then chill.

1½ cups pear nectar or apple juice
1 tablespoon sugar
2 tablespoons pear liqueur or kirsch
3 pounds (about 16) pears
3 eggs
½ cup cream
⅛ teaspoon cinnamon
2 tablespoons butter, cut into pieces

5. Serve 2 halves per guest, filling the cavity with pear custard; pass extra custard.

Cooking Ahead: Both the poached pears and the custard can be prepared 1 or 2 days in advance and kept refrigerated. In this case, once the cooking syrup is cold, pour it over the pears before refrigerating them.

⇓⇓⇓

Tomatoes with Green Sauce

This is another example of what good use can be made of pesto. Yogurt contributes a mild tartness to this sauce, but pesto gives it muscle. The color contrast of pale green and bright red makes this an appealing garnish for any number of pâtés.

Plunge the tomatoes, a few at a time, into boiling water for a few seconds, remove, cool, and peel. Cut the tomatoes into ¼-inch slices. Mix the yogurt and pesto together in a small bowl, and spoon the mixture over the center of each tomato slice, allowing the sauce to spread over most of the surface. The dish looks prettiest if some red tomato edge is allowed to show.	2 pounds (7 or 8) tomatoes 1½ cups yogurt ⅓ cup Pesto (page 231)

Cooking Ahead: The sauce can be mixed together several days in advance. As much as 3 or 4 hours ahead, tomatoes can be peeled, sliced, placed in a bowl, covered, and refrigerated. At serving time, lift the tomatoes from the bowl, leaving behind any juices that have collected, and add the sauce.

A Three-Act Play of Palate Pleasures

SERVES 8

Double Mushrooms on Puffy Fried Noodles
Scallop Terrine
Broccoli Purée on Endive Spears
Icy Oranges with Hot Orange-Ginger Sauce

This pure white Scallop Terrine is the simplest of all fish terrines to make, yet by being presented in a shallow pool of red tomato sauce, plus a sprig of watercress, it takes on very glamorous airs. Because of the sauce, however, a garnish cannot be placed on the dish. The answer turns out to be a thick coriander-scented Broccoli Purée on Endive Spears and eaten out of hand. The spears can be placed on the bread-and-butter dish, perched along the edge of the dinner plate, or enjoyed immediately. The terrine is preceded by dried oriental and fresh mushrooms in a brown sauce over warm oriental noodles—a triple contrast in textures. The finale is in perfect sophisticated tempo with the rest of the meal—chilled orange slices under a hot gingery sauce. White wine is the natural choice—a California Chardonnay, white Burgundy, or Riesling.

Scallop Terrine

2½ pounds
calories per serving—170

The fish section begins with the simplest terrine, and, to my taste, most delicate. Scallop Terrine is subtle, with the pure flavor of the sea, definitely not to be served after a three-martini cocktail hour. The mold can be lined with crêpes before baking, covered with blanched spinach leaves a few hours before serving, or, as below, sliced and arranged on individual dishes with its sauce and garnish. Chilling the food processor bowl and steel blade is essential.

1. Place the food processor bowl in the refrigerator and the steel blade in the freezer. Put the shallots and white wine in a small pot, place on high heat, and boil to reduce the wine to 2 tablespoons. Scrape the shallots and wine into a small bowl, cool, add the vermouth, and chill. Meanwhile, break the bread into large pieces, soak in a bowl with the milk, and let stand for 5 to 10 minutes. Squeeze out the bread, and chill.

Preheat oven to 250 degrees.

2. Place in the chilled processor bowl the scallops, shallots with wines, bread, salt, pepper, and a few drops of Tabasco. Process with the on/off switch to chop the scallops into coarse pieces. Then, with the motor running, slowly pour in the cream, and process until the mixture is smooth. Scrape down the sides, and with the motor running, add the egg whites. Poach a spoonful, cool, taste for seasonings, and correct if necessary.

3. Cut parchment or wax paper to fit the bottom and top of a 6-cup loaf dish. Butter the dish, fit in the paper, and butter it. Spoon in the scallop purée; tap the mold sharply on the counter several times to settle the mixture well into the dish. Butter the second piece of paper, and place it, buttered side down, over the terrine. Cover closely with aluminum foil, and pierce a small hole in the foil. Put the mold in a water bath (page 9), and bake for about 1 hour, or until the terrine reaches an internal temperature of 150 degrees. The terrine should feel firm to the touch. Leave it in the water bath, but remove the foil. Cool for 30 minutes; remove from the water bath; then lightly

- 2 shallots, chopped coarse
- ½ cup white wine
- 3 tablespoons dry vermouth
- 2 slices white bread, crusts removed
- ½ cup milk
- 2 pounds scallops
- salt and pepper
- Tabasco
- 1 cup heavy cream
- 2 egg whites
- butter
- Light Tomato Sauce (page 224)
- watercress

weight it with no more than 2 pounds; remove the weights after 2 hours. Refrigerate the terrine for at least 1 day; 2 days are better.

4. Remove the terrine from the refrigerator about 1 hour before serving time; unmold it onto a platter, removing both pieces of paper. Pour about ¼ cup of Light Tomato Sauce onto chilled individual serving plates. Rotate the dish to coat its surface evenly and place a slice of the Scallop Terrine in the center. Add a few sprigs of watercress.

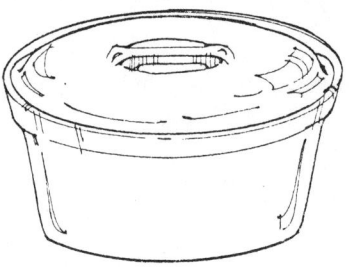

Broccoli Purée on Endive Spears

The haunting flavor behind the broccoli in this purée is fresh coriander, a well-used herb in Asian and Spanish kitchens. Also known as cilantro, coriander belongs to the parsley family and has a light lemon flavor with a hint of licorice. Coriander seeds, dried or ground, cannot be substituted. Devoid of the pungency of the fresh leaves, coriander seeds are mild and slightly sweet. If fresh coriander is not available, mint can be substituted for a very good but different purée.

Makes about 1½ cups

1. Separate the stalks from the broccoli florets. Peel the stalks, and cut them into 2-inch lengths. Boil the pieces in lightly salted water until almost tender, about 6 minutes. Add the florets, and cook for 2 minutes more. Drain well.

2. Put the broccoli in the food processor, and chop with the on/off switch until it is reduced to coarse pieces. Add the coriander, ¼ cup of the chicken stock, salt, and pepper. Process until fairly smooth but not completely puréed. Some tiny pieces should remain. This purée should be stiff enough to stand up on a spoon. Depending on the proportion of stalks to florets, a little more stock may be needed to reach the right consistency. If you are using a blender, at least the full amount will be necessary.

3. Spread about 1½ tablespoons of the purée into the curve of the endive spears, and smooth the tops. Place on a dish in a radiating pattern.

Cooking Ahead: Broccoli Purée can be prepared 1 or 2 days before and refrigerated.

½ pound broccoli (stalks and florets)
salt
3 tablespoons fresh coriander, chopped
¼ to ½ cup Chicken Stock (page 218)
pepper
16 endive spears

Double Mushrooms on Puffy Fried Noodles

There are several reasons why two mushrooms are better than one in this preparation. The oriental dried mushroom permeates the dish with its exotic flavor, while the fresh white mushroom brings a last-minute crispness and light color note.

1. Rinse and put the dried mushrooms in a small pot. Bring the water to a boil; pour it over the mushrooms; cover it; put aside to soak for at least 30 minutes. Always keeping the pot covered, simmer the mushrooms in their soaking water for 15 minutes, add the soy sauce, and simmer for another 15 minutes. Strain the mushrooms over a bowl to reserve the cooking liquid; there should be about 1 cup; add water to fill out if not. Cool the mushrooms, and remove the stems, right up to the cap; scissors work very well here. No amount of cooking will soften the stems. Cut the mushrooms into ¼-inch slices.

2. Pour the mushroom cooking water into a saucepot, add beef stock and celery, cover, and simmer for 15 minutes. Add both the Chinese and fresh mushrooms and the Madeira, and bring back to a simmer. Stir water into the cornstarch to make a thin paste, pour it into the bubbling sauce, and cook it for about 15 minutes, or until the sauce thickens and turns from opaque to clear. Transfer to a warm serving bowl.

3. To serve, place mounds of Puffy Fried Noodles on warmed individual plates. Pass Double Mushrooms at the table.

Cooking Ahead: The Chinese mushrooms can be cooked, stemmed, and sliced 1 or 2 days in advance and refrigerated in their cooking water. The fresh mushrooms can be sliced 1 hour in advance, dipped in acidulated water, drained, tightly covered, and refrigerated. (There really are so few mushrooms to slice that it seems less trouble to prepare them at the last minute, as is preferable.) Adding the fresh mushrooms to the hot liquid and making the sauce must be done just before serving. Cornstarch-thickened sauces cannot be held.

- 2 ounces dried Chinese mushrooms
- 3 cups water
- 1 tablespoon soy sauce
- 1½ cups Beef Stock (page 219)
- 1 celery rib, cut in half lengthwise and sliced thin
- 1 tablespoon Madeira or port
- ¼ pound mushrooms, sliced thin
- 3 tablespoons cornstarch
- Puffy Fried Noodles (page 216)

Icy Oranges with Hot Orange-Ginger Sauce

Savory dishes are served in Britain at the very end of the meal—following dessert—to freshen the palate after the sweet dish. Powerful ginger certainly takes care of that, even when incorporated in the dessert, and pity anything that would follow it. Preserved ginger in syrup is available in most fine shops, the gourmet sections of supermarkets, or Asian, Dutch, and English specialty stores.

1. Use a sharp stainless steel knife to remove the skin and pith from the oranges: First slice off the top and bottom ends of each orange; stand it on a cutting board; position the knife where the orange flesh begins; and using vertical strokes, cut away the peel and white pith. No white pith should cling to the orange; if any remains, trim it off. Cut the oranges crosswise into ¼-inch slices, place them in a covered bowl, and chill well.

2. In a saucepan stir together the cornstarch, sugar, and powdered ginger. Gradually pour in the orange juice, cream, and ginger syrup, while stirring to keep the mixture smooth. Place on medium fire, and cook, stirring constantly, until the liquid thickens, about 3 or 4 minutes. Do not allow the temperature to exceed 167 degrees, at which point the thickening power of cornstarch begins to break down. Add the chopped ginger, and reheat briefly. Remove the pot from the fire, add the butter, and stir to dissolve the butter.

3. Divide the sliced oranges among the 8 plates, garnish the center with a slice of ginger if used, and present the plates to the diners. Pass the hot sauce separately to retain as much of its heat as possible.

Cooking Ahead: The day before serving, the sauce can be made without the butter addition and refrigerated. Reheat over low to medium heat, stirring often, and again, do not let the temperature exceed 167 degrees. Add the butter. The oranges should be sliced at least 3 hours before serving, and as much as 6.

6 seedless oranges
2 tablespoons cornstarch
½ tablespoon sugar
½ teaspoon powdered ginger
½ cup orange juice
1 cup light cream
2 tablespoons preserved ginger syrup
2 tablespoons preserved ginger, chopped
2 tablespoons butter, cut into pieces
OPTIONAL:
8 slices preserved ginger

Decidedly Different and Delicious

SERVES 8

Paprika Mushroom Nests
Spinach-Garnished Scallop Terrine
Hot Blue Cheese Packets
Strawberries with Kiwi Sauce

The very special and varying presentation of every course in this menu will mark the dinner as one of distinction. First, a mound of white puffy noodles awaits a covering of mushrooms in a pink sauce. On to the Scallop Terrine with an interior green garnishing and flanked by two colorful sauces—one red, one yellow. Next, the second hot course. It is not a vegetable this time, but a cheese course—a sauce of blue-veined cheese and ground walnuts spooned onto lettuce leaves or into endive spears. If a restrained amount of sauce was served with the terrine, the same dish can be used; otherwise, small dishes should be provided. Finally, kiwi shells hold the dessert—sliced strawberries under a green kiwi sauce to be eaten with a spoon. The mix of flavors and the style of this menu will long be remembered. A light Moselle or Rhine wine could carry through the meal, or for extra panache, change to port at the cheese course.

Spinach-Garnished Scallop Terrine

3 pounds
calories per serving—172

The preceding Scallop Terrine is taken a step further here by the addition of a green mousseline garnish made of spinach and sole. The procedure for making the green mousseline is exactly the same as that for the plain scallop—all in the food processor. One could provide a simpler garnish than the one described below by simply making two layers of green, one on the bottom and the other on top. The green bull's-eye center takes just a few extra minutes. Small price for the great visual payoff.

1. Place the food processor bowl in the refrigerator and the steel blade in the freezer. Put the shallot and white wine in a small pot, place on high heat, and boil to reduce the wine to 2 tablespoons. Scrape the shallot and wine into a small bowl, cool, add the vermouth, and chill. Meanwhile, break the bread into large pieces, soak in a bowl with the milk, and let stand for 5 to 10 minutes. Squeeze out the bread, and chill.

2. Squeeze all liquid from either the blanched fresh or the defrosted spinach; chop into coarse pieces.

Preheat oven to 250 degrees.

3. Place in the chilled processor bowl the scallops, shallots with wines, three-fourths of the bread, salt, pepper, and a few drops of Tabasco. Process with the on/off switch to chop the scallops into coarse pieces, then, with the motor running, slowly pour in ¾ cup of the cream, and process until the mixture is smooth. Scrape down the sides, and with the motor running, add 2 of the egg whites. Poach a spoonful, cool, taste for seasonings, and correct if necessary. Scrape the scallop mousseline into a bowl, and chill.

4. Process the sole, spinach, and remaining bread until they are reduced to coarse pieces. Sprinkle with salt, pepper, and a touch of nutmeg. With the motor running, slowly pour in the remaining 6 tablespoons of cream. Scrape down the sides, and again with the motor running, add 1 egg white. Poach a spoonful, cool, taste for seasonings, and correct if necessary. Chill.

1 shallot, chopped coarse
¼ cup white wine
2 tablespoons dry vermouth
2 slices white bread, crusts removed
½ cup milk
1 pound fresh spinach, blanched, or 10 ounces frozen spinach, defrosted
1½ pounds scallops
salt and pepper
Tabasco
1⅛ cups heavy cream
4 egg whites
¾ pound fillet of sole or flounder
nutmeg
butter
Light Tomato Sauce (page 224)
Örebro Saffron Sauce (page 225)

5. Cut parchment or wax paper to fit the bottom and top of an 8-cup loaf mold. Butter the mold, fit in the paper, and butter it. Spoon in about one-third of the spinach-sole mousseline, and with a rubber spatula, smooth it to an even layer. Tap the mold on the counter to settle the mixture well into the dish and brush it with part of the remaining egg white. Spoon in about two-thirds of the scallop mousseline, and smooth it to an even layer. With a tablespoon, scoop out the center, leaving a round trough about 1 inch wide. Brush the hollow with egg white. Carefully spoon the remaining spinach mousseline into the space, tapping it lightly to fit it well into the trough. With a spoon or your fingers, round the green mousseline on top to create a completely round shape. Brush it with egg white.

6. Along both sides of the center stripe, spoon in scallop mousseline level with the spinach mousseline. Spoon in 3 or 4 mounds of the rest of the scallop mousseline over the top of the mold, and smooth it into an even layer with a rubber spatula. Tap the mold lightly on the counter several times to settle the mixture well into the dish. Butter the second piece of parchment paper, and place it, buttered side down, over the terrine. Cover closely with aluminum foil and pierce the foil with a skewer. Put the mold in a water bath. Bake it for about 1½ hours, or until the terrine reaches an internal temperature of 150 degrees; it should feel firm to the touch. Leave in the water bath, but remove the foil. Cool for 30 minutes; remove from the water bath; then lightly weight the terrine with no more than 2 pounds; remove the weights after 2 hours. Refrigerate the terrine for at least 1 day; 2 days are better.

7. Remove the terrine from the refrigerator about 1 hour before serving time; unmold onto a platter, removing both pieces of paper. Slice at the table, and spoon a little Light Tomato Sauce on one side of the terrine slice and a little Örebro Saffron Sauce on the other. Do not pass extra sauces; they should not overwhelm the delicacy of the terrine.

Hot Blue Cheese Packets

This is the only separate cheese course presented in the book, and it is an unusual one. Guests spoon hot cheese sauce onto lettuce leaves and roll, or fold, it into small bundles for finger eating. Some guests are not comfortable handling the lettuce, so I always offer crisp endive leaves as well. It is a simple matter to fill the natural container of each spear. Use any good blue-veined cheese—Roquefort, French blues, Gorgonzola, or Stilton.

Makes about 1½ cups

1. Remove and discard any crust from the cheese, and cut it into pieces. Pour the cream into a heavy saucepot, place on very low heat, and add a few pieces of cheese. Stir until that batch melts; then add more, and continue in the same fashion until all the cheese is melted. Grind in lots of pepper, add 3 or 4 drops of Tabasco, and the nuts, stirring to mix it all together. Finally, add the brandy, and mix again. Transfer to a warm serving dish.

2. Fill a bowl with lettuce leaves, and stand endive spears around the edge of the bowl. Pass the hot blue cheese sauce.

Cooking Ahead: The sauce can be made several days in advance. To reheat, pour a little water into a small, heavy pot, add the sauce, and reheat slowly, stirring often.

½ pound blue cheese
¼ cup light cream
pepper
Tabasco
¾ cup ground nuts, preferably walnuts
2 teaspoons brandy
Boston lettuce leaves and Belgian endive spears

↡↡↡

Paprika Mushroom Nests

This dish offers a pleasing color contrast between the pink sauce and the white Puffy Fried Noodles. The pink comes from paprika and tomato paste; the latter is included to avoid an overuse of paprika, which could result in a bitter taste and bite.

1. Melt the butter in a skillet that will hold all the ingredients except the fried noodles. Add the onions, cover, and cook over gentle heat for about 10 minutes, or until very soft. Do not allow the onions to brown.

2. Meanwhile, rinse the mushrooms, and cut any large ones in half. All mushrooms should be of approximately equal size. Add the mushrooms, lemon juice, salt, and pepper, and cover. Simmer for about 5 minutes to allow the mushrooms to render their copious juice.

3. Sprinkle flour over the mushrooms, and stirring constantly, cook for 2 minutes. Pour in chicken stock, mix the cream with the paprika, and add it to the skillet. Stir in the tomato paste. Season with the thyme and brandy, re-cover, and simmer 10 minutes.

4. Present the reheated Puffy Fried Noodles on individual plates, preferably also warmed. Spoon the Paprika Mushrooms into a bowl to be passed at the table. This presentation, rather than preparing each individual dish in the kitchen, retains the warmth of all the components for a longer period and keeps the noodles crisper.

Cooking Ahead: Paprika Mushrooms can be made a day before and refrigerated.

4 tablespoons butter
2 onions, sliced thin
1½ pounds mushrooms
juice of 1½ lemons
salt and pepper
⅓ cup flour
1 cup Chicken Stock (page 218)
½ cup light cream
½ tablespoon paprika
1 tablespoon tomato paste
1½ teaspoons thyme
1 tablespoon brandy
Puffy Fried Noodles (page 216)

Strawberries with Kiwi Sauce

Just because this is a cookbook for the 1980s, please don't think kiwi is included just for its faddishness. This delicious fruit undeservedly became associated with all the eccentricities of *nouvelle cuisine* during its heyday. Now the kiwi has settled back into its proper role as a thoroughly refreshing and piquant fruit that also happens to be very pretty.

1. Cut the kiwis in half lengthwise, and with a teaspoon, scoop out the flesh into a blender. Some specimens of the fruit have a tough stem core; cut it out with small, sharp scissors. Add 1 tablespoon of the kirsch, and purée; there will be about 2½ cups of purée. Chill. Reserve the kiwi shells.

2. No more than 2 hours before serving, cut the strawberries in 3 or 4 lengthwise slices, and toss them with the sugar and the remaining 1½ tablespoons of kirsch. Cover and put aside in a cool spot, not the refrigerator.

3. To serve, lift the strawberries from the marinade, and use them to fill the kiwi shells. Spoon cold kiwi purée over them, and serve 2 halves to each person. There will be extra kiwi sauce to pass separately if you wish.

Cooking Ahead: The kiwi sauce can be prepared 1 day or even 2 days in advance. As indicated above, the strawberries cannot marinate too long, or their flesh will become somewhat mushy. This fast operation can be done just before the cocktail hour.

- 8 kiwis
- 2½ tablespoons kirsch
- 3 cups strawberries
- 2 tablespoons confectioners' sugar

A Striking Palette of Savory Pleasures

SERVES 8

Mushroom Flan

Terrine Neptune

Spiced Radishes

Curried Cauliflower and Snow Peas

Mango Sherbet

The palette of this menu is singularly striking. The first-course mushroom custard is covered with a golden creamy sauce that contrasts with the deep honey color of the flan. This time simple fish terrine is turned into a tricolor flourish. The delicate stripes of white, pink, and green can be wrapped in crêpes, or not, as you like, but the thin pancakes do complete the picture-pretty look of the terrine. The main-course garnish is marinated cooked radishes that have been spiced and strewn with sesame seeds. Next comes a sharp note—the vibrant yellow of curry in a sauce tossed with cauliflower and bright green snow peas. The last color is the beautiful golden orange of mango in a sherbet that is as velvety rich as ice cream. This meal for grand occasions deserves a similar wine—white Châteauneuf-du-Pape, Graves, or California Chardonnay.

Terrine Neptune

3 pounds
calories per serving—243

For sheer good looks this tricolor fish terrine is tops. There are layers of green, pink, and white mousseline. The recipe calls for a row of spinach-wrapped scallops in the center and a covering of crêpes. Both these steps can be eliminated if you wish. The flavor won't change a bit. Terrine Neptune is a very colorful affair even without the embellishments; they are included for a touch of show biz. If you decide to stud the center with whole scallops, they must be sea scallops, not the small bay variety. If the fish are processed in the order given below, the food processor bowl does not have to be cleaned or rinsed between steps. Chill all ingredients.

1. Place the food processor bowl in the refrigerator and the steel blade in the freezer. Select 8 or 10 of the nicest and largest spinach leaves; remove the stems but not the ribs. Pour about ¼ cup water in a nonreactive pot, bring to a boil, add the spinach, re-cover, and steam for 10 seconds. Cool under cold running water, drain, lift the leaves out separately, and spread them between paper towels to dry. Stem and rib the remaining spinach, pour another ¼ cup of water into the pot, and blanch and cool as before. A handful at a time, squeeze as much water as possible from the spinach, and chop it into coarse pieces. There should be just a few tablespoons of chopped spinach; chill.

2. Select 6 or 8 scallops, just enough almost to fill the length of an 8-cup loaf dish. Place the scallops in a small enamel or copper pot, pour on the white wine and vermouth, and marinate for at least 15 minutes. Place the pot on medium heat, cover, and as soon as the liquid comes to a boil, remove the scallops with a slotted spoon and place them on a paper towel-lined dish. Cool and chill. Reduce the liquid to about 1 tablespoon; chill.

3. Break the bread into pieces, and soak in the milk for about 5 minutes. Squeeze out as much milk as possible, and chill.

4. Put the remaining ¾ pound scallops in the chilled food processor with one-third of the bread; process briefly; then add 6 tablespoons of the cream with the motor running. Scrape down the sides of the bowl. Add the reduced wines and salt and pep-

½ pound spinach
1 pound scallops or ¾ pound scallops if not used for center garnish
¼ cup white wine
2 tablespoons dry vermouth
2 slices white bread, crusts removed
½ cup milk
1⅛ cups heavy cream
salt and pepper
5 large egg whites
2 oil-packed anchovy fillets
¾ pound salmon, cut into chunks
Tabasco
¾ pound halibut, flounder, or sole, cut into chunks
oil
6 or 7 5- or 6-inch Crêpes (page 215)
Green Sauce (page 228) or Niçoise Mayonnaise (page 227)

per; with the motor running, add 1 egg white, and process until smooth. Poach a small spoonful, cool, taste for seasonings, and correct if necessary. Scrape the mousseline into a bowl, and chill.

5. Rinse the anchovies under cold water, pat dry, and place in the processor with the salmon, half the remaining bread, a good dash of Tabasco, salt, and pepper. Process briefly; then, with the motor running, add 6 tablespoons of cream. Scrape down the sides of the bowl, and add 1 egg white with the motor running. Process until smooth. Poach, taste for seasonings, and correct if necessary. Scrape into a bowl, and chill.

6. Place the halibut in the processor with the remaining bread, salt, and pepper. Process briefly; with the motor running, add first the spinach, then the remaining cream. Scrape down the sides of the bowl, and add 1 egg white with the motor running. Process until smooth. Poach a spoonful to taste. Chill.

Preheat oven to 250 degrees.

7. Oil an 8-cup loaf dish, line with a piece of parchment or wax paper, and oil it as well. Line the dish with overlapping Crêpes, always brushing egg white on any overlapping parts (page 17). Brush the entire inside of the crêpe-lined dish with egg white. Spoon in all of the spinach-halibut mousseline, and spread it into a smooth layer with a rubber spatula, making certain that the batter fills the corners. Brush with egg white.

8. Layer in about one-third of the salmon batter. On the counter, spread out the blanched whole spinach leaves in an overlapping row. Place the poached scallops along one end of the spinach, spreading a thin layer of salmon batter between them; this is just to seal the scallops into one long line. Roll the scallops in the spinach, lift carefully, and place in the center of the dish, seam side down. Brush with egg white. Carefully spoon in the remaining salmon mousseline alongside and over the scallops, and smooth into an even layer. Brush with egg white.

9. Spoon in the scallop batter, smooth into an even layer, and brush very generously with egg white. Pull the crêpes taut over

THE PÂTÉS, TERRINES, AND THEIR ACCOMPANIMENTS · 151

this final layer; again brush well with egg white any overlapping sections. Brush whites over the top, and cover. Put the dish in a water bath, and bake for about 1½ hours, or until a thermometer registers 150 degrees. Remove the dish from the water bath, cool it for about 30 minutes, and weight it lightly for 2 hours. Refrigerate the terrine for at least 1 day; 2 days are better.

10. To serve, unmold the terrine onto a serving platter. Cut with a serrated knife, using a sawing motion. Pass Green Sauce separately.

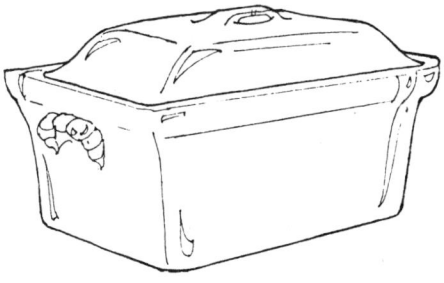

Mango Sherbet

More than almost any other fruit, the juicy flesh of the mango seems to hold all the lush flavor of the tropics. Though delicious eating just plain, it can be churned into an incomparable sherbet, so rich it rivals ice cream. For best results the mango must be very ripe. Also, buy the red-blushed variety, which has a more intense flavor and aroma than the green.

Makes 1½ quarts

1. Pour the sugar and water into a pot, stir for a minute or so, and put aside for about 15 minutes. Place the pot on medium heat, stir several times, cover, and bring to a boil. Remove cover, and boil for 5 minutes. Pour the syrup into a bowl, and cool.

2. Meanwhile, peel the mangoes over a bowl to catch dripping juices. Cut the flesh into chunks, and put them in the bowl of a blender or food processor with the juice. Add the lime juice, and purée. Push the purée through a nonreactive sieve to remove any of the fruit fibers; some mangoes are heavy in fibers. There should be 2 cups of purée. Add it, as well as the egg white and liqueur, to the sugar syrup. Chill.

3. Pour the mixture into an ice cream maker or a 9-inch cake pan, and place it in the freezer. As ice crystals begin to form, beat the mixture in the pan, reducing it almost to the liquid stage. Refreeze, and repeat the beating a few more times. The more often you beat the sherbet, the smoother it will be.

1 cup sugar
2 cups water
1 or 2 mangoes, enough for 2 cups of purée
juice of 1 lime or lemon
1 egg white, lightly beaten
½ tablespoon orange liqueur or kirsch

↯↯↯

Spiced Radishes

Anyone who has never cooked red radishes has a surprise in store. The first thing you see is the red in the skin leaching into the water as if it were a bad dye. As the water turns red, the radishes become pink. The cooking also takes away all sharpness in the taste, leaving a morsel that resembles young sweet turnips.

1. Put the ginger slices in a large pot of water, add salt, and bring to a boil. Meanwhile, snip off the top and stem ends of the radishes, and rinse well. Dump the radishes into the boiling water, and cook for about 20 minutes, or until they are tender. Do not overcook. Drain well.

2. While the radishes are cooking, sprinkle the sesame seeds into a small, heavy skillet, and toast over medium heat, stirring almost constantly. Toast only to a dark golden color, a matter of a minute or so. Put the olive oil, lemon juice, ground ginger, basil, salt, and pepper into a jar, and shake well.

3. Put the hot radishes into a mixing bowl, pour the dressing over them, and toss to coat all surfaces with the sauce. Cover, and put aside to cool; then refrigerate.

4. Remove the radishes from the refrigerator at least 2 hours before serving, mixing them once or twice. Just before serving, sprinkle the sesame seeds over the radishes, and transfer them to a bowl.

Cooking Ahead: Spiced Radishes can be prepared as much as 2 or 3 days in advance.

6 slices fresh ginger
5 cups (4 6-ounce packages) radishes
¼ cup sesame seeds
½ cup olive oil
juice of 1 lemon or lime
¼ teaspoon ground ginger
3 tablespoons basil, chopped, or 2 tablespoons dried basil with 2 tablespoons chopped parsley
salt and pepper

Curried Cauliflower and Snow Peas

This is a particularly colorful dish composed of white cauliflower, bright green snow peas, and golden curry sauce. If fresh snow peas are not available, substitute string beans.

1. While melting the butter in a saucepot, trim and cut the scallions with their green tops into ¼-inch pieces. Add the scallions to the butter, cover, and sauté for about 5 minutes, or until they are soft. Add the flour and curry, and stir with a wire whisk to make a paste; cook for a minute or so. Slowly add chicken stock while whisking to keep the sauce smooth. Add the cream cheese in small pieces, whisking vigorously to dissolve it into the sauce. Simmer for a few minutes.

2. Trim the cauliflower, and break into florets. Cook the florets in a large pot of boiling salted water for about 5 minutes, or until crisply tender. Drain well. Meanwhile, cook the snow peas in a small pot of water for just 1 minute, and drain well.

3. Mix the two hot vegetables together in a serving bowl, pour the curry sauce over them, and carefully mix to distribute the sauce. Wipe the edge of the bowl, and serve.

Cooking Ahead: Since the snow peas require a minimal amount of cooking time, it is more efficient to cook them when needed. Because of cooking odors, you may want to precook the cauliflower, even the day before. If so, cool the cooked florets in cold water, drain well, cover tightly, and refrigerate. Reheat the florets in boiling water for about 1 minute. The sauce can be prepared several days in advance and refrigerated.

- 3 tablespoons butter
- 4 scallions
- 3 tablespoons flour
- 1½ teaspoons curry or to taste
- 2¼ cups Chicken Stock (page 218)
- ¼ cup cream cheese
- 1 head cauliflower
- salt
- 2 ounces (about 1 cup) snow peas

Mushroom Flan

A dish full of finesse and delicacy does not necessarily require intricate preparation. These small custards are a case in point. However, it is important to keep the seasoning well balanced. Don't overdo it; always taste as you go along. I particularly like to make individual flans in small French oval ramekins, but any shape, even custard cups, is fine.

Preheat oven to 350 degrees.

1. Melt the butter in a large skillet while rinsing the mushrooms. Discard any dark stem ends, and cut extra-large ones to equalize the size. Add the mushrooms to the skillet, and season them with the lemon juice, nutmeg, salt, and pepper. To force the mushrooms to render their juice, cover the skillet, and simmer over medium heat for about 5 minutes.

2. While the mushrooms are cooking, break the eggs into a bowl, and beat them lightly. Add the heavy cream, and beat again. Also butter 8 1-cup molds.

3. With a slotted spoon, transfer the mushrooms to the container of a blender or food processor. Reserve the juice in the skillet. Process the mushrooms until they are chopped into coarse pieces. Scrape down the bowl, and with the motor running, pour in the egg-cream mixture and process it until a very smooth purée is achieved. Taste for seasonings, and correct if necessary.

4. Pour the purée into the buttered molds, and place them on a rack in a baking pan. Pour in enough water to reach halfway up the sides of the molds. Bake for about 30 minutes, or until the custard is set. Test by inserting a small, sharp knife into the custard; it should emerge almost dry.

5. While the custards are baking, prepare the sauce. There should be about 1 cup of reserved mushroom juice in the skillet. Pour it into a small pot, and boil briskly to reduce it to ½ cup. Spoon the sour cream into the bowl used for the egg-cream mixture, and slowly pour in the hot liquid while whisking to achieve a smooth sauce. Taste for salt and pepper; correct if necessary. Pour the sauce back into the small pot, and reheat a little, but do not allow it to boil.

4 tablespoons butter plus butter for greasing molds
1 pound mushrooms
juice of ½ lemon
about ¼ teaspoon nutmeg
salt and pepper
4 eggs
½ cup heavy cream
¾ cup sour cream

6. To serve, run a knife around each custard, and reverse it onto a warm individual serving dish. Spoon a little sauce over the custard, and pass the remaining sauce separately.

Cooking Ahead: Although I find the custards are at their most delicate when fresh-baked, they can be prepared in advance with very little loss of texture. If they are baked the day before, cover and refrigerate them in their molds. Place them in a baking dish without a rack, pour in about ¼ inch of hot water, cover with aluminum foil, and place in a 375-degree oven for about 10 minutes, or until a knife plunged into the center comes out hot. The sauce keeps well tightly covered and refrigerated; gently reheat it at serving time.

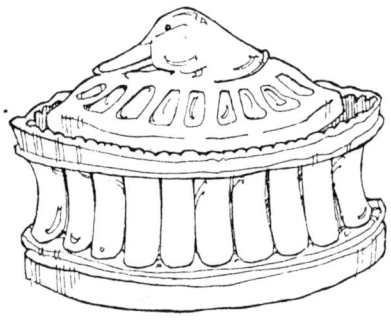

Easy Panache

SERVES 8

Mushroom Compote

Shrimp Terrine

Shoestringed Turnips and Zucchini

Apricot Soufflé

A grand meal is anticipated anytime shrimp are served, and here is a menu that will not disappoint. Mushroom Compote may not sound terribly exciting, but its presentation and flavoring quickly change thoughts about that. This first course can be served two ways: on a salad plate heaped with Puffy Fried Noodles (page 216) or in small bowls or consommé cups with toast triangles on the saucer. Either way, the brandy-laced sauce and crisp vegetables will be an eyeopener for what can be done with simple ingredients. Since the pink Shrimp Terrine contains a spattering of tiny carrot pieces and nuggets of shrimp, its garnish is a contrasting pale green and white. A hint of raspberry vinegar sparks the dressing for the thin strips of turnip and zucchini. A meal that ends with the flourish of a soufflé will long be remembered. But that grand finale needn't chain the cook to the kitchen. This soufflé can be prepared several hours in advance. It will patiently await baking time. The white wine to carry this menu would be a Sancerre, a Pouilly-Fumé, or a California Fumé Blanc.

Shrimp Terrine

3¼ pounds
calories per serving—190

Shrimp mousseline is made precisely the same way as all the preceding ones in this section; only the garnishing is different. In this recipe pieces of carrot and shrimp are randomly strewn throughout the terrine rather than in a restrained layer. I have included a thin green mousseline layer at the top, and again it is completely expendable if you prefer. Reduce the weight by a half pound if the extra layer is omitted.

1. Chill the food processor bowl in the refrigerator and the steel blade in the freezer. Dice the carrot half into tiny pieces about ⅛ inch square, truly small. Cook them in boiling salted water for about 5 minutes, or until just tender but with some crispness. Drain at once, cool under cold water, drain well, and chill on a paper-towel-lined plate. Drop the tomatoes into boiling water for a few seconds, and peel. Cut in half, squeeze out the seeds and juice, chop into coarse pieces, and chill.

2. In a small pot boil the shallots and ½ cup of the wine together until only about 2 tablespoons of wine remain. Rinse the anchovy fillet under cold water, pat dry, and add to the shallots for the last minute of cooking; stir to dissolve it completely. Break the bread into pieces, and soak them in the milk for 5 minutes; squeeze dry, and chill. Squeeze all juices out of the spinach, chop into coarse pieces, and chill.

3. In a small covered pot boil together for 5 minutes the remaining ¼ cup wine, the water, parsley, celery, juice of the lemon quarter, salt, and pepper. Add ½ pound of the shrimp, reduce the heat, cover, and cook for 1 minute. Drain at once, set aside to cool, and peel. Cut the cooked shrimp into ½-inch pieces, and chill on a paper-towel-lined plate.

Preheat oven to 250 degrees.

4. In the chilled food processor bowl place the sole, remaining peeled raw shrimp, two-thirds of the bread, shallots-wine mixture, juice of ½ lemon, few drops of Tabasco, salt, and pepper. Drain the tomatoes of any juices that have collected, and add the pulp to the processor. Process briefly with the on/off switch; then, with the motor running, add 2 of the egg whites. Scrape

½ carrot
salt
2 medium tomatoes
2 shallots, chopped coarse (about ¼ cup)
¾ cup white wine
1 oil-packed anchovy fillet
3 slices white bread, crusts removed
½ cup milk
½ pound fresh spinach, blanched, or 5 ounces frozen spinach, defrosted
1 cup water
2 parsley sprigs
3-inch piece celery rib or ¼ teaspoon celery seeds
1¼ lemons
pepper
¾ pound shelled (about 1 pound with shells) raw shrimp
1 pound sole or flounder, cut into pieces
Tabasco
salt and pepper

down the sides of the bowl; again with the motor running, add 1 cup of the cream, and process until smooth. Poach to taste, and correct seasonings if necessary. Transfer to a bowl, and chill.

5. Briefly process together the spinach, remaining bread, juice of ½ lemon, nutmeg, salt and pepper. With the motor running add the remaining egg white and the remaining ¼ cup cream; process until smooth; chill.

6. Cut parchment or wax paper to fit the top and bottom of an 8-cup mold. Butter the mold, fit one paper piece in the bottom, and butter it. Spoon the spinach mousseline into the mold, making certain it reaches into the corners. Tap the dish sharply on the counter several times. Carefully fold the diced carrots and cooked shrimp pieces into the shrimp mousseline. If any liquid has collected in the carrot or shrimp dishes, drain it off before adding the garnishes. Scoop the shrimp mousseline into the mold, smooth it into an even layer, and tap the mold sharply on the counter. Butter the other piece of paper, and place it, greased side down, over the mousseline, and cover.

7. Put the mold in a water bath, and bake it for about 1½ hours, or until a thermometer registers 150 degrees. The terrine should feel firm to the touch. Leave in the water bath, but remove the cover. Cool for 30 minutes; remove from the water bath; then lightly weight the terrine with no more than 2 pounds; remove the weights after 2 hours. Refrigerate the terrine for at least 1 day; 2 days are better.

8. Remove the terrine from the refrigerator about 1 hour before serving time. Unmold onto a platter, removing both pieces of paper. Cut into slices with a serrated knife, using a sawing motion. Pass Örebro Saffron Sauce separately.

3 egg whites
1¼ cups heavy cream
nutmeg
butter
Örebro Saffron Sauce (page 225) or Green Sauce (page 228)

↯↯↯

Shoestringed Turnips and Zucchini

It's surprising what contrast there is between thin strips of turnip and zucchini once they are cooked. The turnips remain snowy white, but the green-edged zucchini take on a soft yellow tone and some translucency. Tossed together, they complement each other nicely.

Makes about 4 cups

1. Cook the turnips and zucchini separately in lightly salted water just to the crisply tender stage, about 2 minutes for the turnips and less than 1 minute for the zucchini. Drain; cool under cold water; drain well again.

2. Prepare the dressing by shaking together in a small jar the oil, vinegar, bitters, salt, and pepper. Just before serving, pour the dressing over the vegetables and toss.

Cooking Ahead: The vegetables can be cooked as much as a day in advance and refrigerated separately. The sauce can be prepared several days before. Do not dump the vegetables into the mixing bowl, but lift them out of their storage containers. Some liquid probably will have exuded, and it should be left behind; otherwise, it will dilute the dressing.

½ pound turnips, cut into thin strips
¾ pound zucchini, cut into thin strips
salt
1 cup oil
1½ tablespoons raspberry vinegar
2 teaspoons aromatic bitters
pepper

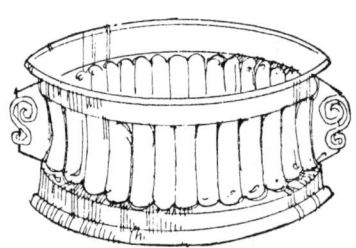

Apricot Soufflé

A soufflé always ends a meal with a flourish. Do not be concerned that you'll be locked in the kitchen at the last minute, beating egg whites. This is a do-ahead soufflé that calls for no more laborious effort than pushing a button on the blender. It can also be prepared in the food processor. Either way, it will patiently wait for hours before going into the oven.

1. Put the apricots in a small pot, pour the boiling water over, cover, and put aside for 1 hour. Stir in the sugar, bring to a simmer, and cook, covered, for 20 minutes. Cool for at least 15 minutes.

Preheat oven to 375 degrees.

2. Break the eggs into the blender; add the extra whites, the cream, lemon juice, and alcohols. Process to blend. Scrape in the cooked apricots, and process to purée the fruit. Finally, add the cream cheese, breaking it into chunks as you add it. Thoroughly incorporate each piece of cream cheese before adding more. Give a final burst at high speed.

3. Smear the butter in a 6-cup soufflé mold. Pour in the batter to about the three-fourths level; do not fill to the top. Bake for about 50 minutes, or until the top is lightly browned and puffy. This should produce a soufflé that is still soft in the center. The custardy center serves as a sauce to spoon over the fully baked outer portions. To test for doneness, shake the dish a little; if the center is soft, it will jiggle. A fully baked soufflé will be firm throughout when shaken and the top will be convex. Serve at once.

Cooking Ahead: As noted above, this soufflé can be prepared several hours in advance, placed in its mold, and kept in a cool spot. If the kitchen is very hot, put it in the refrigerator, but allow an extra 5 minutes for the baking.

½ pound dried apricots
2½ cups boiling water
½ cup sugar
6 eggs
2 egg whites
½ cup heavy cream
juice of ½ lemon
1 tablespoon kirsch
1 tablespoon orange liqueur
11 ounces cream cheese
1 tablespoon butter

⇂⇂⇂

Mushroom Compote

It starts simply enough—some scallions, mushrooms, and tomatoes. Then this Mushroom Compote is helped along with a good slug of brandy, and things become more interesting. The strength of the brandy is greatly diminished by other additions, but it's the single ingredient, not often used with vegetables, that gives this dish its undefinable punch.

1. Melt the butter in a large skillet, add the scallions, cover, and cook over medium heat for 5 minutes. Add the brandy, and cook over high heat, uncovered, to reduce the brandy in half. Add the mushrooms, tomatoes, wine, and ¾ cup of chicken stock, and sprinkle with salt and pepper. Cover and cook for 3 minutes over medium heat.

2. In a small bowl mix the sour cream with about ½ cup of the hot cooking stock; then pour it back into the skillet. Cover and keep it warm over a low fire. Make a thin paste by stirring the remaining ½ cup stock into the cornstarch. Add the paste to the bubbling sauce, and stir for about 3 minutes, or until the sauce thickens. Serve at once on Puffy Fried Noodles or with the toast.

Cooking Ahead: Mushrooms and tomatoes cannot be cooked ahead, or they become limp. An hour or 2 hours before serving, fry the scallions, add the brandy, and reduce it. Then finish the dish, in about 5 minutes' time, when you are ready for it. This means you dirty the skillet only once.

3 tablespoons butter
about 15 scallions, cut 1 inch long, some green included (1½ cups)
½ cup brandy
1¼ pounds mushrooms, sliced
24 cherry tomatoes or 2 tomatoes, cut into eighths
¾ cup white wine
1¼ cups Chicken Stock (page 218)
salt and pepper
⅓ cup sour cream
¼ cup cornstarch
Puffy Fried Noodles (page 216) or 16 toast triangles

Brunch with an Emphatic Difference

SERVES 8

Cocktailed Spaghetti Squash

Smoked Haddock Pâté

Gingered Tomato Relish

Pumpkin Surprise

This would make an excellent weekend brunch or Sunday night supper, as well as a small dinner party. It is a light menu that could even serve for after-theater entertaining with a change of dessert, which would require less baking time. The spaghetti squash is served piping hot and imitates real pasta since it is cooked in a tomato sauce and given a final sprinkling of cheese at the table. Smoked Haddock Pâté is gutsy, so be sure your guests are adventurous, and perhaps you'll make some converts for this exceptional fish product. The snappy tomato relish served with the pâté stands up to it admirably. The meal ends with a hot pumpkin dessert that is a knockout. The "surprise" is that the whole pumpkin comes to the table full of steaming baked fruits. The fruits are served with the baked pumpkin flesh. This is a recipe to keep in mind for Thanksgiving and Christmas time, when pumpkins are available. When fresh pumpkins cannot be bought for this menu, substitute Gratinéed Blueberries (page 184) or Baked Pears with Caramel Sauce (page 83). A chilled Beaujolais would do very well here, as would a Tavel, Zinfandel rosé, or even a chilled small Bordeaux.

Smoked Haddock Pâté

3½ pounds
calories per serving—161

Until now the terrines in this fish section have been rather delicate in flavor. Smoked haddock abruptly changes that. Smoked haddock is an admirable product, one that, I believe, is underutilized. It has a big, robust flavor and costs less than most other fish. In this recipe it is first poached in flavored milk. Save the milk and onions, and turn them into the base of hearty soup by adding potatoes and, if you like, a strong-flavored fish.

I do not put any interior layers into this particular terrine. It can be decorated quite simply with blanched spinach leaves (page 17) or crisscrossed with strips of pimiento. My favorite topping is vermouth-laced chicken aspic (page 222) encasing a row of very thin lemon slices overlapped down the center.

1. Slice the onions, and place half of them in a nonreactive pan that will hold the haddock snugly. Rinse the haddock, place it in the pan, and scatter the rest of the onions over it. Pour in enough milk almost to cover the fish; fill out with water, if necessary. Break the bay leaf in half, and tuck in the pieces, sprinkle very lightly with salt and very generously with pepper. Cover and very slowly bring it to a simmer; then cook for 5 minutes. Remove the pan from the heat, and allow the haddock to steep for 5 minutes, still covered. Lift the haddock out of the milk, and pick it over to remove any bones or tough skin. Flake the fish, cool, and chill. Drain ½ cup of the cooked onion slices, add to the fish, cool, and chill. Reserve ½ cup of the milk, and chill.

Preheat oven to 375 degrees.

2. Chill the food processor bowl in the refrigerator and the steel blade in the freezer. Soak the bread in the reserved milk for 5 minutes, squeeze dry, and place in the chilled processor bowl. Add the smoked haddock, cardamom, nutmeg, mace, cayenne, and vermouth. Process until the fish is fairly smooth. With the motor running, add first the eggs, then the cream. Process until very smooth. Poach a spoonful, cool, taste for seasonings, and correct if necessary.

3. Cut parchment or wax paper to fit the bottom and top of an 8-cup mold. Butter the mold, fit a paper in, and butter it.

2 onions
2 pounds smoked haddock
3 to 4 cups milk
1 bay leaf
salt and pepper
4 slices white bread, crusts removed
1 teaspoon ground cardamom
½ teaspoon nutmeg
½ teaspoon ground mace
¼ teaspoon cayenne
¼ cup vermouth
4 eggs, beaten
¾ cup heavy cream
butter

Spoon in the haddock mousse, pushing it well into the corners; then smooth the top. Tap the mold sharply on the counter several times, and cover. Place in a water bath, and bake for about 1½ hours, or until a thermometer registers 170 degrees. The terrine should feel firm to the touch. Leave in the water, but remove the cover. Cool for 30 minutes; remove from the water bath; then lightly weight the terrine with no more than 2 pounds; remove the weights after 2 hours. Refrigerate the terrine for at least 3 days.

4. To serve, unmold the terrine onto a serving platter, and slice with a serrated knife, using a sawing motion.

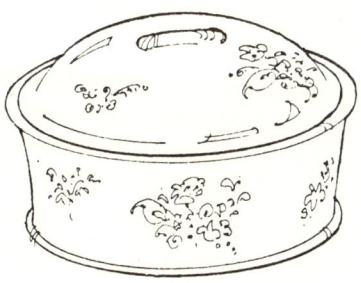

Pumpkin Surprise

The surprise within the pumpkin can be as variable as you like, within reason. Choose firm-fleshed fruits with flavors that complement each other. Even a few raisins can be tossed in. I've added candied orange peel simply because some happened to be on hand.

Preheat oven to 350 degrees.

1. With a strong, sharp knife, cut off a lid from the pumpkin, and put it aside. Use a heavy spoon to scrape out the seeds and fibers until the inside of the pumpkin is smooth. Place it on a baking dish or large pie dish, one that can be taken to the dining table.

2. Crumble 3 of the cookies into the bottom of the pumpkin; then layer in one-third of the apples and bananas. Drain the juice from the pineapple into a bowl, and reserve. Place one-third of the pineapple over the bananas. Sprinkle with 1 tablespoon of the brown sugar. Repeat again with two more layers of the alternating fruits, cookies, and sugar. The final layer should be cookies and sugar. Do not completely fill the pumpkin shell; leave about 1 inch at the top.

3. To the reserved pineapple juice, add the orange juice or apple cider, liqueur, cinnamon, nutmeg, and ginger. Beat the liquid and spices together, and pour over the fruit and cookies; the liquid should be barely visible through the top layer of crumbled cookies. If necessary, add a little more orange juice. Replace the lid on the pumpkin, making certain it fits well; follow the cutting line. Pour the oil onto a paper towel, and rub it over the surface of the pumpkin to give it a shine.

4. Place the baking dish in the oven, and bake it for about 3 hours, or until the pumpkin flesh is soft. If the fit of the lid is not tight and too much steam escapes, place a piece of aluminum foil over the top. Test by removing the pumpkin lid and inserting a small, sharp knife into the pulp, which should be soft.

5. The baked pumpkin should be served very warm but not piping hot. Present it at the table as is, remove the lid for the

4- to 5-pound pumpkin, preferably with stem intact
9 coconut cookies or ginger snaps
1 large apple, unpeeled, quartered, cored, and sliced thin
1 banana, peeled and sliced
½ cup pineapple tidbits
3 tablespoons brown sugar
1 cup orange juice or apple cider
2 tablespoons orange or other fruit liqueur
¼ teaspoon each cinnamon, nutmeg, ginger
1 teaspoon oil
OPTIONAL:
lightly whipped cream

guests to see the steam rise, and provide two long spoons for serving. The fruit and pulp are scooped out together. Pass the optional cream.

Cooking Ahead: Pumpkin Surprise is best served about ½ hour after it has been baked. If prebaked and held, the shell will become wrinkled and be far less attractive. The pumpkin can be filled early in the day and refrigerated until baking time, but allow an extra 15 minutes or so to compensate for the chill. The fruits will not turn dark because of the acid in the fruit juice.

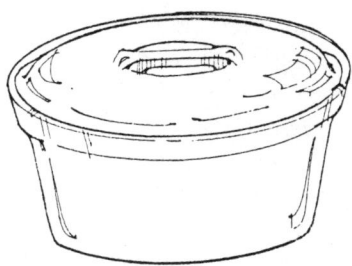

Cocktailed Spaghetti Squash

Spaghetti with tomato sauce and Parmesan cheese is an old standby. Here it's been updated by substituting low-calorie spaghetti squash for the pasta and by using a vegetable cocktail juice more as a flavoring than a true sauce. Who can improve on Parmesan cheese?

1. Instructions for splitting the squash are on page 127, Spaghetti Squash and Peas. Place the squash, cut sides down, in a pot or skillet large enough to hold the halves side by side. Pour in the vegetable cocktail, add Tabasco to your taste for hotness, and sprinkle lightly with salt and pepper. Bring the juice to a boil, cover, and simmer for about 20 minutes, or until a knife will cut through the skin rather easily. Do not overcook, or it will turn mushy and not separate into strands.

2. Boil the juice in the skillet to reduce it by one-third. Lift the strands out of the squash with a fork, and put them in a large bowl. Pour the juice over the squash, and toss with two forks. Pile the spaghetti squash on warm individual plates and serve at once. Pass the Parmesan cheese at the table.

Cooking Ahead: The spaghetti squash can be cooked the day before, the strands pulled out of the shell, closely covered, and refrigerated. Reduce the juice in the skillet only slightly; then, at serving time, reheat the squash in the juice.

2- to 2½-pound spaghetti squash
2 cups vegetable cocktail juice
Tabasco
salt and pepper
grated Parmesan cheese

↡↡↡

Gingered Tomato Relish

Tomatoes in yogurt—now there is an innocent-looking concoction. But look out. Under it lurks the tingling bite of fresh ginger and the power to turn this relish into a real palate awakener. Summer tomatoes, you will find, give off more juice in the marinade than out-of-season varieties. That's about the only good thing one can say for the latter, but even their pallid flesh is enhanced with this dressing.

Makes about 4 cups

1. Plunge the tomatoes into boiling water for a few seconds, remove them, cool, and peel. Cut the tomatoes in half, squeeze out the seeds and juice, and cut the flesh into ¼-inch pieces. Place the tomatoes in a bowl, and sprinkle them with the ginger, chopped mint, olive oil, salt, and pepper. Mix with your hands to coat the tomatoes thoroughly with the flavorings. Put aside until serving time or for at least ½ hour.

2. Just before serving, drain the tomatoes, which will have exuded more juice. Stir in the yogurt, and transfer to a serving bowl. A sprig of mint planted in the center adds a nice touch.

Cooking Ahead: The tomatoes and flavorings can be mixed together as much as 2 hours ahead. Marinating longer than that would rob the tomatoes of any fresh flavor and texture, which are essential to the final balance of the relish. If need be, prepare the tomatoes, chop them, cover, and refrigerate without the other ingredients. Add the marinating flavorings 1 to 2 hours before serving.

4 tomatoes
1 tablespoon peeled, fine-chopped ginger
1 tablespoon fine-chopped mint
3 tablespoons olive oil
salt and pepper
½ cup yogurt
mint sprig

Regally Russian

SERVES 10

Omelette Rustique (Rustic Omelet)

Kulebyaka

Acorn Squash Purée

Palais de Glace (Ice Palace, a Maple Mold)

Kulebyaka is a hot Russian fish pâté that should be served on very special occasions. It's an elegant affair that takes a lot of work, none of it complicated, just time-consuming. Still, every single step, including the final assembly, can be prepared well in advance, even in the evenings after work. Only the baking must be done just before serving. The Rustic Omelet that precedes the Kulebyaka is called that only because it is not the traditional rolled style of omelet. It's a very fine dish that can be sliced into wedges and served at room temperature during the cocktail hour or slightly warmer at the table. Acorn Squash Purée has a pleasing orange color and delicacy that marry well with the pâté. The finale is what I like to call Palais de Glace, really a molded maple-flavored dessert. It has as much eye appeal as the Kulebyaka, is equally good, and is a light note to finish the gala dinner. The meal deserves a good white wine—Chablis, Meursault, or a California Chardonnay.

Kulebyaka

6 pounds
calories per serving—335

There are nine different preliminary steps in the making of a proper Russian Kulebyaka. Even so, this is not a 100 percent authentic version since *vesiga*, sturgeon spinal marrow, is rarely available here. Adjustments have been made in the recipe to make up for this lack of binding material. Though this is a time-consuming operation, all the preliminary steps fortunately can be done the day before, leaving only the final assembly for Dinner Day. Obviously Kulebyaka is a pâté for very special occasions. If you find this extravaganza a bit daunting, there is a streamlined, nonauthentic version on page 210. By the way, the word is pronounced "kool-lĕh-be-ăh-kah" and derives from *kulyok*, the Russian word for bag. Indeed, the pâté has been put in a pastry bag.

I. *Yeast Dough*—*similar to dough for kulitch, or "poor" French brioche*

Put the flour in a large mixing bowl, and make a well in the center. Sprinkle the yeast, plus the hot water, in the well. Meanwhile, punch the butter to soften it, folding it over a few times; then add it to the center of the bowl along with the salt and eggs. Working with your fingertips, blend together the eggs and butter; then slowly incorporate the flour. When all the flour has been worked in, sprinkle on 2 tablespoons of warm water, and work the dough until it forms a ball; if necessary, add 1 or 2 more tablespoons of warm water. Knead well for at least 2 or 3 minutes; then throw the dough against the floured table—the pounding will give more body to the dough. Put the ball of dough in the bowl, lightly dust with flour, cover, and place in a warm area for about 1 to 1½ hours, or until it doubles in bulk. Flour the board, and knead the dough lightly. Flour the bowl and the dough lightly, cover with a barely damp cloth or plastic wrap, and refrigerate until needed.

5 cups flour (about 1½ pounds)
2 packages (½-ounce) yeast
2 tablespoons almost hot water
1 cup (8 ounces) butter, at room temperature
½ teaspoon salt
4 eggs, at room temperature
about 2 to 4 tablespoons warm water

II. *12 Crêpes* (page 215)

III. Poached Salmon

Place the fish in a heavy pot that holds it snugly. Pour on fish stock barely to cover. Place on a medium flame, and bring to a simmer; partially cover. Cook gently until the fish flakes, about 10 minutes per inch of thickness, but undercook a little since it will also be baked. Cool in stock, and refrigerate.

1½ pounds fresh salmon or half salmon and a firm-fleshed white fish, such as cod or haddock

approximately 4 cups cool Fish Stock (page 220)

IV. Two Hard-Boiled Eggs

V. Duxelles

A food processor makes fast work of this step. Melt butter in a large, heavy skillet while chopping the onion. Scrape the onion into the skillet, stir, reduce the heat, and cover. Chop the mushrooms, and add to the softened onion, sprinkle with salt and pepper, stir, and cook over high heat to cook off most of the moisture. Remove from heat, and cool. Stir in the chopped dill and parsley.

3 tablespoons butter
1 medium onion, chopped fine
1 pound mushrooms, chopped fine
salt and pepper
½ cup dill, chopped
1 cup parsley, chopped

VI. Rice

Melt butter in a small, heavy pot, add unwashed rice grains, and stir until they turn opaque white. Pour in chicken stock, sprinkle with salt and pepper, cover, reduce heat, and cook about 15 minutes, or until barely tender. Cool, and stir into duxelles.

1 tablespoon butter
¼ cup rice
½ cup Chicken Stock (page 218)
salt and pepper

VII. Kasha (Toasted Buckwheat Kernels)

Put kasha in a small, heavy pot or skillet, and stir in the egg. Put on medium-high heat, and stir until grains become dry and separated. Add chicken stock, salt, and pepper; cover; reduce heat; and simmer for about 15 minutes, or until the liquid has been almost completely absorbed; there will be 2 cups of cooked kasha. Cool, and stir into duxelles.

½ cup kasha
1 egg, beaten
1 cup Chicken Stock (page 218)
salt and pepper

VIII. Dill Butter

In a small bowl cream together the butter and dill. Cover and refrigerate.

¼ cup soft butter
¼ cup chopped dill

IX. Optional: Clarified Dill Butter

Stir the dill into the clarified butter, cover, and refrigerate.

½ pound butter, clarified (page 222)
½ cup chopped dill

Dinner Day

Assembling the Kulebyaka

1. Remove all ingredients except the dough from the refrigerator, and bring to room temperature. The dough should warm up just enough to roll easily (about fifteen minutes). Peel and slice the hard-boiled eggs. Drain the salmon, remove skin and bones, and break into large chunks.

flour
¼ cup butter
1 well-beaten egg
watercress for garnish

2. On a well-floured board, roll out the dough to a rectangle approximately 19 × 15 inches and about ¼ inch thick, leaving a central rectangle of about 6 × 12 inches a bit thicker; keep the board well floured. Cut off edges to make a straight rectangle, and reserve the dough for decoration.

Preheat oven to 450 degrees.

3. Work quickly to prevent the yeast dough from rising. Lay 6 Crêpes in two overlapping parallel rows in the center rectangle. Use about one-third of the duxelles-rice-kasha mixture to make a smooth, approximately ½-inch layer over the crêpes. Do not extend this filling layer to the edges of the crêpes.

4. Melt ¼ cup of butter. Place half the flaked salmon over the filling. Pat all edges to keep smooth. Sprinkle on half the melted butter; then make a layer of half the sliced eggs.

5. Repeat again, layering in this order: half the remaining duxelles mixture, the salmon, melted butter, egg slices, and the last of the duxelles mixture. Keep tapping edges to keep them firm and smooth. Finally, cover the construction with the remaining 6 crêpes. Then, to ensure a firmer, easier-to-cut loaf, press all the ingredients together ever so lightly.

6. Cut a small rectangle from the four corners, taking care not to reach all the way to the filling, (page 11). Brush a well-beaten egg all over the dough, and pull one long side over the filling; brush with egg. Repeat with the other long side and finally with the two shorter ends. Brush with egg at each step.

7. Heavily butter a baking sheet. Carefully lift the kulebyaka off the board with the aid of a long spatula, slipping your right arm under it. Reverse the loaf to the baking sheet; all the seams are now underneath. Brush entire surface with egg. Cut out two holes.

8. Using leftover dough, take pieces, and rub them between your floured hands to form a rope; tuck this rope close in under the loaf, all around, thus providing a support for the heavy filling. Brush this foundation with egg. Decorate the loaf with leftover dough, or simply score lightly with the tip of a sharp knife. Make two chimneys from parchment paper or aluminum foil, and place in the holes. Fill each chimney with the chilled dill butter. Place in the preheated oven. When the dough begins to appear to firm up and change color a little (about 10 to 15 minutes), reduce heat to 375 degrees, and finish baking for about 45 minutes, or until the crust is a nice brown. During the baking add more dill butter in the chimneys. Test interior heat with a skewer. The filling should be very warm but not simmering hot, about 140 degrees.

9. While the kulebyaka is baking, melt the clarified dill butter, and pass it at the table. Other sauce possibilities: plain clarified butter; sour cream; hollandaise sauce.

10. The finished kulebyaka must rest at least ½ hour before being served. Cut into slices, and present on warm dishes.

Cooking Ahead: The prepared kulebyaka can wait for several hours in a cool spot; if kept in a warm area, the yeast dough will begin to rise again. It may even be refrigerated until the next day, but in that case bring it to almost room temperature before baking it.

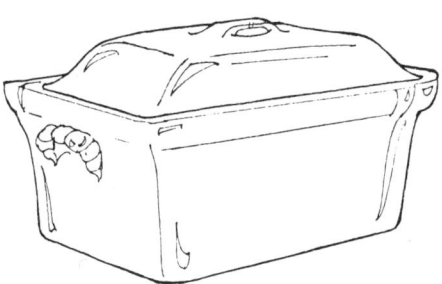

Acorn Squash Purée

The toughest thing about cooking with acorn squash is its skin. One has to possess a very sturdy knife and be steady of hand to cut through the defiant outer layer. Boiling until both skin and flesh are soft solves the problem completely. It also presents the opportunity of boiling potatoes along with the squash, for this or other uses. Although I am rather fond of the flavor of cold purées, acorn squash, I find, cannot be served this way. Its delicate flavor is further diminished by the lack of warmth.

Makes about 4 cups

2-pound acorn squash
1 pound (about 3) potatoes
½ cup Chicken Stock (page 218)
½ cup heavy cream
nutmeg
salt and pepper

1. Bring about six quarts of water to a boil in a deep pot. Meanwhile, scrub the potatoes, and pierce the acorn squash in several places with a sturdy fork. Place the squash and the potatoes in the boiling water, and cook for about 30 minutes, or until the squash is soft and the flesh can be easily pierced with a knife. Drain the vegetables.

2. When they are cool, peel the potato and cut it into chunks; split the squash in half, spoon out the seeds and fibers, and scoop out the flesh from the shell, putting it into a blender or food processor. Add the potato pieces to the blender, and pour in chicken stock, ¼ cup of the cream, and a large pinch of nutmeg. Purée. If the blender labors, it may need the remaining ¼ cup of cream; food processors will work fine with the smaller amount. Scrape the purée into a pot, add salt and pepper, and reheat.

Cooking Ahead: Acorn Squash Purée can be made 1 or 2 days in advance and reheated with just a little cream.

Palais de Glace (Ice Palace, A Maple Mold)

The name of this splendid dessert has roots in Paris, specifically from the Palais de Glace skating pavilion tucked behind the Champs-Elysées, now converted into a theater. That enchanting building has a glass-domed roof that reflected the ice rink below, giving double duty to the word *glace*, which means both ice and mirror as well as ice cream. Once unmolded, this imitation ice palace has a glistening layer of jelly on top that, in a small way, reminds me of the French original. But since this dessert concludes a meal that starred a Russian centerpiece, one could pretend that Leningrad's glorious Winter Palace was the inspiration.

1. Pour the maple syrup into a small pot, and heat over a low fire. Sprinkle the gelatin over the water, and put aside to soften.

2. Use either a standing electric mixer or a portable hand mixer for beating the egg whites. Begin beating the whites, and add the cream of tartar after the whites have been broken down and softened a little. Continue beating until the whites are quite firm. Keep an eye on the maple syrup; as soon as it comes to a boil, remove it from the heat, add the gelatin, and stir for a few moments to dissolve it. While beating the whites, add the hot maple syrup, turn the speed to high, and beat for ½ minute. Add the vanilla and rum, and beat for 1 minute more.

3. Lightly oil a 10-cup bowl; a mixing or large salad bowl is perfect. Scoop the mixture into the bowl, smooth the top, and refrigerate for at least 3 hours or overnight.

4. To unmold, run a hot, flexible knife around the dessert, first reaching halfway down the sides of the bowl; then go around again, reaching all the way to the bottom. Dip the bottom of the bowl in hot water for a few seconds, place the serving dish over the bowl, and invert. The serving dish should be a little shallow to accommodate some sauce. Pour a little of Light Chocolate Sauce around the mold, and pass the rest separately.

Cooking Ahead: Ice Palace can be made the day before; it is best not to prepare it any longer in advance.

¾ cup maple syrup
1½ tablespoons gelatin
½ cup water
9 egg whites
⅛ teaspoon cream of tartar
1 teaspoon vanilla
1 teaspoon rum
oil
1¾ cups cold Light Chocolate Sauce (page 232)

Omelette Rustique (Rustic Omelet)

This is not a classic rolled or folded omelet, but a flat, thick one that more closely resembles the Italian frittata or Spanish tortilla. It can, indeed, be served hot, but I often use it as a cold first course. It can even play that role during the cocktail hour. In this case cut the omelet into slices or wedges that can easily be picked up with fingers, and garnish each with a dab of sauce on top. A small piece of lettuce under each piece facilitates handling.

1. Sauté the ham quickly in ½ tablespoon of the butter, remove the pieces with a slotted spoon, and place them in a mixing bowl. If a red pepper is used, sauté it over medium heat in the fat remaining in the skillet; if necessary, add ½ tablespoon butter; remove it with the slotted spoon, and add to the prosciutto with the peas, parsley, coriander, cheese, a good dash of Tabasco, cream, salt and pepper. Beat together lightly, add the eggs, and beat lightly again. If pimiento is used, add it directly to the egg mixture.

2. Put 2 tablespoons butter in a 10- or 11-inch omelet pan or other nonstick skillet. When the butter is foaming hot, pour in the egg mixture, which should fill the skillet to about the three-fourths level. Immediately begin stirring with a fork, lifting the edges to allow some of the batter to run underneath. Reduce the heat to medium-low, cover, and cook for about 10 minutes. Occasionally repeat the process of lifting the edges and allowing more batter to run underneath. Test after 10 minutes by cutting near the center with a small, sharp knife. The omelet should be moistly cooked—that is, still soft and not solid and dry. Remove the cover, and place the pan under the broiler to finish cooking the thin layer of egg batter on the surface.

3. Carefully pull the edges of the omelet away from the pan, place a serving dish over the pan, and invert. The bottom of the omelet, which is now the top, should present a nicely browned surface. Cut into wedges or slices, and pass Avocado Sauce separately when served at the table.

Cooking Ahead: If served hot, the omelet must be cooked at the last minute. The mixture, however, can be prepared a few hours in advance and refrigerated.

3 ounces cured prosciutto-style ham, cut into ¼-inch pieces (about ¾ cup)
3 tablespoons butter
¼ cup red pepper or pimiento, chopped
½ cup peas, cooked
¼ cup parsley leaves, chopped
½ teaspoon ground coriander
2 tablespoons grated Parmesan cheese
Tabasco
¼ cup light or heavy cream
salt and pepper
10 eggs
Avocado Sauce (page 230) or Niçoise Mayonnaise (page 227)

↓↓↓

Stellar Sunday Lunch

SERVES 8

Macaroni and Gorgonzola

Carrot Pâté

Prune Timbale

Gratinéed Blueberries

The question arises when to serve a vegetable pâté as a main course. Easy. Perfect for luncheon or brunch or after-theater supper. But take another look at the menu, and you will notice the pâté is surrounded by substantial fare. The menu is indeed meant for informal dinners. Furthermore, this is a vegetable pâté with a walloping flavor, the sort of taste wine connoisseurs refer to as "big." Macaroni and Gorgonzola is a new twist on our old stand-by macaroni and cheese. A small plate of it kicks off the meal with a snap. Stuffed prunes march through the center of the Carrot Pâté, making a striking design when sliced, and of course, the Prune Timbale echoes that garnish. Cool blueberries under a bubbling hot topping closes the meal that will be remembered for its delicious flavors as well as for its surprises. The red wine for this menu should have some muscle—Chianti Classico, Barbaresco, Côtes du Rhône, or a light Zinfandel.

Carrot Pâté

3½ pounds
calories per serving—226

Carrot Pâté sounds like health food. This version will change your mind. I remember presenting it at a tasting session together with several meat pâtés. To my utter amazement everyone, including the men, was more enthusiastic about this one than about the meats. I think that was because they knew what to expect of the meat pâtés, but the big flavor of the Carrot Pâté was totally unexpected.

1. Select an 8-cup mold, and place enough prunes and whole carrots to make a single row down the center. When measuring the space the prunes take, allow some room for their expansion in cooking. Rinse the prunes, and place them in a small nonreactive pot. Add ¼ to ½ cup of the Madeira, or enough to cover them. Cover the pot, and soak the prunes for 1 hour. Add ¼ teaspoon of the nutmeg and the lemon slice, bring to a simmer, cover, and cook gently for 10 minutes. Drain and reserve the Madeira. Cut the whole carrots in half lengthwise, and cook in boiling water until just barely tender. Cool.

Preheat oven to 350 degrees.

2. The order for shredding and chopping the ingredients in a processor is: nuts (chop with on/off switch), Parmesan, onion, mushrooms, parsley, and carrot shreds. Melt the butter in a large skillet; add the onion; cover; and stirring occasionally, sauté gently for about 10 minutes, or until it is soft and translucent. Add the garlic, mushrooms, lemon juice, 2 tablespoons of the cooking Madeira, salt, and pepper. Cover, and simmer for 5 minutes to draw out the mushroom juices. Uncover, and stirring often, cook over high heat to boil off the juices. Cool for 5 minutes; then season with the remaining ¼ teaspoon nutmeg, and stir in the parsley. Scrape the mixture into a large mixing bowl.

3. To the mushrooms add the shredded carrots, 1¼ cups of the nuts, Parmesan, bread crumbs, mace, and ginger. Beat together in a small bowl the eggs, 2 tablespoons of the cream, 2 teaspoons of salt, and pepper. Pour over the carrot mixture, and blend together thoroughly. Poach a spoonful to taste for

about 6 large pitted prunes
½ to ¾ cup Madeira or port
1¾ pounds carrots, about ¼ pound whole, the remainder shredded
½ teaspoon nutmeg
1 lemon slice
1½ cups walnuts or pecans, ground
1 cup grated Parmesan cheese
1 large onion, chopped
1 pound mushrooms, chopped
½ cup parsley leaves, chopped
3 tablespoons butter plus butter for greasing paper
3 garlic cloves, minced
juice of ½ lemon
salt and pepper
½ cup bread crumbs
½ teaspoon mace

seasonings; correct if necessary. The mixture will not hold together, so remove with a slotted spoon to get some idea of how well seasoned the pâté is.

4. Make a paste of ¼ cup of walnuts with 1 tablespoon of the cooking Madeira, the remaining 1 tablespoon of cream, and a pinch of nutmeg. Stuff the prunes with this paste.

5. Cut parchment or wax paper to fit the top and bottom of an 8-cup mold. Fit in one paper, and butter it. Scoop half the carrot mixture into the mold, pushing it well into the corners. Tap the mold on the counter sharply several times. Place the stuffed prunes in a row down the center, and press them into the pâté a little. About 1 inch away from both sides of the prunes, make a row of the cooked carrot halves. Place the carrots rounded sides down since you are working in reverse for a pâté that will be unmolded. Spoon the rest of the carrot mixture alongside and over the prunes and carrots. Tap the mold on the counter several times. Butter the other piece of paper, and place it, greased side down, over the pâté. Cover. Place the mold in a water bath, and bake it for about 1½ hours, or until a thermometer registers 170 degrees. Leave the pâté in the water bath, but remove the cover. Cool for 30 minutes, lift out of the water, and place about 3 pounds of weights on it for 3 hours. Refrigerate the pâté for at least 2 days.

6. Unmold Carrot Pâté onto a serving platter, removing the two sheets of paper. Garnish the top with Carrot Flower Garnish and chives or scallions, according to the pattern on page 18, or any fanciful design you choose. To pick up on the nuts in the pâté, nut halves can be added as leaves beneath the carrot flower.

½ teaspoon ground ginger
4 eggs
3 tablespoons heavy cream
GARNISH: Carrot Flower Garnish (page 18), and 2 walnut halves

⇟⇟⇟

Macaroni and Gorgonzola

That all-American classic macaroni and cheese has an Italian counterpart in *Penne con Gorgonzola*. *Penne* (pens) are straight tubes of pasta with diagonally sliced ends. Though macaroni are a bit smaller than *penne*, they make a fine substitute. If you have fresh pasta, by all means use it.

1. Add the oil to a large pot of salted boiling water, and boil the macaroni until *al dente*, tender but with a touch of bite in the center, about 6 minutes. Meanwhile, heat the milk and butter together in a saucepot. Add the Gorgonzola gradually, stirring until it is completely melted before adding more. Grind in plenty of pepper; add the brandy and, at the very end, the Parmesan.

2. Place the well-drained macaroni in a large warm serving bowl. Pour on the sauce, and toss well to mix. Serve on warm plates, and do not pass any grated cheese.

Cooking Ahead: The sauce can be prepared well in advance and even refrigerated for several days. Reheat over a flame deflector pad with a few tablespoons of water stirred in. The pasta must be cooked at the last minute.

2 tablespoons oil
salt
8 ounces macaroni
⅔ cup milk
2 tablespoons butter
10 ounces Gorgonzola, broken into pieces
pepper
1 tablespoon brandy
⅓ cup grated Parmesan cheese

⇊⇊⇊

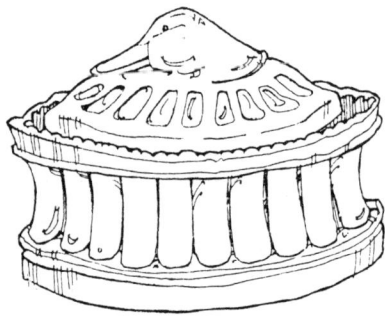

Prune Timbale

Although specifically devised for the prune-studded Carrot Pâté, these little molds would also be good company for light meat pâtés or a fruit salad plate.

1. Put the prunes in a small pot, pour on enough boiling water to immerse them, cover, and put aside for at least 30 minutes.

2. Drain the prunes, add chicken stock, port, orange juice, lemon rind, ginger, and nutmeg. Bring to a simmer, cover, and cook gently for 30 minutes.

3. Discard the ginger slice and lemon rind. With a skimmer remove the prunes to a blender or food processor, sprinkle the gelatin on the hot syrup, and let stand for a few minutes. While stirring constantly, reheat the syrup to almost the boiling point. Pour it over the prunes, and process to a smooth purée. Add the yogurt, and process again.

4. Lightly oil 8 small baba, or similar, molds, and fill with the purée. Chill to set the mixture. Though metal molds are the easiest to unmold, custard cups, small glasses, or even demitasse cups could also be used.

5. At serving time, run a hot knife around the inside of each mold, dip the bottom in hot water, and reverse onto a serving dish.

Cooking Ahead: Prune Timbales can be made 1 or 2 days in advance and unmolded several hours in advance.

½ cup (about 4 ounces) pitted prunes
½ cup Chicken Stock (page 218)
¼ cup port or Madeira
¼ cup orange juice
2-inch strip lemon rind
1 ginger slice, lightly crushed
⅛ teaspoon nutmeg
1 tablespoon gelatin
½ cup yogurt
oil

Gratinéed Blueberries

An old well-loved American dessert is simply a mixture of fresh blueberries, sour cream, and brown sugar. There is something unctuously delicious about biting into juicy blueberries bathed in the satiny cream. I find this hot version even more intriguing, though, because it adds the unexpectancy of cool berries beneath the piping hot topping.

Preheat broiler.

Distribute the berries among 8 individual gratin dishes or into 1 large baking dish. In a bowl mix together the sour cream, kirsch, and brown sugar. Spoon the cream over the berries, and just before serving, place under the hot broiler for about 1 minute, or until the cream browns lightly and bubbles.

Cooking Ahead: Place the berries in the dish, and mix the cream topping. Do not combine, but refrigerate them separately if they are to be held more than 2 hours. Spoon the cream over the berries just before broiling.

1½ pints blueberries
1½ cups sour cream
2 tablespoons kirsch
½ cup firm-packed dark brown sugar

A Dinner Salute to Italy

SERVES 8

Riso al Limone (Rice with Eggs and Lemon)

Tricolor Vegetable Terrine

Cucumbers in Mustard Sauce

Pears in Red Wine with Broccoli Purée

Biscuit Tortoni

The preceding vegetable pâté was all vegetable. This one and the next use chicken breast as the base for the mousse, a procedure that produces a lighter result and allows for more intricate garnishing within. This is a menu with flair that can be served at any dinner party of importance. One begins with a small dish of a northern Italian specialty—Rice with Eggs and Lemon—not often encountered here. The crisp lemony flavor begins the meal smartly. The terrine contains layers of pink, green, and white, each distinctively seasoned, but harmonious throughout. Cucumbers in Mustard Sauce is the perfect accompaniment—mildly assertive, but not too much so. The next is a hot and stunning dish, one for which you may want to change to small dishes instead of serving it on the dinner plate. Pear halves are poached in a snappy red wine broth, turning a deep ruby red. Each half appears with a small mound of delicately scented Broccoli Purée in the center. Keep it in mind at Christmas time, and surprise a lot of people. An old friend, frozen Biscuit Tortoni, completes this very special dinner. Pair the menu with a small red Bordeaux, a non-monster California Cabernet, or a dry California Sauvignon Blanc.

Tricolor Vegetable Terrine

3 pounds
calories per serving—145

The pale ribbons of orange, green, and pink in this terrine create a temptingly delicate picture. Each vegetable filling is sparked with different flavorings, all carefully balanced to make an overall harmonious blend. Extra time is necessary to put it all together, but both the eye and the palate are rewarded. One can gild this lily even further with the carrot and chive decoration illustrated on page 18. If the cook follows the steps as outlined, only one pot is needed for cooking both the broccoli and the carrots, and the food processor bowl needs no rinsing between steps since the color progression is from white to green. If you like, buy a full pound of broccoli, use only eight ounces of the peeled stems for the terrine, and save the florets for a separate presentation. I like this Tricolor Vegetable Terrine best after two or three days in the refrigerator.

1. Place the food processor bowl in the refrigerator and the steel blade in the freezer. Bring a pot of water to a boil, add the carrots, and boil for about 10 minutes, or until soft. Add only the white parts of 4 scallions for the last 2 minutes of cooking. Lift the carrots and scallions out with a skimmer, place in a strainer, and cool under cold running water. Drain very well, and chill. Cook the broccoli for about 7 minutes in the same water; add 3 or 4 whole scallions for the last 2 minutes of cooking. Cool the vegetables under running water, drain very well, and chill.

2. While the vegetables are cooking, prepare the chicken mousse. Place the cold chicken pieces in the chilled processor bowl, and chop with an on/off pulse into coarse pieces. Add the whole eggs, salt, and pepper, and process until smooth. With the motor running, slowly add first the egg whites and then the cream; process until very smooth. Scrape into a bowl, and chill. There should be about 24 ounces of chicken mousse.

Preheat oven to 300 degrees.

3. Place in the processor the tomato, ⅓ cup of the ricotta, one-third of the chicken mousse (about 8 ounces), a large pinch of cayenne, the coriander, salt, and pepper. Process until the mixture is very smooth. Poach a small spoonful, cool, and taste for seasonings; correct if necessary; then scrape into a bowl, and chill.

6 ounces (2 or 3) carrots, cut into chunks
1 bunch scallions
½ pound broccoli, peeled and cut into chunks
1 pound skinless, boneless chicken breasts or turkey scallops, cut into 1½-inch pieces and chilled
2 eggs
salt and pepper
2 egg whites
¾ cup heavy cream
1 tomato, peeled, seeded, and cut into chunks (about ½ cup)
1 cup ricotta
large pinch of cayenne
½ teaspoon ground coriander
6 tablespoons white wine

4. Now prepare the carrot mousse, using an on/off pulse to process the carrots and scallions with ¼ cup of the white wine until the vegetables are chopped into coarse pieces. Add ⅓ cup of the ricotta, one-third of the chicken mousse, the mace, ginger, bitters, salt, and pepper. Poach to taste, and correct if necessary. Use the same procedure to make the broccoli mousse, using the cooked broccoli and scallions, 2 tablespoons of white wine, the remaining ⅓ cup ricotta, the remaining third of the chicken mousse, parsley, basil, nutmeg, salt, and pepper.

5. Cut parchment paper to fit the top and bottom of a 6-cup mold; place one piece of paper in the bottom; then butter the paper. Put the tomato mousse into the dish, using a very flexible rubber spatula to smooth it into an even layer. Tap the mold on the counter, put large spoonfuls of the broccoli filling on top of the tomato, and smooth it into an even layer.* Tap the mold again; finally, add the carrot filling, and tap one last time. Butter the second piece of parchment paper, and place the greased side on top of the carrot mousse. Cover the mold with aluminum foil, pierce a hole in it, and place in a water bath. Bake for about 1½ hours, or until a thermometer registers 150 degrees. Remove the foil at once, but allow the mold to cool in the water bath for 30 minutes. Remove the terrine from the pan, and place a light weight on it for 6 hours. Chill. Drain before unmolding.

¼ teaspoon mace
½ teaspoon ground ginger
¼ teaspoon aromatic bitters
¼ cup parsley leaves
1 tablespoon fresh or dried basil
¼ teaspoon nutmeg
butter
OPTIONAL:
2 hard-boiled egg yolks

*If you use the optional hard-boiled egg yolk garnish, slip the yolks into a small pot of boiling water when you separate the eggs to gather the whites needed in the chicken mousse. Simmer the yolks for 6 or 7 minutes, or until firm; cool; chill; and chop into coarse pieces. Layer only half the broccoli mousse into the dish; then sprinkle a stripe of the chopped yolks down the center. Carefully add the remaining broccoli filling by first spooning some of it along both sides of the yellow stripe, thus supporting the feather-light yolks; gently tap the yolks with your finger to press them into the filling. Finally, cover the yolks with the last of the filling. The yolks provide a pretty golden touch in a sea of green. For a bolder stripe, use 3 or 4 hard-boiled egg yolks.

Biscuit Tortoni

Some years ago Biscuit Tortoni and spumoni were all the rage. Then chocolate mousse came along, and now it's chocolate truffles, either in candy or ice cream form. Like many a forgotten old friend, Biscuit Tortoni has many admirable qualities, number one being that it's delicious. It's also simple to make. Originally the recipe was based on good crisp macaroon cookies, as rare to find now as real truffles on these shores. Fortunately amaretto cookies are popular and readily available. These almondy cookies are expensive, but very little is needed, less than a half cup when they are ground. The exact number of cookies will vary since they differ in size.

1. Chill beaters and bowl for whipping the cream. In a food processor grind the cookies until they turn into crumbs; there should be 7 to 8 tablespoons; reserve 1 tablespoon. Pour the crumbs into a small bowl, add the sugar and milk, and let stand for 1 hour. The crumbs will absorb most of the milk and become mushy. Stir in the corn syrup.

2. Place 8 paper-lined 2½-inch foil cups on a small baking sheet or flat dish that can go into the freezer. Using the chilled bowl and beaters, beat the cream until very thick; add the vanilla and amaretto, and beat for another 10 seconds.

3. Scoop about one-third of the whipped cream over the crumbs, and fold in the cream very thoroughly to lighten the mushy mixture. Scrape the crumbs and cream over the whipped cream, and fold together thoroughly but lightly.

4. Use a small ladle or a pitcher to pour the cream into the cups to the two-thirds level. Sprinkle with the reserved crumbs, and freeze for at least 5 hours. Remove from the freezer about 10 minutes before serving.

Cooking Ahead: If the dessert is made a day or so in advance, freezer-wrap the frozen Biscuit Tortoni so it will not absorb other odors.

Note: A frozen cream, quite different but resembling Biscuit Tortoni, can be made with graham cracker crumbs. Follow the same procedure, but increase the crumbs to ½ cup, and do not sprinkle any on the surface.

2½ ounces amaretto cookies
2 tablespoons sugar
6 tablespoons milk
1 tablespoon corn syrup
¾ cup heavy cream
¼ teaspoon vanilla
¼ teaspoon amaretto liqueur or ⅛ teaspoon almond extract

Pears in Red Wine with Broccoli Purée

Pears as a vegetable? Why not? There is enough tartness in the poaching liquid to create the sweet-sour balance that is admired in many cuisines. This is a very pretty dish of dark red pears holding a mound of bright green purée. The purée is the same as that used with Broccoli Purée in Endive Spears, but the amount of coriander is reduced. Seasonings in cold dishes are less intense than when served hot.

1. Pour the wine into a large, flat nonreactive skillet; add the vinegar, basil, salt, and pepper, and bring to a boil. Cover, and simmer for 10 minutes.

2. Meanwhile, peel the pears, cut in half lengthwise, scoop out the seeds and core, and drop into acidulated water. Slip the pears into the skillet. Turn the pears several times, using wooden spoons so as not to damage the flesh. Cover and simmer for 5 minutes, turning several times during the cooking. Test for doneness with a knife; the pears should be soft but not mushy. The cooking time will depend on the size and ripeness of the fruit.

3. Warm the Broccoli Purée, drain the pears well, and fill the center cavity with a mound of about 2 tablespoons of the purée. Serve hot, ½ pear per diner.

Cooking Ahead: It is strongly recommended to cook the pears at least 1 day, even 2 days in advance. Keep turning them in the flavored wine, and watch the red color deepen. Reheat the pears in the wine carefully, so as not to overcook. Broccoli Purée can be prepared 1 or 2 days in advance and warmed at serving time.

3 cups red wine
¼ cup raspberry vinegar
¼ cup fresh basil leaves or 2 tablespoons dried basil
salt and pepper
4 Anjou, Bartlett, or Bosc pears
1 cup Broccoli Purée (page 139) made with 2 tablespoons coriander leaves

Cucumbers in Mustard Sauce

Since mustard is the dominating seasoning in this sauce, its quality is important. The grainy French type works best, but any Dijon-style mustard is fine.

Makes about 4½ cups

1. While bringing a large quantity of water to a boil, peel the cucumbers, cut in half lengthwise, and scoop out the seeds; a grapefruit knife works well for this. Cut the cucumber halves diagonally into ¼-inch slices, add to the boiling water with a little salt, and cook for about 5 minutes, or until they are just soft and translucent. Drain at once, and cool under running cold water. Drain well again; then squeeze the cucumbers, a handful at a time, to extract as much water as possible.

2. In a medium-sized bowl beat together mayonnaise, yogurt, mustard, lime juice, salt, and pepper. Add the cucumbers, and mix to coat all pieces. Cut the mint into small pieces with scissors (scissors work better than chopping with a knife), scatter them over the cucumbers, and mix again.

Cooking Ahead: The cucumbers can be cooked, and the sauce prepared, the day before, and both can be refrigerated separately. Mix together 1 or 2 hours before serving, adding the mint at the same time. Lift the cooked cucumbers out of their storage bowl to leave behind any water that has exuded.

4 cucumbers
⅓ cup Mayonnaise (page 226)
⅓ cup yogurt
1 tablespoon French-style mustard
juice of 1 lime
salt and pepper
¼ cup mint

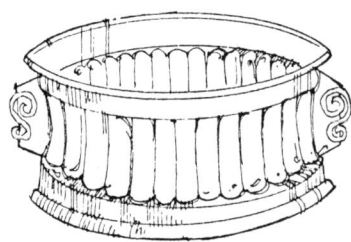

Riso al Limone (Rice with Eggs and Lemon)

Piedmont, the rice-growing region of northern Italy, makes a specialty of cooking rice in imaginative combinations. This is one of the simplest and one of the best.

1. Bring a large pot of water to the boil, add salt, and to maintain a rolling boil, add the rice in a thin stream. Stir briefly with a long wooden spoon to guarantee that no rice sticks to the bottom, and cook for about 15 minutes, or until it is crisply tender. Bite into a grain to test for doneness.

2. While the rice is cooking, beat together the eggs, lemon juice, and pepper. Drain the rice thoroughly, and working quickly, transfer it to a large warm bowl, pour the egg-lemon juice combination over the rice, add the butter and ⅔ cup of the Parmesan, and toss with large forks. The heat of the rice should be sufficient to melt the butter and cheese and barely cook the eggs; if not, place in a warm oven for a few minutes, stirring often. If you prefer a moister rice, slowly pour in the cream until you arrive at the consistency you prefer. Serve at once with the remaining Parmesan cheese.

Cooking Ahead: Served hot, rice is at its best only when freshly cooked. If it must be cooked ahead, drain well, and refrigerate. Bring back to room temperature, place in a well-buttered heat-proof casserole, put a damp dishcloth directly on top of the rice, cover, and warm in a 375-degree oven for 10 to 15 minutes. Stir once or twice. The final additions must be done at serving time.

salt
2 cups Italian Arborio rice or long-grain rice
6 eggs
⅓ cup lemon juice
pepper
¼ cup butter, cut into ½-inch pieces
1½ cups grated Parmesan cheese
OPTIONAL:
¼ to ½ cup heavy cream, hot

⇊⇊⇊

Artistic Flair
Frames a Stylish Menu

SERVES 6

Oysters Bercy

Mosaic Vegetable Terrine

Stuffed Apricots in Aspic

Chocolate Omelet

The vegetable terrine that stars in this menu is a specialty of many world-famous chefs and the same one shown in so many food magazines. It is picture-pretty and more delicate than the two preceding vegetable terrines. For this reason a sauce is suggested alongside. To complete the studied effect of the plate, a new fruit garnish was created—apricots plumped with a stuffing and encased in shimmering aspic. The two make a handsome couple. The meal begins with fried oysters in a winy sauce and ends with another hot dish, Chocolate Omelet. Once beyond the oysters, every dish has a shape and coloring that let guests know this was a carefully planned meal. The oysters don't need good looks; they are here just for their delicious selves. A white wine from beginning to end is one possibility—Burgundy, Mâcon-Villages, Rioja, or a California Chardonnay. For a special occasion, switch to a syrupy Sauternes for the hot omelet.

Mosaic Vegetable Terrine

2½ pounds
calories per serving—238

As vegetable terrines go, this one is a *Ziegfeld Follies* number. It's a very showy affair with brightly colored vegetables parading in a field of snowy chicken mousseline. Chefs on both sides of the Atlantic compete to see who can create the most sensational effect. Too often they go overboard. I prefer more restrained garnishing. For all its good looks, you will find this a mild terrine, one that benefits from being served with a sauce. Avocado Sauce (page 230), Niçoise Mayonnaise (page 227), or Rosy Cream Sauce (page 225) would be a harmonious choice.

1. Place the food processor bowl in the refrigerator and the steel blade in the freezer. Carefully remove all fat, membranes, and tendons from the chicken; cut into 1-inch pieces; and place in the refrigerator for at least ½ hour. Have egg whites and cream thoroughly chilled.

2. Put the chicken in the chilled processor bowl; add the parsley, tarragon, coriander, salt, and pepper. First process with the on/off switch to chop the chicken into coarse pieces; then process until smooth. With the motor running, slowly pour in first the egg whites and then the cream, scraping down the bowl between additions. Do not use all the cream if there is the risk of making the mousseline too thin; it is best to reserve ¼ cup. Poach a spoonful of mousseline to test for taste and consistency. If the mousseline feels too firm, add the remaining ¼ cup of cream. Scrape the mousseline into a bowl, and chill.

3. Prepare the vegetables. Top and tail the string beans; break off the tough asparagus ends, but do not peel; peel the turnip, and cut into thick strips, about ½ inch wide and 1 to 1½ inches long; peel the carrots, and cut in half lengthwise. To use a single pot, cook the vegetables in the following order in lightly salted boiling water until crisply tender: string beans, asparagus, turnips, and carrots. Place the vegetables in a single layer on a plate lined with several thicknesses of paper towels, and chill.

Preheat oven to 325 degrees.

2 pounds boneless, skinless chicken breasts
2 egg whites
2 cups heavy cream
2 tablespoons parsley
½ teaspoon tarragon
½ teaspoon ground coriander
salt and pepper
about 4 string beans
¼ pound asparagus
1 large turnip
2 carrots
butter
OPTIONAL GARNISH:
1 asparagus, 1 carrot

4. Cut parchment or wax paper to fit the top and bottom of a 6-cup loaf dish. Butter the dish, fit in one paper, and butter it. Spoon in one-third of the mousseline, smooth it with a wet rubber spatula, and tap the dish sharply on the counter. Make a layer of the asparagus spears, alternating top and bottom ends. Press the asparagus lightly into the mousseline, and cover with half the remaining mousseline. Tap the dish on the counter. Place the string beans in a row in the center of the mold. Next comes a row of turnips on each side of the string beans, and finally come two rows of carrots, rounded sides down. Press these vegetables lightly into the mousseline, and spoon the remaining mousseline over them. Smooth the top, and tap the dish on the counter. Butter the other sheet of paper, and place it, greased side down, on the mousseline. Cover, place in a water bath, and bake it for 30 to 40 minutes, or until a thermometer registers 140 degrees. Remove the cover, and cool the terrine in the water bath for 30 minutes. Lift from the pan, and weight it lightly for no more than 2 hours. Remove the weights, and refrigerate for at least 2 days.

5. Unmold the terrine onto a serving dish, removing the two pieces of paper. If you wish to decorate the terrine, cut the carrot into julienne strips, and cook until they are crisply tender. Cook the asparagus for about ½ minute, cool under cold running water, and cut diagonally into long, thin slices. Make a fan in the center of the terrine by alternating the carrot and asparagus slices. Cut with a very sharp knife, using a sawing motion. Pass the sauce separately.

⇊⇊⇊

Stuffed Apricots in Aspic

Some dried fruits have long been used with the main course—prune with pork, for one; dried figs with duck, for another. But the dried apricot, despite its natural tartness, is generally reserved for dessert dishes. Here is one way to make the most of it in an unusual way. After being plumped in water, the apricots are stuffed, set in a bed of aspic, and given a glistening aspic coating. Broccoli stuffing makes a pretty green stripe in the center, but the nut stuffing provides a nice crunch. Take your pick.

1. Rinse the apricots, put them in a small pot, cover with boiling water and a lid, and put aside for 30 minutes. Add the coriander, bring to a simmer, and cook gently, still covered, for 10 minutes. Immediately remove the apricots from the hot water with a skimmer, and spread them out on a dish to cool. Turn the fruit over after about 10 minutes to cool both sides faster. Handled this way, the apricots will retain a little firmness and not go limp.

2. Select a serving dish that can hold the apricots in a single layer with space around each one. The dish should also be about ¼ inch deep. Pour enough aspic into the dish to make a generous coating on the bottom; chill to set the aspic.

3. Meanwhile, stuff the apricots with enough Broccoli Purée or nut paste to make them plump; scrape off excess stuffing to make a smooth center stripe; chill.

4. Pour about 1 cup of the aspic into a small bowl, and chill until syrupy. When the aspic-coated dish is ready, one at a time, place a stuffed apricot on a fork, immerse it in the syrupy aspic, and set it on the dish. Arrange the apricots in concentric circles, straight or radiating lines, or whatever you fancy. Chill to set the aspic.

5. Use a tablespoon to dribble more of the syrupy aspic over each apricot, and chill. This can be repeated one more time. While in the syrupy stage, some of the aspic will slide off the apricot; it doesn't matter. Pour all remaining aspic into a flat dish, and chill to set.

6. At serving time, dice the aspic (page 18), sprinkle a little on each apricot, and scatter the rest between the pieces. Use a spoon and small spatula to serve, reaching under each apricot to include the aspic base.

6 ounces dried whole apricots, the larger the better
½ teaspoon ground coriander
3 cups clarified chicken aspic (page 222)
½ cup Broccoli Purée (page 139) or nut paste in Carrot Pâté (page 180), the quantity doubled

Oysters Bercy

Plump oysters lend themselves to a tantalizing array of easy, fast preparations. This one is particularly appealing because its light flour coating gives a tinge of crispness and color to the morsels. The oysters can be served without the slice of toast, but I find it markedly improves the presentation. Not only does the toast act as a pillow lifting the oysters off the plate, but it also guarantees that every drop of the sauce will be absorbed and enjoyed.

1 quart shucked oysters
12 tablespoons butter
4 tablespoons oil
about 1 cup flour
salt and pepper
2 large shallots, chopped fine (about ½ cup)
¾ cup white wine
juice of ½ lemon
¼ cup chopped parsley
8 slices toast

1. Drain the oysters in a sieve suspended over a bowl. Sharply shake the sieve a few times to force out as much of the liquor as possible. Reserve the liquor; there should be about 1 cup.

2. Place 1 large or 2 medium-sized frying pans over medium-high heat, and melt together 8 tablespoons of the butter and the oil. Meanwhile, spread the flour in a large dish or on wax paper, and scatter the drained oysters over the flour. With your hands toss the oysters to coat them with the flour. This flouring must be done at the last minute so that the light coating remains dry. When the fat is hot and foamy, lift the oysters from the flour, and add them to the pan. Do not overcrowd the oysters, or they will not brown. After about ½ minute turn the oysters to fry them on the other side for about another ½ minute. Sprinkle with salt and pepper, lift the oysters from the pan to a heated dish, and keep them warm.

3. If using two pans, prepare the sauce in only one. Discard the frying fat, reduce the heat to medium, and add the shallots to the pan. With a wooden spoon, scrape up the juices from the bottom of the pan, and stir together with the shallots. Cook for about ½ minute. Add the white wine, increase the heat to high, and boil briskly to reduce the wine to about half. Add the oyster liquor, lemon juice, salt, and pepper. Again boil briskly to reduce the liquid by about one-third. Remove the pan from the heat, and a bit at a time, stir in the remaining 4 tablespoons of butter. Add the parsley.

4. Place a slice of toast on each of 8 warmed plates, and divide the oysters over the toasts. Add to the sauce any juices that collected in the oyster dish, and spoon the sauce over the oysters.

Chocolate Omelet

Cooks who worry about rolling an omelet out of a skillet perfectly will have no problem with this one—it's baked. A light, airy, soufflélike omelet, this winning dessert is child's play to concoct.

Preheat oven to 350 degrees.

1. Place the butter in a deep 10-inch pie dish, about a 5-cup capacity, and place in the oven. Beat the egg yolks with 2 tablespoons of the sugar until light and frothy. Add the orange liqueur and rum, and beat again.

2. Beat the egg whites until a little foamy, add the cream of tartar, and continue beating until frothy. Gradually add the remaining 3 tablespoons of sugar, and beat until stiff peaks are formed. Fold about one-third of the beaten whites into the yolks, and blend together well. Add the remaining whites to the yolk base, and begin folding them in delicately. Before the whites are completely incorporated, sprinkle on the cocoa, and fold it into the batter with the whites.

3. Use potholders to remove the pie dish from the oven, and rotate the dish to grease the entire surface with the melted butter. Scrape the omelet batter into the pie dish, and place in the oven for about 10 minutes, or until the omelet is nice and puffy. Serve at once, preferably on warmed plates. Pull the omelet apart with two large spoons for individual portions. Pass the Light Chocolate Sauce separately.

Cooking Ahead: The egg yolk-sugar base can be beaten together several hours in advance and kept in a cool spot, covered. Whisk once or twice before continuing with the recipe. The whites must be beaten just before baking.

1 tablespoon butter
4 eggs, separated
⅓ cup sugar, sifted
1 tablespoon orange liqueur
2 teaspoons rum
pinch of cream of tartar
2 tablespoons cocoa
Light Chocolate Sauce (page 232), at room temperature

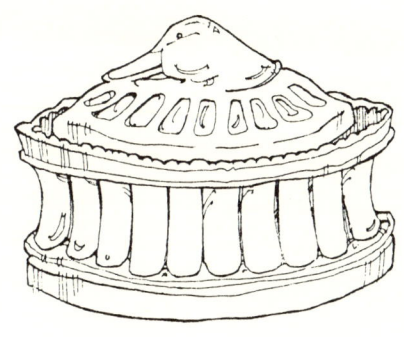

PART THREE

⇟⇟⇟

Serendipities

CHAPTER FIVE

More Innovative Pâtés and Terrines and One Old Favorite

Chicken Terrine

3½ pounds
calories per serving—365

The tastiest meat on poultry is the dark meat; that is why it is included in the forcemeat of this recipe. Since most of the dark meat is on the legs and thighs, it means a little work removing tendons and gristle. Don't be tempted to use all white meat instead; results will not be as good.

1. Slice the chicken breasts in half lengthwise; remove any skin, tendons, and cartilage; and flatten lightly with a meat pounder or the bottom of a heavy skillet. Place the breasts in a bowl, sprinkle with salt and pepper, and pour the brandy, plus 2 tablespoons of the Madeira, over them. Turn the chicken pieces with your hands to coat all surfaces, cover, and put aside to marinate for about 2 hours.

2. Trim all fat from the ham, and cut the meat into long strips, about ½ inch wide. Place the strips in a bowl, mix together the rest of the Madeira and the bitters, and pour them over the ham. Mix to coat all pieces, cover, and put aside to marinate.

3. Remove the skin, gristle, and tendons from the white and dark chicken meat, and cut into pieces. If salted fatback is used instead of fresh, trim it of any rind, rinse, boil for 10 minutes, and rinse again. Cut the fatback into 1-inch pieces. Grind the meats, or chop in a food processor, in this order: chicken; fatback; pork and veal together. Grind twice or process to a fairly smooth consistency.

2 boneless and skinless chicken breasts
salt and pepper
2 tablespoons brandy
½ cup Madeira or port
½ pound ham, about ½ inch thick
1 teaspoon aromatic bitters
¾ pound boneless chicken meat, dark and white
¾ pound fatback or salted fatback
½ pound veal, cut into 1-inch pieces
½ pound pork, cut into 1-inch pieces
⅛ teaspoon allspice
½ teaspoon ground coriander

4. Put the chopped meats in a mixing bowl, and season with 1 teaspoon of salt, ½ teaspoon of pepper, the allspice, coriander, thyme, nutmeg, shallots, white wine, and the alcohols drained from the two marinades. Mix all together very well with your hands. Add the bread crumbs, and mix again. Finally, add the eggs, and mix all together very well. Fry a small piece of the forcemeat, cool, taste for seasonings, and correct if necessary.

¼ teaspoon thyme
⅛ teaspoon nutmeg
2 shallots, chopped
½ cup white wine
½ cup bread crumbs
2 eggs, beaten
oil, fatback or caul for terrine dish

Preheat oven to 350 degrees.

5. Oil an 8-cup mold, or line it with fatback or caul, allowing excess to hang over the edges. Put in one-third of the forcemeat, and tap the dish sharply on the counter. Place 2 of the chicken breast halves between strips of ham, and press them lightly into the forcemeat. Repeat with another layer of forcemeat, the remaining breast meat and ham, and a final layer of forcemeat. Smooth the top, and tap the dish sharply on the counter several times. Pull the extra fatback or caul over the meat, or smear oil over the surface. Cover with aluminum foil, put on the lid, and poke a small hole in the foil. Bake in a water bath for about 1½ hours, or until a thermometer registers 160 degrees.

6. Lift the mold from the water bath, let it rest for 30 minutes, and weight it. When it is cool, refrigerate the mold overnight with the weights in place. Remove the weights, cover well, and refrigerate the terrine for 3 or 4 days before serving.

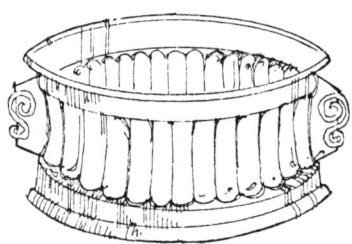

Pâté Panaché en Aspic
(Mixed Pâté in Aspic)

3 pounds
calories per serving—164

A few meats, a few vegetables, and a well-flavored aspic add up to an admirable pâté, low in both cost and calories.

1. Place the chop in a small pot, pour in chicken stock, and add the carrots, onion, garlic, basil, bay leaf, pepper, and a pinch of salt. Cover the pot, put on medium fire, and bring the stock to a simmer. Reduce the heat, and simmer gently for 1 hour. Add the peas for the last 5 minutes of cooking. Remove from the heat, and cool the meat and vegetables in the stock.

2. Strain the stock; then return it to the rinsed pot, and put it on the fire. Bring back to the boiling point. While the stock is heating, soften the gelatin in the wine, and add to the hot stock. Remove from the heat, and stir until the gelatin is dissolved. Cool; then chill until slightly syrupy.

3. Meanwhile, discard the bay leaf from the meat and vegetables. Select an 8-cup loaf dish, and make a decorative pattern on the bottom with the carrot slices and peas. Carefully pour in ½ cup of the stock so as not to disturb the pattern. It is best to pour against the side of the dish rather than over the vegetables. Refrigerate until the aspic sets.

4. Remove the fat and bone from the chop, shred the meat coarsely, and place in a mixing bowl. Add the remaining peas, carrots, and onion, squashing the onion somewhat between your fingers as you do. Cut the ham into cubes, about ¼ to ½ inch, and add to the bowl. Mix the meat and vegetables together gently with your hands, and carefully place them in the loaf dish so as not to disturb the set layer of aspic. Smooth the top of the filling, and pour in the aspic. Refrigerate for at least 3 hours; overnight is better.

5. To serve, run a hot knife around the pâté, dip the bottom of the pan in hot water; place a chilled serving dish over the pâté, and reverse the two together.

1½-pound veal or pork chop (1 double chop)
2½ cups Chicken Stock (page 218)
3 carrots, sliced
1 onion, quartered
1 garlic clove, mashed
1 teaspoon basil
1 bay leaf
pepper and salt
1 cup fresh or frozen peas
2 tablespoons gelatin
½ cup white wine
½ pound (1 thick slice) ham

Creamy Chicken Liver Pâté

3 pounds
calories per serving—296

The creaminess of this pâté comes from an unexpected source—velvety ricotta cheese.

Preheat oven to 350 degrees.

1. Carefully pick over the chicken livers, removing all fat and membranes. Put in a bowl, and season with the mace, ginger, salt, and pepper. Pour on the wine and brandy, mix with your hands, cover, and refrigerate overnight.

2. Lift the livers out of the marinade, and place them in the food processor with the pork. Pour the marinade into a small skillet, and reduce it over high heat until only 2 tablespoons remain; there will also be some solids. Scrape the reduced marinade into the processor bowl, add salt and pepper, and process until smooth. Beat the eggs, ricotta, and bitters together, add to the meats, and process to blend well. Poach a spoonful to taste for seasonings; correct if necessary.

3. Oil an 8-cup mold, fit a sheet of parchment or wax paper in the bottom, and fill with the pâté mixture. Cover, place in a water bath, and bake for about 1½ hours, or until a thermometer registers 160 degrees.

4. Lift the mold from the water bath, let it rest for 1 hour, and lightly weight it with no more than 3 pounds. When the mold is cool, refrigerate it overnight with the weights in place. Remove the weights, cover well, and refrigerate the pâté for 2 or 3 days before serving. Unmold, and remove the paper before serving.

1½ pounds chicken livers
½ teaspoon ground mace
½ teaspoon ground ginger
salt and pepper
¾ cup white wine
2 tablespoons brandy
1½ pounds fatty pork, ground
3 eggs
¾ cup ricotta
1 teaspoon aromatic bitters
oil

⇊⇊⇊

Petits Pâtés Chauds (Individual Hot Pâtés)

10 10-ounce pâtés
calories per serving—780

Just as it takes longer to make many little cookies instead of one large cake, the same is true with pâtés. These individual pâtés are essentially the same presentation as Hot Veal and Ham Pâté (page 123) but take longer to do because of separate operations. Still, I find the individual servings more festive in a way since each person receives a complete pâté, decorations and all. Another thing to keep in mind is that small pâtés eliminate slicing at serving time, something that is always a little trickier with hot pâtés which cannot be weighted for firm texture. Since it is difficult to make truly small, attractive pâtés, these individual servings weigh in at 10 ounces, more than twice the usual amount. Obviously, the calorie count is correspondingly heavy. Keep the rest of the meal very light.

1. Cut the ham, bacon, and half the veal into ¼-inch pieces, and put in a mixing bowl. Add to the meats the onion, 2 tablespoons each of the white wine and brandy, plus the Madeira, ¼ teaspoon of the thyme, oil, and pepper. Mix the meats and seasonings well, break the bay leaf in half, and tuck into the bowl.

2. Remove the rind from the salt pork, cover with cold water in a pot, bring to a boil, and simmer for 10 minutes; then rinse with cold water. Cut the salt pork and lean pork into chunks, and separately grind each to a fine consistency. Put the pork in a large mixing bowl. Cut the remaining veal into 1-inch pieces, grind to a smooth consistency, and add to the pork.

3. Remove any fat or membranes from the chicken livers, and place them in the processor with the garlic. Process until smooth, and add to the pork. Season the forcemeat with the remaining 2 tablespoons white wine and 1 tablespoon brandy, ¼ teaspoon thyme, allspice, cayenne, salt, and pepper, and mix well. Cover both bowls closely, and refrigerate overnight or leave at room temperature for at least 2 hours, mixing one or two times.

4. The diced meats should have absorbed most of the marinade; if not, drain the alcohols into a small skillet, reduce to 1 tablespoon over high fire, and add to the ground meats along

8 ounces lightly smoked ham
4 ounces bacon
8 ounces lean veal or turkey breast
1 onion, chopped
¼ cup white wine
3 tablespoons brandy
2 tablespoons Madeira or port
½ teaspoon thyme
2 tablespoons oil
pepper
1 bay leaf
4 ounces salt pork
8 ounces lean pork
4 ounces chicken livers
2 garlic cloves, chopped coarse
1 teaspoon allspice
⅛ teaspoon cayenne
salt
2 eggs
⅓ cup bread crumbs

with the diced meats. Beat 1 egg; add it to the meats with the bread crumbs. Mix the meats very well with your hands. Fry a spoonful to taste for seasonings; correct if necessary.

Preheat oven to 375 degrees.

5. Depending on your working space, make either 1 pâté or several at a time. For each pâté you will need 5 ounces of Pastry rolled to 10 × 8 inches. Use about ¾ cup of the forcemeat, patted into an oblong about 3 × 4 inches in the center of the pastry sheet. Follow instructions for wrapping forcemeat in pastry on page 11. Use the extra egg for brushing the pastry and pastry scraps for decorating. Cut a hole in the center of each pâté, and fit with a parchment paper chimney. Place them on a buttered baking sheet.

6. Bake the pâtés for about 10 minutes, or until the pastry whitens a little; reduce the heat to 350 degrees; bake for an additional 40 minutes, or until a thermometer registers 160 degrees. Allow the pâtés to rest for 10 minutes before serving. Reheat Orbec Sauce, pour a tablespoon into each chimney hole, and garnish with a few parsley sprigs in the hole. Pass the rest of the sauce separately.

Cooking Ahead: The pâtés can be baked 1 or 2 days in advance and refrigerated. The flavor will be improved for standing. Bring back to room temperature, pour 1 tablespoon of Madeira into the vent hole of each one, and reheat in a 325-degree oven for about 25 minutes, or until a thermometer registers 130 degrees.

3 pounds Pastry (page 217)
Orbec Sauce (page 223)
parsley sprigs
dollop of butter

Spinach-Fish Terrine

2½ pounds
calories per serving—169

1. Chill the food processor bowl in the refrigerator and the steel blade in the freezer. Cook the carrot halves in boiling water for 6 or 7 minutes, or until just crisply tender. Drain at once, cool under cold running water, pat dry, wrap in paper towels, and refrigerate.

2. Chop the scallions into coarse pieces, and sauté in the 2 tablespoons butter for about 5 minutes, or until soft; do not allow them to brown. Scrape the scallions into a small bowl; cool; then chill. Meanwhile, place the anchovy fillets in a small pot with ¼ cup of the cream, bring to a simmer, and cook for about 1 minute. Stir until the anchovies dissolve, pour into a small cup, cool, and chill. Squeeze all liquid from the spinach, chop into coarse pieces, and chill. Cut the pimiento into ½-inch strips, place on paper towels, and chill.

Preheat oven to 350 degrees.

3. Put the fish, eggs, anchovy-cream, and the remaining ¾ cup of cream into the chilled processor bowl, and process until the fish is chopped to a smooth purée. Scrape the fish into a mixing bowl. Put the spinach into the processor with the cooked scallions, vermouth, basil, dill, coriander, cayenne, salt, and pepper, and purée. Beat this herb mixture into the fish. Poach a spoonful of the mousse, cool, taste for seasonings, and correct if necessary.

4. Cut parchment or wax paper to fit the top and bottom of a 6-cup loaf dish. Butter the dish, place the paper in, and butter it. Spoon in half the mousse, smooth into an even layer, and tap the dish sharply on the counter. Make a double-thick row of pimiento slices down the center; then flank the pimiento with carrot halves, rounded sides down. Leave about ½-inch space between the rows. Lightly press the vegetables into the mousse. Spoon the remaining mousse in 3 or 4 mounds on top of the vegetable garnish, and smooth it into an even layer with a rubber spatula. Butter the second piece of paper, and place

- 1 long carrot, cut in half lengthwise
- 4 scallions, including green tops
- 2 tablespoons butter plus butter for greasing mold
- 2 oil-packed anchovy fillets
- 1 cup heavy cream
- 10 ounces frozen spinach, defrosted, or 1 pound fresh spinach, blanched
- 2 or 3 pimiento halves
- 1 pound fillets of flounder, cod, or haddock, cut into 1-inch pieces, chilled
- 2 eggs
- 2 tablespoons vermouth
- 2 teaspoons fresh basil or 1 teaspoon dried basil
- 1 tablespoon dill
- 1 teaspoon ground coriander
- ¼ teaspoon cayenne
- 2 teaspoon salt
- ½ teaspoon pepper

it, greased side down, over the terrine. Cover closely with aluminum foil, and pierce a small hole in the foil.

5. Put the dish in a water bath, and bake for about 1 hour, or until a thermometer registers 150 degrees. Leave the dish in the water bath, but remove the foil. Cool for 30 minutes; then remove from water bath and lightly weight it with no more than 2 pounds; remove the weights after 2 hours, and refrigerate the terrine for at least 1 day; 2 days are better.

6. Remove the terrine from the refrigerator about 1 hour before serving time. Unmold onto a serving platter, removing both pieces of paper. A sauce to accompany the terrine could be Rosy Cream Sauce (page 225), Avocado Sauce (page 230), or Niçoise Mayonnaise (page 227).

⇓⇓⇓

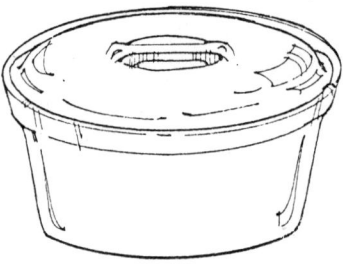

Crab Pâté

2 pounds
calories per serving—335

This pâté is adapted from a famous recipe popular in western England, where crab used to abound. The original, though called Buttered Crab, is really Potted Crab. England's potted dishes are meant to be spread on toast. This version cuts like a true pâté. A spot of color can be added to the center with a strip of lightly poached salmon or tightly rolled smoked salmon. The floral decoration of carrots and chives (page 18) could dress the top with one or two coatings of aspic (page 18).

1. Pick over the crab to remove any bones or cartilage. Pour the wine into a saucepot; add the anchovy paste, nutmeg, butter, salt, and pepper; and bring to a simmer, stirring until the butter melts. Remove from the fire; add the crab and finally the bread crumbs.

2. Cut a piece of parchment or wax paper to fit the bottom of a 6-cup mold. Oil the mold, fit the paper in the bottom, and oil it. Spoon in the crab pâté, smooth the top, cover, and refrigerate for 2 days.

3. To serve, unmold, remove the paper, and slice. Niçoise Mayonnaise (page 227) would be a nice sauce with Crab Pâté.

1 pound crab meat
⅔ cup white wine
1 teaspoon anchovy paste
½ teaspoon nutmeg
10 ounces (2½ sticks) butter, cut into pieces
salt and pepper
2 cups fresh, dry, white bread crumbs*
oil

*Packaged bread crumbs cannot be used because their dark tan color gives an unpleasant look to this pâté. Crumbs must be made from a firm-textured bread, not from soft sandwich bread. Remove the crusts, process into crumbs, spread on a baking sheet, and dry out in a 250-degree oven for 10 minutes. These crumbs will keep indefinitely in a tightly covered container. This is an excellent way to use up leftover baguettes after a dinner party.

Streamlined Kulebyaka

4 pounds
calories per serving—306

The recipe for authentic Russian Kulebyaka (page 171) goes on through nine different preparations. Here is its short cousin. I think you will find it equally attractive and delicious—almost. The only thing missing from this recipe is time and a sinkful of pots and pans.

1. Melt the butter in a large skillet, add the onion, reduce the heat, cover, and simmer for 5 minutes. Add the kasha and rice, increase the heat, and while stirring, cook for 2 or 3 minutes, or until you can see some of the rice grains turn opaque white. Add chicken stock and a little salt and pepper, cover, reduce the heat, and simmer for 5 minutes. Stir the chopped mushrooms into the grains with the vermouth and 2 teaspoons of dill. Re-cover and cook for another 5 minutes. Fluff with a fork, transfer to a mixing bowl, cool, and refrigerate.

2. Meanwhile, poach the salmon in fish stock, according to the directions for Kulebyaka, page 172.

Preheat oven to 450 degrees.

3. Beat 1 egg with the sour cream, season lightly with salt and pepper, and add to the grain and mushroom mixture. Stir well to incorporate the cream completely into the filling. Stir the remaining 2 teaspoons of dill into the melted butter. Remove all skin and bones from the salmon, and break into large chunks. Slice the hard-boiled eggs. Most chefs disdain the small egg slicer with wire cutters, but I find that for uniformly thin slices nothing works better.

4. Roll out pastry as for Hot Veal and Ham Pâté, page 123. Use about one-third of the grain-mushroom filling to make a rectangle about 4×8 inches in the center of the dough. Scatter half the salmon pieces over the filling; cover the fish with half the egg slices; then dribble half the dill butter over the eggs and salmon. Repeat with another layer of filling, salmon, egg, and dill butter, finishing the loaf with the final one-third of the grain-mushroom filling. Keep patting the loaf at the sides to keep it firm and straight. Enclose the kulebyaka loaf in the pas-

2 tablespoons butter
1 onion, chopped (about 1 cup)
½ cup kasha (toasted buckwheat kernels)
½ cup rice
2 cups Chicken Stock (page 218)
salt and pepper
½ pound mushrooms, chopped
¼ cup vermouth
4 teaspoons dill
1 pound salmon
2 to 3 cups Fish Stock (page 220)
2 eggs
½ cup sour cream
2 tablespoons melted butter
2 hard-boiled eggs
1½ pounds Pastry (page 217)
OPTIONAL:
Clarified Butter (page 222) or dill butter

try according to the directions on page 173, using the remaining egg to paint all overlapping surfaces and to give a final coating over the surface of the completed kulebyaka.

5. Bake for about 10 minutes, reduce the heat to 375 degrees, and bake for about another 45 minutes, or until a thermometer registers 140 degrees. Cover the loaf with aluminum foil if the pastry begins to darken too deeply. Let the baked loaf rest for at least 20 minutes before slicing. Pass the optional clarified butter or dill butter.

↓↓↓

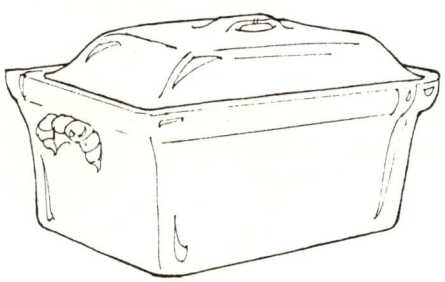

Spinach-Zucchini Terrine

3 pounds
calories per serving—132

Once puréed, zucchini adds both green and white flecks to the terrine, ensuring attractive slices. However, if further interior garnishing is desired, tiny diced carrots would add an extra note of interest; see Shrimp Terrine (page 158). Either Pink Horseradish Sauce (page 229) or Light Tomato Sauce (page 224) would go well with Spinach-Zucchini Terrine.

Preheat oven to 325 degrees.

1. In a covered skillet over medium heat, sauté the zucchini and scallions in olive oil until they are soft, about 15 minutes. Stir from time to time. Add the garlic, turn up the heat, and cook, uncovered, until most of the vegetable juices have evaporated, 5 to 8 minutes. Scrape the sautéed vegetables into a food processor.

2. Squeeze all the liquid from the spinach, chop it into coarse pieces, and add to the zucchini. Purée the vegetables. Add the tarragon, dill, cayenne, salt, and pepper, and purée again briefly. Beat the eggs and bitters together, and add to the processor with the motor running. Sprinkle in the bread crumbs, and process very briefly, just enough to incorporate them into the mixture.

3. Cut parchment or wax paper to fit the top and bottom of a 6-cup mold. Butter the mold, fit a paper in, and butter it. Scoop in the terrine mixture, and smooth the top. Butter the other sheet of paper, and place it, greased side down, over the filling. Cover the mold, place in a water bath, and bake for 1½ hours, or until a knife plunged in the center comes out clean. Uncover the mold; turn off the heat; let the terrine cool in the oven.

4. Remove the terrine from the water bath, and lightly weight it with no more than 2 pounds. Remove the weights after 3 hours; cover and refrigerate the terrine for 1 or 2 days.

2 pounds zucchini, thinly sliced
2 bunches (16 to 20) scallions, chopped, greens included
¼ cup olive oil
3 garlic cloves, chopped coarse
1 pound fresh spinach, blanched, or 10 ounces frozen spinach, defrosted
1 tablespoon tarragon
1 teaspoon dill
¼ teaspoon cayenne
2 teaspoons salt
pepper
4 eggs
1 tablespoon aromatic bitters
1 cup dry bread crumbs
butter

Broccoli Terrine

2¼ pounds
calories per serving—155

The broccoli floret garnish in the center of this terrine can be done two ways: chopped and spread into a layer, as below, or left whole and placed in rows. The first is easier to slice; the second demands an impeccably sharp knife.

1. Chill the food processor bowl in the refrigerator and the steel blade in the freezer. Bring a pot of water to a boil while preparing the broccoli. Cut off the florets, and reserve; peel the stems, and cut them into 1½-inch pieces. Add salt to the boiling water, and cook the stem pieces for about 7 minutes. Add the florets, and cook for 1 minute more. Drain at once, and cool under cold running water. Drain well again. Take out about 3 cups of florets, and place on a dish between paper towels. Measure the stem pieces. There should be about 2 cups; if not, fill out with florets. Place the stems between paper towels in a dish, and chill both dishes.

2. Sauté the onion in the 4 tablespoons butter over medium heat in a covered skillet. When the onion is soft, about 10 minutes, transfer it to a bowl, cool, and chill. Remove all tendons and cartilage from the chicken, cut into ½-inch pieces, and chill. If the pimiento is used for garnish, place it between paper towels, and chill.

Preheat oven to 300 degrees.

3. Put the chicken and onion in the chilled processor bowl, and process with the on/off switch until they are chopped into coarse pieces. Add the broccoli stems and parsley, and process for about 20 seconds. Add the ricotta, whole egg, egg white, nutmeg, cayenne, salt, and pepper, and process until very smooth. With the motor running, slowly add the cream. Poach a spoonful of the mousse, cool, taste for seasonings, and correct if necessary. There should be about 4 cups of mousse.

4. Cut parchment or wax paper to fit the top and bottom of a 6-cup mold. Butter the mold, fit in a paper, and butter it.

5 cups (about 1 pound) broccoli stems and florets
salt
1 onion, chopped coarse
4 tablespoons butter plus butter for greasing mold
½ pound skinless, boneless chicken breast
½ cup parsley leaves
½ cup ricotta
1 egg
1 egg white
¼ teaspoon nutmeg
large pinch of cayenne pepper
½ cup heavy cream
OPTIONAL GARNISH:
3 or 4 pimiento halves

Spoon in half of the broccoli mousse, smooth the top, and tap the mold sharply on the counter. Chop about half the reserved florets into coarse pieces, and sprinkle them in the center to make a layer. If using the pimiento garnish, cut the halves into ½-inch strips, and use double thick as a stripe down the center. Lightly press the vegetables into the mousse, spoon in the remaining mousse, smooth the top, and tap the mold sharply on the counter. Butter the other piece of paper, and place it, greased side down, over the mousse. Cover the mold closely.

5. Place the mold in a water bath, and bake for about 1 hour, or until a thermometer registers 140 degrees. Remove from the oven, uncover, but leave in the water bath for 15 minutes. Cool another 15 minutes; then lightly weight it with no more than 2 pounds. Once the mold is cool, remove the weights, cover the mold well, and refrigerate for 1 or 2 days.

6. To serve, unmold the terrine onto a serving platter, chop the reserved florets, and scatter over the top.

CHAPTER SIX

Basic Recipes for Use in Many Menus

Crêpes

There are many recipes for preparing crêpe batter in a blender. Don't do it, unless you like tough crêpes. Even at the slowest speed, a blender overdevelops the gluten in the flour for perfect rubbery crêpes or any kind of pancake. Making the batter by hand is easily done in a matter of minutes. The resting time of the batter is very important for achieving thin crêpes. When left to stand, the flour absorbs some of the liquid and makes the batter thick. More milk is then added, and the resulting crêpes are as delicate as one could want.

Makes about 12 crêpes

1. Put the flour in a mixing bowl, and make a well in the center. Place the eggs, salt, and about ½ cup of the milk in the well. Using a wire whisk, blend together the eggs and milk; then slowly incorporate the flour. Beat the batter until it seems to pull and makes an occasional bubble. Beat in another ½ cup milk, and season with the black pepper. Cover and put bowl aside at room temperature to rest for at least ½ hour; 1 hour is better.

¾ cup (3 ounces) flour
1 egg plus 1 egg yolk
pinch of salt
1¼ cups milk, at room temperature
pinch of black pepper
4 tablespoons butter

2. Melt 2 tablespoons of the butter in the crêpe pan, and stir into the batter; if the mixture seems too thick, add the remaining ¼ cup milk.

3. To fry the crêpes, pour about 3 tablespoons of batter into the hot greased pan, and swirl immediately to cover the bottom surface with a film. When it has fried to a golden brown, turn and fry the other side for a few seconds. Slide the crêpe onto a plate, and continue frying more, greasing the pan each time. When using the crêpes, remember that the presentation side is the first side fried; it is more evenly colored.

↯↯↯

Puffy Fried Noodles

Modestly priced oriental restaurants often feature what appears to be a remarkable bargain: an order of shrimp toast for somewhere between $1.50 and $2. The menu stretches the language a bit. What arrives is not the carefully prepared, fine-chopped shrimp batter fried on bread but something resembling potato chips. These shrimp "toasts" or fritters are really sliver-thin starch-based dried chips that explode impressively on contact with hot oil. Puffy noodles follow the same expansive journey in the deep fryer. For many dishes, I find them much prettier and lighter-looking on the plate than rice or toast. Small pieces of the dry noodles will fly about when being cut. To minimize the scattering, cut the strands inside a deep bowl.

Makes 8 to 10 servings

2 ounces bean thread or rice noodles
oil for deep frying

1. Cut the noodles with scissors into 4- or 5-inch lengths, and line a large cookie sheet with double-thick paper towels. Heat the oil to 375 degrees, and a handful at a time, toss in the noodles. They will immediately puff up with a loud, sizzling noise. Using a wide slotted spoon or skimmer and a long fork, turn the noodles over, and fry for another few seconds. Lift the noodles out of the oil; hold for a few seconds over the pan to allow excess oil to drip; then place them on the paper-lined sheet. Skim any stray noodles out of the oil. Repeat with successive batches, and when a complete layer of noodles has filled the cookie sheet, place double-thick paper towels over them to receive more fried noodles. Keep the noodles in a cool, dry spot in the kitchen.

2. At serving time, heat the oven to 350 degrees, change the paper towels in the bottom of the cookie sheet, but do not cover the noodles, and warm them for 10 minutes. To prevent the crisp noodles from going limp under a hot saucy garnish, put just the noodles on warm plates and pass the garnish at the table, or prepare the individual dishes at the last moment.

Cooking Ahead: Once thoroughly drained, Puffy Fried Noodles can be stored in a brown paper bag in a dry place for several days.

Pastry

When pastry covers forcemeat for baking, certain requirements are made of it. It must be pliable enough to wrap easily around the loaf without cracking. It must also be sturdy enough to withstand the pressure of the steaming juices as the pâté bakes. This is particularly important for pâtés baked without a mold. The following recipe fills both requirements admirably. The egg is critical for both pliability and sturdiness. Although many recipes for pâté dough call for butter or part butter and lard, I much prefer just lard. It is 100 percent fat, contains no solids as butter does, and produces a very tasty and flaky crust with a smaller proportion of fat than most recipes. Puff pastry is often used for decorating the top or even for the crust itself. It strikes me as too delicate and fussy a dough for something as substantial as pâté en croûte.

Makes 1½ pounds

1. Put the 4 cups flour, salt, and lard in the food processor. Use the on/off switch to cut the lard into fine pieces. If necessary, let the motor run a few seconds to produce a mealy texture.

2. Beat the eggs with 2 tablespoons of water, and with the motor running, pour it into the bowl. Add water, a tablespoon at a time, until the dough begins to cohere. Stop the machine after each water addition, gather a little of the dough with your fingertips, and press it gently; if it stays together, it is ready. Do not allow the dough to pull together into a ball; this overdevelops the gluten in the flour and toughens the pastry.

3. Gather the dough into a ball, and transfer to a lightly floured pastry board. With the heel of your hand, push small sections of dough away from you, pushing about 6 inches. Reassemble the dough, and repeat one more time. (In French this thorough blending of fat and flour is called *briser* [to break].) Gather the dough into a ball, cover closely with plastic wrap, and chill for at least 1 hour. The pastry will keep in the refrigerator for several days.

4 cups flour plus flour for pastry board
1 teaspoon salt
10 tablespoons lard, diced and chilled
2 eggs, chilled
6 to 8 tablespoons cold water

Alternative Method

Put the flour on a pastry board. Make a well in the center, into which you put the salt, lard, egg, and 2 tablespoons of water. Mix these ingredients together very well with your fingertips; then gradually incorporate the flour until the mixture becomes mealy. Add water, a little at a time, until the pastry holds together; then *briser*.

Chicken Stock

Makes about 2 quarts

1. Put the chicken in a stockpot, and pour in the water, which should cover the pieces by about 2 inches. Over low heat, bring to a boil, skimming off the scum as it rises to the surface. When all the scum has ceased, add the carrots, onions, celery, tomato, and parsley. Add just a little salt, partially cover, and simmer for about 2 hours. Occasionally skim any fats that collect on the surface. Taste for seasonings, and add salt and pepper, if necessary.

2. Strain the stock through a colander into a large bowl, cool, and refrigerate the stock. The next day lift off the layer of fat that will have congealed on the surface.

Cooking Ahead: Chicken Stock can be refrigerated or frozen. If it is being frozen, it is best to decant it into several-sized containers for different uses. If it is being refrigerated, bring it to the boiling point every 2 days.

- 4 pounds chicken pieces, cooked or raw, with necks, gizzards, and trimmings
- 4 quarts water
- 4 carrots, sliced
- 2 onions, sliced
- 1 celery rib
- 1 tomato
- 6 sprigs parsley
- salt and pepper

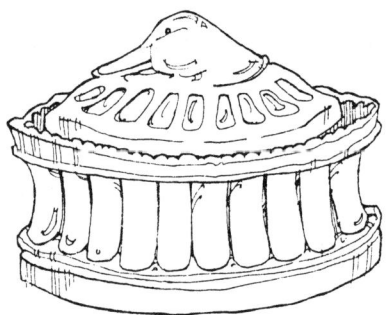

Beef Stock

Makes about 2 quarts

Preheat oven to 450 degrees.

1. Scatter the beef bones; the carrots; 2 of the onions, cut into quarters; and the celery in a roasting pan. Roast the bones and vegetables until they become dark brown. Turn and baste the browning ingredients several times. A lot of smoke is inevitable, but this is an essential step for arriving at a good color in the finished stock. The browning will take about 40 minutes. Transfer the browned bones and vegetables to a large stockpot, leaving behind all the fat. Pour off the fat, add 1 cup or so of water to the roasting pan, and deglaze by scraping up all the juices solidified on the bottom. Placing the pan over a flame helps the deglazing. Add these juices to the stockpot with the beef.

2. Add the remaining water to the stockpot; there should be enough to cover the ingredients by at least 2 inches. Push the cloves into the remaining onion; add to the pot with the herb bouquet, garlic, and a little salt. Bring the water to a simmer, and skim off any scum that rises to the surface. Partially cover, and simmer for about 5 hours, occasionally skimming any fats that collect on the surface. The lean beef can be removed after 2 hours and used in salads and such. Add the pepper for the last 15 minutes of cooking. Taste the stock seasonings, and correct if necessary.

3. Strain the stock through a colander into a large bowl, cool, and refrigerate the stock. The next day lift off the layer of fat that will have congealed on the surface.

Cooking Ahead: Beef Stock can be refrigerated or frozen. If it is being frozen, it is best to decant it into several-sized containers for different uses. If it is being refrigerated, bring it to the boiling point every 2 days.

about 2 pounds beef bones, sawed into 2-inch pieces
4 carrots, sliced thick
3 large onions
1 celery rib, broken in half
about 2 pounds lean beef
about 4½ quarts water
2 cloves
1 large herb bouquet containing 10 sprigs parsley, 2 bay leaves, 1 leek
4 garlic cloves, unpeeled
salt and pepper

Fish Stock

These proportions produce a well-flavored stock that is preferable for making sauces, such as Örebro Saffron Sauce (page 225). For poaching fish, this stock could be lengthened a little with a small quantity of water.

Makes 1 quart

1. Place the fish and vegetables in a pot, add salt and pepper, and cover with water. Bring to a simmer, and skim any scum that rises to the surface. When no more scum appears, partially cover the pot, and simmer for 15 minutes.

2. Add the wine, and simmer for another 15 minutes, adding a little pepper for the final 10 minutes of cooking. Strain through a fine sieve, and correct seasoning if necessary.

Cooking Ahead: Fish Stock can be refrigerated or frozen. If it is being frozen, it is best to decant it into several-sized containers for different uses. If it is being refrigerated, bring it to the boiling point every 2 days.

2 pounds lean fish heads, bones, and trimmings
1 onion, sliced thin
1 carrot, sliced thin
4-inch piece celery rib
salt and pepper
1 cup dry white wine

⇓⇓⇓

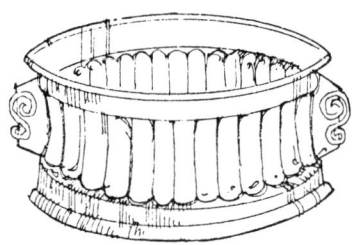

Clarifying Stocks

Before being turned into aspics to garnish terrines or pâtés, stocks must first be clarified of all particles suspended in the liquid to make them brilliantly clear and sparkling. The procedure is very simple and requires nothing more than egg whites and shells to seize the floating specks in the stock. During the clarification there is a small loss of flavor and quantity, both of which can be rectified. Many cooks add extra meat, vegetables, or seasonings during the clarification to replace some of the lost intensity. As for quantity, if you want to have a quart when finished, start with an extra cup of stock.

Makes about 1 quart clarified stock

1. Pour the cold stock into a large saucepan, and set on medium heat. As the stock warms, lightly beat the egg whites, and whisk them into the stock. Crush the eggshells, and add them as well. Continue whisking to keep the egg whites circulating throughout all the stock. When the stock reaches the boiling point, turn off the heat, and allow to stand for 10 minutes. Repeat the boiling and standing one more time.

2. Thoroughly wet and wring out 4 layers of cheesecloth or a perfect kitchen towel (a single hole would ruin the effort). Line a colander with the cloth, and set it in a large bowl. Carefully ladle the stock with the floating egg whites into the colander, and allow it to drain for 5 or 10 minutes.

- 5 cups stock, thoroughly degreased
- 2 egg whites and their shells

Aspics

Homemade clarified beef, fish, and chicken stocks (pages 219, 220, and 218) can be turned into aspics for garnishing pâtés and terrines. Both beef and chicken stocks should already be somewhat gelatinized from the bones and meats used in the stock. The more bones and gelatinous meats used originally, the less commercial gelatin need be added. If split calf's feet are included in the stock, there will probably be no need at all for additional jelling power.

Before proceeding, test the consistency of the stock by chilling a few tablespoons in a saucer for about 15 minutes. For the purposes of this book the chilled jelly should be firm and remain separated when cut into pieces. Though less satisfactory in flavor, commercial canned broths can also be jelled.

You need 1 tablespoon of powdered gelatin to jell 2 cups of liquid. If the stock is somewhat jellied, use ½ tablespoon, and retest. For 1 tablespoon of gelatin, sprinkle onto ¼ cup of cold water, and put aside to soften. Bring the stock to the boiling point, add the gelatin, turn off the heat, and stir until the gelatin is completely dissolved.

Clarified Butter

The clear butter served with lobsters and such has been rid of milky solids to produce a finer-looking sauce. In many cooking operations clarified butter is preferred since it is the milk solids that burn first and take on an unpleasant character. Well-covered and refrigerated, clarified (or drawn) butter has a storage life of several weeks. Begin with about one-third more butter than you need when clarified.

Cut the butter into pieces, and melt them over medium heat. Put aside and let stand for 10 minutes, spoon off the white foam on top, and let stand for at least another 15 minutes. Slowly pour off the clear melted butter into a bowl, leaving behind all the milky residue. The solids at the bottom can be stirred into cooked vegetables or sauces as a flavoring.

CHAPTER SEVEN

Sauces, Sweet and Savory

Orbec Sauce

This light red wine sauce goes especially well with hot meat pâtés. My name for the sauce is a salute to fond memories of excellent meals in that picturesque village in the heart of Normandy apple country in France.

Makes 1⅔ cup

1. In an enamel or copper saucepot boil the wine and stock together, uncovered, for 10 minutes. Meanwhile, quarter and core the apple but do not peel. Add the apple to the wine and cook another 15 minutes, or until the apple is soft.

2. With a skimmer, remove the apple and, when cool enough to handle, pull off the skin. Place the apple in the blender with about ½ cup of the cooking liquid and process briefly. Do not overprocess or the purée will become very pale and foamy and will not blend well with the rest of the sauce. Return the purée to the pot and add the bitters. Make a paste of the cornstarch and Madeira and stir it into the sauce. Cook for 2 or 3 minutes, remove from the heat and whisk in the butter pieces. Transfer to a warm sauce boat.

Cooking Ahead: A day or so in advance, cook the sauce, purée it, and add the bitters. Keep it refrigerated. At serving time, complete the sauce with the cornstarch paste and butter additions.

- 1 cup red wine
- 1 cup Beef Stock (page 219)
- 1 small tart apple (about 4 ounces)
- ½ teaspoon aromatic bitters
- 1 tablespoon cornstarch
- 1 tablespoon Madeira or port
- 4 tablespoons butter, cut into pieces

⇊⇊⇊

Light Tomato Sauce

Do not use a blender or food processor instead of the sieve called for in the recipe. The tomato's fibers and stringy pulp will be puréed into the sauce instead of discarded, and the sauce will not be red but will churn into a frothy pink.

Makes 1½ cups

1. In a covered saucepot simmer the oil and onion together for about 5 minutes. Add the tomatoes with their juice and all the spices; partially cover, and simmer for 30 minutes.

2. Pour the sauce into a sieve, and push the tomato pulp through with a pestle or the back of a wooden spoon. Discard the fibers and pulp remaining in the sieve. Add the butter to the still-hot sauce, and stir until it melts.

Cooking Ahead: Light Tomato Sauce can be made several days in advance and refrigerated. It will keep for months in the freezer.

2 tablespoons olive oil
¼ cup coarse-chopped onion
14-ounce to 1-pound can tomatoes, preferably Italian plum
¼ teaspoon oregano
¼ teaspoon basil
¼ teaspoon fennel seeds
salt and pepper
½ tablespoon butter, at room temperature

Örebro Saffron Sauce

This beautiful sauce should not be confined to the recipes in this book. It will complement any poached fish in an important manner. From its velvety texture and bright yellow color, few would guess how easy it is to make. When served with fish terrines, it should be barely lukewarm; for other hot fish presentations, it should, of course, be hot.

Makes 1 cup

In a small nonreactive saucepot boil together fish stock, cream, wine, and saffron until reduced by half. If the saffron flavor and color need intensification, add a pinch more during the reduction. Season lightly with salt and pepper. Remove from the heat; cool for ½-minute; then whisk in the butter, a few pieces at a time, until the sauce is thick and velvety.

Cooking Ahead: The sauce cannot be completely prepared in advance since in reheating, butter melts and destroys the sauce's consistency. The reduction can certainly be done ahead; then, just before serving, reheat it, and add the butter. This final step takes only a minute or so.

½ cup Fish Stock (page 220)
½ cup heavy cream
½ cup white wine
large pinch of powdered saffron
salt and pepper
8 tablespoons (1 stick) butter, diced

Rosy Cream Sauce

Makes 1¼ cups

Place all ingredients in a blender, and process until smooth.

Cooking Ahead: This sauce can be prepared as much as 3 days in advance. Beat it with a wire whisk before serving.

1 cup sour cream
½ cup tomatoes, peeled, seeds and juice extracted, and chopped coarse
1 tablespoon aromatic bitters
salt and pepper

Mayonnaise

Mayonnaise is a basic ingredient in many sauces and preparations in this book. When these recipes were developed, only homemade mayonnaise was used. A jarred product will, of course, produce different results. But there is no mystery about making mayonnaise. All the "technique" is in the temperature. As long as *all* ingredients are at room temperature, it is child's play to produce the egg-oil emulsion. Today you have a choice of four different ways to make it: wire whisk; electric portable beater; blender; food processor. All are fast. One adjustment must be made for blender and processor: A whole egg rather than 2 yolks is used.

Makes about 1½ cups

1. Put the egg yolks in a warmed mixing bowl, or break the whole egg into the blender or processor container. Add the mustard, salt, and pepper. Beat or process until the eggs turn thick and look almost opaque; this will be a matter of seconds in a processor. While beating or with motor running, slowly begin adding oil, a drop at a time at the beginning. Increase the flow of oil to a thin stream, and beat or process until the mayonnaise thickens.

2. Put the vinegar or lemon juice in a large metal spoon, and hold it over a flame or electric grid to heat the liquid almost to the boiling point. Add the hot vinegar to the mayonnaise, and blend or beat again at high speed until it is mixed into the sauce. Taste for seasonings, and correct if necessary, again blending after any additions. Scrape into a container with a tight-fitting cover, and refrigerate.

1 whole egg or 2 egg yolks
½ teaspoon prepared mustard
½ teaspoon salt
⅛ teaspoon pepper
1 to 1½ cups oil
2 to 3 tablespoons vinegar or lemon juice or a combination*

*The more acidic the vinegar or lemon juice added, the longer the mayonnaise will keep. Use these measurements as a minimum; for some recipes you might like even more. I find that mayonnaise, tightly covered and refrigerated, keeps for a week, not the several days usually stated.

⇊⇊⇊

Niçoise Mayonnaise

Makes 1 cup

1. Dip the tomato into boiling water for a few seconds, cool it slightly, and slip off the skin. Cut in half, and gently squeeze out the seeds and juice. Chop the remaining flesh; there should be about ¼ cup.

2. In a bowl stir together mayonnaise, tomato pulp, liqueur to taste, Tabasco, salt, and pepper. The flavoring and pink color are meant to be subdued, not strident.

Cooking Ahead: Niçoise Mayonnaise can be prepared 1 or 2 days in advance, tightly covered, and refrigerated.

1 medium tomato
1 cup Mayonnaise (page 226)
½ to 1 teaspoon anise-flavored liqueur (Pernod, Ouzo, Arak, etc.)
Tabasco
salt and pepper

Sauce Verte (Green Sauce)

Makes about 1½ cups

1. Blanch the watercress leaves in rapidly boiling water for a few seconds. Immediately drain into a colander or sieve, and cool under cold running water. Squeeze the leaves dry.

2. Prepare the mayonnaise base in either the blender, or the food processor. Break the egg into the container, add the lime juice, salt, and pepper, and process for ½ minute. With the motor running, slowly add the oil, a few drops at a time; then increase the oil flow to a thin stream.

3. Remove about three-fourths of the mayonnaise into a mixing bowl. To the mayonnaise remaining in the container add the watercress leaves, basil, tarragon, liqueur, clam juice, and a few drops of Tabasco. Process until a dark green purée is produced. Stir this purée into the rest of the mayonnaise.

Cooking Ahead: Green Sauce can be prepared several days in advance, covered tightly, and refrigerated.

2 cups watercress leaves
1 egg, at room temperature
juice of ½ lime, at room temperature
salt and pepper
about 1 cup oil, at room temperature
1 tablespoon basil, preferably fresh
1 teaspoon tarragon, preferably fresh
1 tablespoon anise-flavored liqueur (Pernod, Ouzo, Arak, etc.)
1 tablespoon clam juice
Tabasco

Pink Horseradish Sauce

Makes about 1 cup

1. Plunge the tomato into boiling water for a few seconds, remove, cool, and peel. Cut the tomato in half, squeeze out the seeds and juice, and chop the pulp until it has a fine consistency. Reserve ¼ cup of the chopped pulp for this recipe; any remainder can be used in other sauces, stews, or soups or stirred into scrambled eggs.

2. In a bowl whisk together mayonnaise, yogurt, tomato pulp, horseradish, brandy, salt, and pepper.

Cooking Ahead: This sauce can be made as much as 4 or 5 days in advance and refrigerated.

1 medium tomato
½ cup Mayonnaise (page 226)
½ cup yogurt
1 tablespoon horseradish
1 teaspoon brandy
salt and pepper

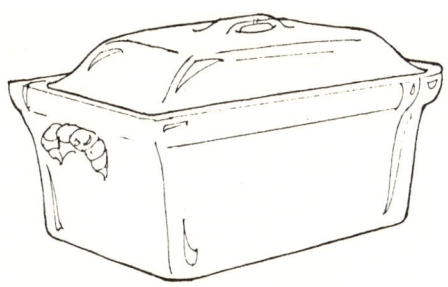

Avocado Sauce

Makes 2 cups

Cut each avocado in half, remove the stones, and scoop out the flesh with a large spoon. Place the avocado flesh in a large bowl, and mash it with a fork; then use a whisk to incorporate the lime juice and oil. Beat until the sauce is light. Stir in the yogurt, and add salt and pepper to taste.

2 avocados
⅓ cup lime juice
2 tablespoons olive oil
½ cup yogurt
salt and pepper

Cooking Ahead: The lime juice will help prevent the avocado flesh from turning dark. For additional insurance against discoloration, place plastic film directly on the surface of the sauce. Thus protected, it can be made a day ahead of time.

Pesto (Basil-Garlic Sauce)

Pungent pesto is classically used over hot pasta or added to thick country soups. Its walloping essence can transform the most timid dish into a powerful gustatory experience. Pesto's strength, of course, is variable. Cooks all over Italy, especially in its home base of Genoa, add and subtract ingredients to suit their style. A recipe is included in this book because I have found pesto an inspired addition to many other sauces. Even a spoonful brings a lot of flavor change with it. Pesto can be bought in small jars, but it is much better, and cheaper, to prepare it at home during the summer months, when basil is in full leaf. Prepare the sauce without cheese, distribute it into small jars, filling only to the two-thirds level, and freeze. Add cheese after defrosting and before stirring the sauce into hot dishes. By the way, the name *pesto* comes from the Italian word for paste since traditionally the ingredients were ground to that consistency in a mortar. The food processor is today's ideal instrument.

Makes about 1½ to 2 cups

1. Put the basil leaves, garlic, salt, and pepper into the food processor container. Process in short bursts to chop the leaves and reduce their volume. Add the nuts, and repeat the chopping for ½ minute. With the motor running, slowly add the oil in a thin stream until the sauce is thin enough to drop easily from a spoon.

2. If you are using the sauce at once with hot foods, add the cheese and process it until smooth. For the purposes of this book, cheese is not added.

Cooking Ahead: Pesto will keep in the refrigerator for several weeks or can be frozen for months.

2 cups fresh basil leaves
2 to 3 teaspoons chopped garlic
1 teaspoon salt
½ teaspoon black pepper
¼ cup pine nuts, walnuts, or cashews
1 to 1½ cups olive oil
½ cup fresh-grated Parmesan or Romano cheese

Yogurt-Pesto Sauce

Makes about 1 cup

1. Plunge the tomato into boiling water for a few seconds, remove, cool, and peel. Cut the tomato in half, squeeze out the seeds and juice, and chop the pulp until fine. Reserve 2 tablespoons of the chopped pulp for this recipe; the remainder can be used in other sauces, stews, or soups or stirred into scrambled eggs.

2. In a bowl whisk together the tomato pulp, yogurt, and pesto.

Cooking Ahead: This sauce can be made as much as 4 or 5 days in advance and refrigerated.

1 small tomato
1 cup yogurt
1½ tablespoons Pesto (page 231)

Light Chocolate Sauce

This easy-to-make pouring sauce is deliberately kept light in chocolate flavor since it is meant to accent desserts, not to dominate them. Besides Ice Palace (page 177) and Chocolate Omelet (page 197), keep it in mind for garnishing crêpes, custards, and puddings.

Makes 1¾ cups

Put all ingredients in the blender, and process for 1 minute. Pour the sauce into a small saucepan, and bring to a slow simmer. Cook for 1 minute. Light Chocolate Sauce may be served hot or cold.

¼ cup sugar
1 cup milk
3 tablespoons cocoa
3 tablespoons butter
2 teaspoons vanilla
1 teaspoon rum

Caramel Sauce

Served hot over ice cream, cold over hot fruit, or as a baking sauce, caramel can be counted on to transform ordinary desserts into unabashed pleasures. It costs very little, takes only minutes to make, and keeps indefinitely. These seem assets enough to encourage its frequent use, but caramel has one drawback: the inexperienced cook's fear of it. Agreed, it is a well-founded fear for the careless cook. Caramel is hotter than hot, climbing to a temperature of about 350 degrees. This is the point where it is used for lining molds, which takes a bit of nimble dexterity. But making a caramel sauce is another matter, an entirely safe one. Just follow the very few, very simple directions below.

Makes 2 cups

1. Fill a mixing bowl with cold water, and place it in the sink. Measure the sugar and cold water into a heavy saucepot large enough so the sugar and water reach a depth of only one-third of the pot. An unlined copper pot is the classic vessel, but an enameled cast-iron pot also works fine. Do not use a lined copper pot because the intense heat will melt the lining. Let the pot stand for about 5 minutes; then cover it, and place it on a very low flame to dissolve all the sugar crystals. Once the mixture is clear, remove the cover and turn up the heat to medium.

2 cups sugar
½ cup cold water
1 cup warm water

2. Let the syrup boil briskly until it begins to color. Never stir at any point; the pot can be swirled, but stirring with a spoon would cause crystallization. It may take 5 to 6 minutes for the syrup to begin coloring. At this point it must be watched carefully, or it will burn and take on a bitter flavor. As soon as the syrup turns a rich brown color, a minute or so, remove it from the heat, and plunge the bottom of the pot into the bowl of cold water to arrest the cooking. Let the pot stand in the water for about a minute; then add the warm water.

3. Return the pot to the heat, and cook over medium fire to boil and dissolve the thick caramel. Scrape the bottom of the pot with a wooden spoon to incorporate all the caramel into the sauce. Cool; transfer to a tightly closed container; then refrigerate.

Note: To give the pot a preliminary cleaning, simply fill it with water, and boil the water to dissolve any trace of caramel clinging to the pot.

Index

Note: Recipes are found on page numbers printed in boldface.

Acorn squash purée, 170, **176**
Advance preparation, 3–4
Aluminum foil seal, 9, 17, 21
Aluminum pots, 22
Anchovies, 22
Appetizers and first courses (*see also* Soups):
    artichoke sunburst, 130, **132**
    cauliflower with shrimp sauce, 40, **43**
    cocktailed spaghetti squash, 163, **168**
    fettucine Orvieto, 108, **112**
    Greek stuffed tomatoes, 65, **68**
    macaroni and gorgonzola, 179, **182**
    mushroom caps, fried stuffed, 100, **106**
    mushroom compote, 157, **162**
    mushroom flan, 108, 148, **155–156**
    mushrooms on puffy fried noodles, 108, 136, **140**
    mussels à la Townshend, 71, **74–75**
    mussels, gratinéed, with saffron sauce, 51, **55–56**
    onion compote, 45, **49**
    oysters Bercy, 192, **196**
    paprika mushroom nests, 142, **146**
    riso al limone (rice with eggs and lemon), 185, **191**
    rustic omelet, 170, **178**
    scallops, sautéed, 92, **99**
    scallops with parmesan, 79, **84**
    shrimp, gingered, on leeks, 85, **88–89**
    shrimp with Pernod, 122, **126**
    snails on toast, 58, **63**
    steamed soft-shell clams, 32, **38–39**
Apple gratin, 51, **57**
Apricot soufflé, 157, **161**
Apricots, studded, in aspic, 192, **195**
Artichoke sunburst, 130, **132**
Asparagus, hot, with herbed vinaigrette, 92, **98**, 108
Aspic, **222**
    as coating, 18, 47, 81, 94

Aspic (*continued*)
    filling holes in pâté with, 13
    as garnish, 18, 94, 195
    lemon-chicken, vermouth-laced, **109–110**, 164
    stock for, 221, **222**
Avocado sauce, 178, 193, 208, **230**

Bacon, 21
Baked pears with caramel sauce, 79, **83**, 163
Baking:
    of pâté, 11–12
    of terrine, 9
Banana puffs, hot, 45, **50**
Bards. *See* Fatback
Basil-garlic sauce. *See* Pesto
Bay scallops with parmesan, **84**
Bean sprout salad, 65, **69**
Beans, string, Singapore, 26, **31**, 92
Beef:
    canned broth, use of, 21
    stock, **219**
    use in terrines and pâtés, 27, 131
Beet relish, 108, 111, **116**
Biscuit Tortoni, 185, **188**
Blueberries, gratinéed, 163, 179, **184**
Blue cheese packets, hot, 142, **145**
Brains, use in pâtés, 59
Bread crumbs, fresh, 22, 209
Broccoli mousse, in tricolor vegetable terrine, **186–187**
Broccoli purée, **195**
    on endive spears, 136, **139**
    pears in red wine and, 185, **189**
Broccoli terrine, **213–214**
Broth, canned, use of, 21
Butter coating. *See* Clarified butter
Buttered Crab, **209**

Calf's feet, for stock, 222
Calories, 3
Canadian meat pie, hot, 130, **131**
Caramel sauce, 44, 83, 233
Caramelized pineapple, 116, **121**
Carrot mousse, in tricolor vegetable terrine, 186–187
Carrot pâté, 179, 180–181
Carrot-pear purée, 58, 61
Caul, as lining and cover, 6, 21
Cauliflower:
    with shrimp sauce, 40, 43
    and snow peas, curried, 148, **154**
Champignons Balzac, 100, **106**
Cheese (*see also* Ricotta):
    goat cheese pâté, 116, 117–118
    gorgonzola sauce, for macaroni, 182
    ham and ricotta terrine, 100, 101–102
    hot blue cheese packets, 142, **145**
Chicken:
    canned broth, use of, 21
    in lemon aspic, 108, 109–110
    stock, 218
    use in terrines and pâtés, 52, 109, 186, 193, 201, 213
Chicken liver parfait, 71, 72–73
Chicken liver pâté, creamy, 204
Chicken liver terrine, 65, 66–67
    with spinach and herbs, 45, 46–47
Chicken livers, use in terrines and pâtés, 41, 46, 52, 66, 72, 204, 205
Chicken terrine, 201–202
Chimney, of parchment paper, as vent, 11, 12
Chocolate omelet, 192, **197**
Chocolate sauce, light, 50, 177, 197, 232
Chou-fleur, sauce crevette, 40, 43
Clams, steamed soft-shell, 32, 38–39
Clarified butter, 222
    as coating, 21, 67, 73
Clarifying of stock, 221
Coatings:
    aspic, 18
    fat, 6, 21
Cocktailed spaghetti squash, 163, **168**
Coconut sherbet, 100, **103**
Cod, use in terrines, 172, 207
Cold pâté, 3
Country pâté (pâté de campagne), 4, 5, 27, 32, 33–34
Crab meat stuffing for fried mushrooms, 106

Crab pâté, 209
Cranberries, ginger-baked, 32, **35**
Cream sauce, rosy, 193, 208, 225
Creamy chicken liver pâté, 204
Crêpes, as garnish, 17, 137, 148, 149–151, 173–174
    basic recipe, 215
Crevettes au Pernod, 122, **126**
Crown of Cognac cream, 58, 62
Cucumbers:
    herbed, 40, **42**
    in mustard sauce, 185, **190**
Curried cauliflower and snow peas, 148, **154**
Custard (*see also* Flan):
    pear, 133
    pecan chiffon, 108, 113–114

Desserts:
    apple gratin, 51, **57**
    apricot soufflé, 157, **161**
    baked pears with caramel sauce, 79, 83, **163**
    biscuit Tortoni, 185, **188**
    blueberries, gratinéed, 163, 179, **184**
    caramelized pineapple, 116, **121**
    chocolate omelet, 192, **197**
    coconut sherbet, 100, **103**
    fruit velvet, 71, **78**
    German wine pudding, 26, 30
    honeydew balls in strawberry sauce, 122, **129**
    hot banana puffs, 45, **50**
    icy oranges with hot orange-ginger sauce, 136, **141**
    mango sherbet, 148, **152**
    Palais de Glace maple mold, 170, **177**
    peach gratin, 40, **44**
    pear gratin, 85, **91**
    pears, poached, with pear custard, 130, 133–134
    pecan chiffon custard, 108, 113–114
    poppy seed flan, 92, 96–97
    pumpkin surprise, 163, 166–167
    raspberry-baked peaches, 65, **70**
    Rosé Snow, 32, **36**
    Snow of Cognac cream, 58, 62
    strawberries with kiwi sauce, 142, **147**
Duck terrine, orange-flavored, 79, 80–81

Earthenware molds, 5
Egg white, 22
Eggs, stuffed, with capers, 85, **90**

Épices fines, 22
Excess juices, 10, 15

Fatback (bard, salt pork):
   lardons of, 7
   as lining and cover, 6, 21
Fat coatings, 6, 21. *See also*
       Clarified butter, as coating; Lard coating
Fettucine Orvieto, 108, 112
Fish stock, 220
Fish terrines and pâtés, 13, 15
   crab pâté, 209
   Kulebyaka, 170, 171–175
      streamlined recipe, 210–211
   scallop terrine, 136, 137–138
      spinach-garnished, 142, 143–144
   shrimp terrine, 157, 158–159
   smoked haddock pâté, 163, 164–165
   spinach-fish terrine, 207–208
   Terrine Neptune, 148, 149–151
Flan:
   mushroom, 108, 148, 155–156
   poppy seed, 92, 96–97
Flavoring, tasting for:
   of forcemeat, 8
   of mousseline, 13
Flounder, use in terrines, 143, 149–150, 158, 207
Freezing of pâté, 4
Fried noodles, puffy, 216
   use of, 140, 146, 157, 162
Fried parsley, 106–107
Fried stuffed mushroom caps, 100, 106
Fruit desserts. *See* Desserts
Fruit garnishes:
   ginger-baked cranberries, 32, 35
   pear-carrot purée, 58, 61
   pears in red wine, 71, 76
   prune timbale, 179, 183
   stuffed apricots in aspic, 192, 195
Fruit velvet, 71, 78

Garlic, 21
Garlic-basil sauce. *See* Pesto
Garnishes:
   accompanying, 4
      acorn squash puree, 170, 176
      bean sprout salad, 65, 69
      beet relish, 108, 111 , 116

Garnishes *(continued)*
   carrot-pear purée, 58, 61
   cucumbers in mustard sauce, 185, 190
   ginger-baked cranberries, 32, 35
   gingered tomato relish, 163, 169
   herbed cucumbers, 40, 42
   lettuce cushions, 79, 82
   marinated onion rings, 116, 119
   marinated red pepper strips, 45, 48
   pears in red wine, 71, 76
   prune timbale, 179, 183
   red rice salad, 26, 29
   shoestringed turnips and zucchini, 157, 160
   spaghetti squash salad, 51, **54**
   spiced radishes, 148, 153
   stuffed apricots in aspic, 192, **195**
   stuffed eggs with capers, 85, 90
   tomatoes with green sauce, 130, 135
   turnip purée, 92, 95
   zesty radish slices, 100, **104**
  decorative, 17–19
  interior, 7, 8
   lardons used for, 7, 8
   layering, 4, 8, 11, 14
German wine pudding, 26, 30
   Ginger-baked cranberries, 32, 35
Gingered shrimp on leeks, 85, 88–89
Gingered tomato relish, 163, 169
Goat cheese pâté, 116, 117–118
Gorgonzola sauce, for macaroni, 182
Gratinéed blueberries, 163, 179, **184**
Gratinéed mussels with saffron sauce, 51, 55–56
Greek stuffed tomatoes, 65, 68
Green sauce, 106, 149, 151, 159, 228
   of pesto and yogurt, 135
Grinding meats, 7, 21

Haddock, use in terrines, 172, 207
Haddock pâté, smoked, 163, 164–165
Halibut, use in terrines, 149–150
Ham:
   use in terrines and pâtés, 33, 46, 52, 66, 93, 101, 117, 123, 201, 203, 205
   in vegetable ragout, 105
Ham and ricotta terrine, 100, 101–102
Ham and tongue pâté, 92, 93–94
Ham and veal pâté in crust, hot, 122, 123–125
   small individual (petits pâtés chauds), 205–206

Herbed cucumbers, 40, 42
Herbed vinaigrette, 98
Herbs:
    dried vs. fresh, 22
    Provençal, 86
Honeydew balls in strawberry sauce, 122, 129
Horseradish sauce, pink, 132, 229
Hot banana puffs, 45, 50
Hot blue cheese packets, 142, 145
Hot Canadian meat pie, 130, 131
Hot pâté, 3
Hot veal and ham pâté in crust, 122, 123–125
    small individual (petits pâtés chauds), 205–206

Ice Palace, 170, 177
Individual hot pâtés, 205–206
Iron pots, 22

Juices, excess, 10, 15

Kiwi sauce, 147
Kulebyaka, 170, 171–175
    streamlined recipe, 210–211

Lamb terrine with Provençal herbs, 85, 86–87
Lard coating, 21, 67, 73, 81
Lardons:
    of fat, 7
    of meat, 7, 8
Lasagna pâté, 51, 52–53
Layering, 4, 8, 11
    lardons for, 7, 8
    in mousselines, 14
Leeks, gingered shrimp on, 85, 88–89
Lemon aspic, chicken in, 108, 109–110
Lettuce cushions, 79, 82
Lettuce soup, shredded, 116, 120
Light chocolate sauce, 50, 177, 197, 232
Light tomato sauce, 27, 137, 138, 143, 144, 224

Macaroni and gorgonzola, 179, 182
Mango sherbet, 148, 152
Maple mold, 170, 177
Marinated onion rings, 116, 119
Marinated red pepper strips, 45, 48
Mayonnaise, 226. *See also* Niçoise mayonnaise
Meat, 7, 21
    grinding, 7, 21

Meat *(continued)*
    lean vs. fat, ratio, 7, 21
    mixing of, 8
    See also Beef; Chicken; Chicken livers; Ham; Pork; Tongue; Turkey; Veal
Meat loaf terrine, 26, 27
Meat pie, hot Canadian, 130, 131
Meat terrines and pâtés:
    chicken in lemon aspic, 108, 109–110
    chicken liver parfait, 71, 72–73
    chicken liver pâté, creamy, 204
    chicken liver terrine, 65, 66–67
        with spinach and herbs, 45, 46–47
    chicken terrine, 201–202
    ham and ricotta terrine, 100, 101–102
    lamb terrine with Provençal herbs, 85, 86–87
    pâté de campagne (country pâté), 4, 5, 27, 32, 33–34
    pâté panaché (mixed pâté), in aspic, 203
    sweetbread pâté with spinach, 58, 59–60
    terrine de canard à l'orange (duck terrine), 3, 79 80–81
    terrine fine, 40, 41
    tongue and ham pâté, 92, 93–94
    veal and ham pâté, in crust, hot, 122, 123–125
        small individual (petits pâtés chauds), 205–206
Melon (honeydew) balls in strawberry sauce, 122, 129
Metal molds, 12
Mixed pâté in aspic, 203
Mixing of forcemeats, 8
Molds, 20
    earthenware, 5
    metal, 12
    lining of:
        with crêpes, 17
        with pastry, 12
    for mousseline, preparing and handling of, 14
    sealing, 9, 21
    unmolding, 15–16
Mosaic vegetable terrine, 192, 193–194
Mousse or mousseline, 13
    baking, 15
    layering of, 14
    preparing mold for, 14
    unmolding, 15–16
    See also Fish terrines; Vegetable terrines

Mushroom compote, 157, 162
Mushroom flan, 108, 148, 155–156
Mushrooms:
    double, on puffy fried noodles, 108, 136, 140
    fried stuffed caps, 100, 106
    paprika nests, 142, 146
    in vegetable compote, 49
    in vegetable ragout, 105
Mussels:
    gratinéed, with saffron sauce, 51, 55–56
    à la Townshend, 71, 74–75
Mustard sauce, 190

Niçoise mayonnaise, 132, 149, 178, 193, 208, 209, 227
Nonreactive pots and pans, 22
Noodles, puffy fried, 216
    uses of, 140, 146, 157, 162
Nut paste, 180–181, 195
Nuts, 4, 7, 8

Oil coating, 21
Olives, 7
Omelets:
    chocolate, 192, 197
    rustic, 170, 178
Onion compote, 45, 49
Onion rings, marinated, 116, 119
Onion soup, mild, 26, 28
Orange-flavored duck terrine, 79, 80–81
Oranges, icy, with hot orange-ginger sauce, 136, 141
Orbec sauce, 123, 206, 223
Örebro saffron sauce, 55, 143, 144, 159, 220, 225
Oregano, 22
Oysters Bercy, 192, 196

Palais de Glace, 170, 177
Pans, nonreactive, 22
Paprika mushroom nests, 142, 146
Parchment paper, chimney vents of, 11, 12
Parfait de foie de volaille, 71, 72–73
Parsley, fried, 106–107
Pasta:
    fettucine Orvieto, 108, 112
    lasagna pâté, 51, 52–53
    macaroni and gorgonzola, 179, 182
Pastry decorations, 19, 217
Pastry wrapping, 5
    basic recipe, 217
    recipes using, 117, 122, 123–125, 130, 131,

Pasta wrapping *(continued)*
    171–175, 205–206, 210–211
    wrapping methods, 11–12
Pâté:
    baking of, 11–12
    defined, 5
    filling holes with aspic, 13
    freezing of, 4
    individual small, 205–206
    pastry wrapping for, 5, 11–12, 217
Pâté chaud de veau et jambon en croûte, 122, 123–125
    petits pâtés chauds, 205–206
Pâté de campagne, 4, 5, 27, 32, 33–34
Pâté de foie gras, 4, 5
Pâté de ris de veau aux épinards, 58, 59–60
Pâté panaché en aspic, 203
Peaches:
    gratin, 40, 44
    raspberry-baked, 65, 70
Pear-carrot puré, 58, 61
Pears:
    baked, with caramel sauce, 79, 83, 163
    gratin, 85, 91
    poached, with pear custard, 130, 133–134
    in red wine, 71, 76
    with broccoli purée, 185, 189
Peas, spaghetti squash and, 92, 122, 127–128. *See also* Snow peas
Pecan chiffon custard, 108, 113–114
Peppers. *See* Red peppers
Pesto sauce, 32, 37, 90, 115, 132, 135, 231
Petits pâtés chauds, 205–206
Pimiento, as garnish, 7, 18
Pineapple, caramelized, 116, 121
Pink horseradish sauce, 132, 229
Poached pears with pear custard, 130, 133–134
Poppy seed flan, 92, 96–97
Pork, use in terrines and pâtés, 27, 33, 41, 46, 52, 59, 66, 80, 86, 101, 131, 201, 203, 204, 205
Pots, nonreactive, 22
Potted Crab, 209
Provence, herbs of, 86
Prune timbale, 179, 183
Pudding, German wine, 26, 30
Puff pastry, 217
Puffy fried noodles, 216
    uses of, 140, 146, 157, 162

Pumpkin surprise, 163, 166–167

Radishes:
    spiced, 148, 153
    zesty sliced, 100, 104
Raspberry-baked peaches, 65, 70
Red peppers:
    as garnish, 7
    marinated strips, 45, 48
    snow peas with, 58, 64
Reheating of pâtés and terrines, 4
Relishes:
    beet, 108, 111, 116
    tomato, gingered, 162, 169
Rice:
    with eggs and lemon, 185, 191
    salad, red, 26, 29
Ricotta, use in terrines and pâtés, 101, 186, 204, 213
Riso al limone, 185, 191
Rosé Snow, 32, 36
Rosy cream sauce, 193, 208, 225
Russian Kulebyaka fish terrine, 170, 171–175
    streamlined recipe, 210–211
Rustic omelet, 170, 178

Saffron sauce, Örebro, 55, 143, 144, 159, 220, 225
Salads:
    bean sprout, 65, 69
    lettuce cushion, 82
    red rice, 26, 29
    spaghetti squash, 51, 54
Salmon, use in terrines, 149–150, 172, 209, 210
Salt pork. *See* Fatback
Sauces:
    avocado, 178, 193, 208, 230
    caramel, 44, 83, 233
    chocolate, light, 50, 177, 197, 232
    gorgonzola, for macaroni, 182
    green (verte), 106, 149, 151, 159, 228
        of pesto and yogurt, 135
    kiwi, 147
    mayonnaise, 226
    mustard, 190
    Niçoise mayonnaise, 132, 149, 178, 193, 208, 209, 227
    orange-ginger, hot, 141
    Orbec, 123, 206, 223
    Örebro saffron, 55, 143, 144, 159, 220, 225

Sauces *(continued)*
    pesto (basil-garlic), 32, 37, 90, 115, 132, 135, 231
    pink horseradish, 132, 229
    rosy cream, 193, 208, 225
    shrimp, 43
    strawberry, 129
    tomato, light, 27, 137, 138, 143, 144, 224
    yogurt-pesto, 135, 232
Sautéed scallops, 92, 99
Scallop terrine, 136, 137–138
    spinach-garnished, 142, 143–144
Scalloped pastry circles, 19
Scallops:
    with parmesan, 79, 84
    sautéed, 92, 99
    in Terrine Neptune, 149–150
Seafood terrines. *See* Fish Terrines
Sherbet:
    coconut, 100, 103
    mango, 148, 152
    Rosé Snow, 32, 36
Shoestringed turnips and zucchini, 157, 160
Shredded lettuce soup, 116, 120
Shrimp:
    gingered, on leeks, 85, 88–89
    with Pernod, 122, 126
Shrimp sauce, 43
Shrimp terrine, 157, 158–159
Singapore string beans, 26, 31, 92
Smoked haddock pâté, 163, 164–165
Snails on toast, 58, 63
Snow peas:
    and cauliflower, curried, 148, 154
    with red peppers, 58, 64
Sole, use in terrines, 143, 149–150, 158
Soups:
    onion, mild, 26, 28
    shredded lettuce, 116, 120
Spaghetti squash:
    cocktailed, 163, 168
    and peas, 92, 122, 127–128
    salad, 51, 54
    splitting, 127
Spiced radishes, 148, 153
Spices, 22
Spinach:
    as garnish, 17, 47, 137
    use in terrines and pâtés, 46–47, 59–60, 143,

Spinach (continued)
    149–150, 158–159, 207, 212
Spinach-fish terrine, 207–208
Spinach-garnished scallop terrine, 142, 143–144
Spinach lasagna, 52
Spinach-zucchini terrine, 212
Squash. See Acorn squash; Spaghetti squash; Zucchini
Steam-baked zucchini, 108, 115
Steamed soft-shell clams, 32, 38–39
Steamed vegetable pesto, 32, 37
Stock:
    beef, 219
    chicken, 218
    clarifying of, 221
    fish, 220
    use in aspics, 221, 222
Strawberries with kiwi sauce, 142, 147
Strawberry sauce, 129
String beans Singapore, 26, 31, 92
Stuffed apricots in aspic, 192, 195
Stuffed eggs with capers, 85, 90
Stuffed tomatoes, Greek, 65, 68
Substitutions, 4
Sweetbread pâté with spinach, 58, 59–60
Sweetbreads, in terrines and pâtés, 41, 59–60

Tasting:
    of forcemeat, 8
    of mousseline, 13
    of stock and sauces, 21
Terrine:
    baking of, 9, 15
    composing and layering of, 8, 14
    defined, 5
    freezing of, 4
    sealing of, 9
    unmolding of, 15–16
    weighting of, 10, 15
Terrine d'agneau aux herbes de Provence, 85, 86–87
Terrine de canard à l'orange, 3, 79, 80–81
Terrine de foies de volaille, 65, 66–67
    aux épinards et herbes, 45, 46–47
Terrine fine, 40, 41
Terrine Neptune, 148, 149–151
Tomato relish, gingered, 163, 169
Tomato sauce, light, 27, 137, 138, 143, 144, 224

Tomatoes:
    cherry, in mushroom compote, 162
    cherry, in steamed vegetable pesto, 37
    Greek stuffed, 65, 68
    with green sauce, 130, 135
    in vegetable compote, 49
Tongue:
    cooking, 94
    use in terrines and pâtés, 52, 93
Tongue and ham pâté, 92, 93–94
Tourin, le, 26, 28
Tourtière, 130, 131
Townshend mussels, 71, 74–75
Tricolor vegetable terrine, 185, 186–187
Truffles, 4, 7
Turkey, use in terrines and pâtés, 33, 52, 186, 205
Turnips, 74
    purée, 92, 95
    in vegetable ragout, 105
    and zucchini, shoestringed, 157, 160

Unmolding, 15–16

Veal, in terrines and pâtés, 41, 59, 80, 123, 201, 203, 205
Veal and ham pâté in crust, hot, 122, 123–125
    small individual (petits pâtés chauds), 205–206
Vegetable terrines and pâtés, 13, 15
    broccoli terrine, 213–214
    carrot pâté, 179, 180–181
    low cost of, 4
    mixed pâté in aspic, 203
    mosaic terrine, 192, 193–194
    spinach-fish terrine, 207–208
    spinach-zucchini terrine, 212
    tricolor terrine, 185, 186–187
Vegetables:
    asparagus with herbed vinaigrette, 92, 98, 108
    broccoli purée on endive spears, 136, 139
    cocktailed spaghetti squash, 163, 168
    compote, 49
    curried cauliflower and snow peas, 148, 154
    as garnishes, 7, 18
        acorn squash purée, 170, 176
        bean sprout salad, 65, 69
        beet relish, 108, 111, 116
        carrot-pear purée, 58, 61
        cucumbers, herbed, 40, 42

Vegetables *(continued)*
    cucumbers in mustard sauce, 185, **190**
    gingered tomato relish, 163, **169**
    lettuce cushions, 79, **82**
    onion rings, marinated, 116, **119**
    radishes, spiced, 148, **153**
    radish slices, zesty, 100, **104**
    red pepper strips, marinated, 45, **48**
    shoestringed turnips and zucchini, 157, **160**
    spaghetti squash salad, 51, **54**
    tomatoes with green sauce, 130, **135**
    turnip purée, 92, **95**
  mushroom compote, 157, **162**
  mushroom flan, 108, 148, **155–156**
  mushrooms on puffy fried noodles, 108, 136, **140**
  pears in red wine with broccoli purée, 185, **189**
  ragout, 100, **105**
  Singapore string beans, 26, **31**, 92
  snow peas with red peppers, 58, **64**
  spaghetti squash and peas, 92, 122, **127–128**
  steamed, in pesto sauce, 32, **37**
  zucchini leaves, 71, **77**, 92
  zucchini, steam-baked, 108, **115**
Vents, during baking of pâté, 11, 12

Vermouth-laced chicken-lemon aspic, 109–110, **164**
Vinaigrette, herbed, **98**

Water bath, 9, 15
Weighting:
  of fish and vegetable terrines, during baking, 15
  of meat terrines, after baking, 10
Wine pudding, German, 26, **30**
Wrapping:
  fat, 4, 6, 21
  pastry, 5, 11–12, 217
  use of crêpes, 17

Yogurt-pesto sauce, **232**
  green, **135**

Zesty radish slices, 100, **104**
Zucchini:
  leaves, 71, **77**, 92
  steam-baked, 108, **115**
  in steamed vegetable pesto, **37**
  and turnips, shoestringed, 157, **160**
Zucchini-spinach terrine, **212**